Exploring International Foods
Travel China, Italy, and Mexico

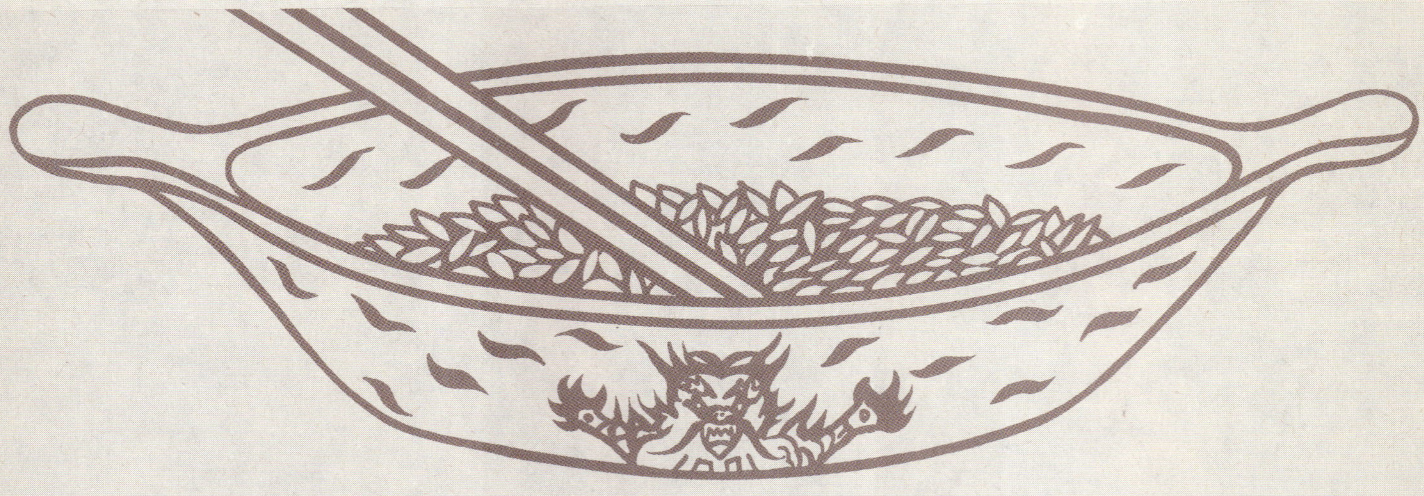

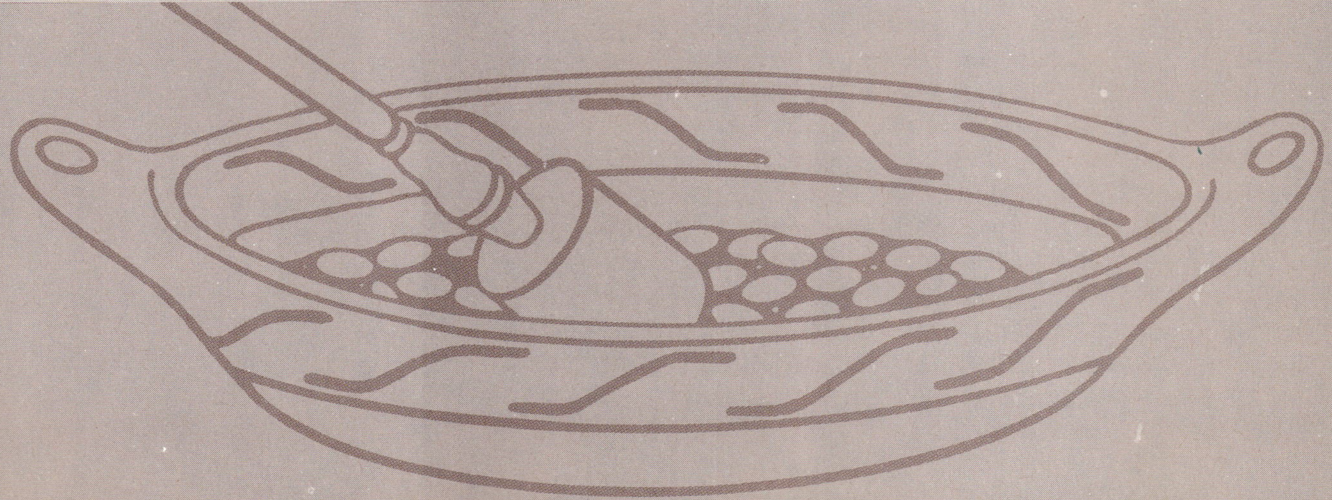

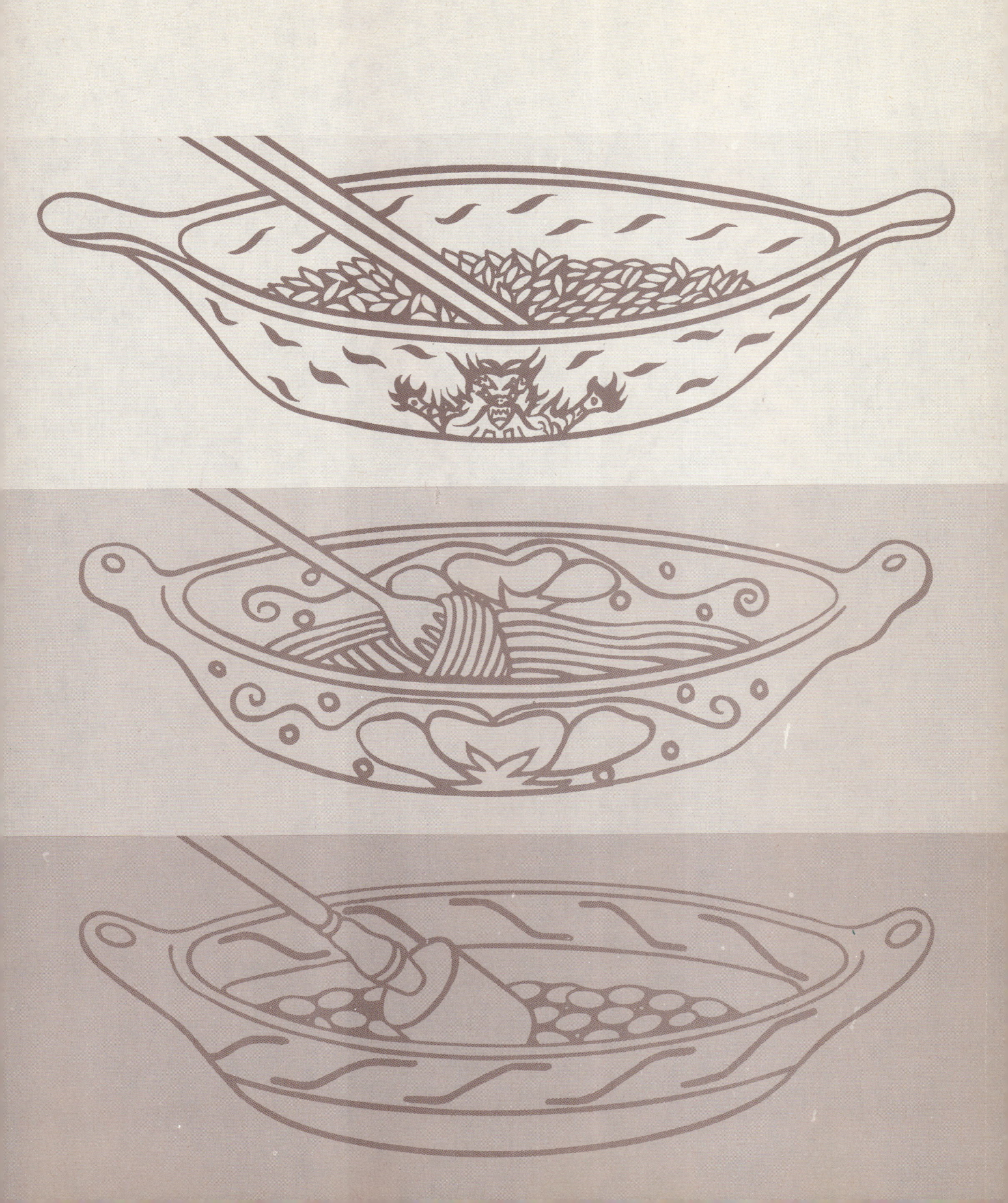

Exploring International Foods
Travel China, Italy, and Mexico

Laura Debus

Department Chairperson Home Economics
Irvington High School
Fremont, California

Robert H. Zedlitz

Department Chairperson Career Education
Irvington High School
Fremont, California

Carol M. Zedlitz

Educational Consultant
Pleasanton, California

Published by
HE62 **SOUTH-WESTERN PUBLISHING CO.**

CINCINNATI WEST CHICAGO, IL DALLAS PELHAM MANOR, NY LIVERMORE, CA

Copyright © 1986
by SOUTH-WESTERN PUBLISHING CO.

ALL RIGHTS RESERVED

The text of this publication, or any part thereof, may not be reproduced or transmitted in any form or by any means, electronic or mechanical, including photocopying, recording, storage in an information retrieval system, or otherwise, without the prior written permission of the publisher.

ISBN: 0-538-32620-4

Library of Congress
Catalog Card Number: 85-62376

2 3 4 5 6 7 8 H 1 0 9 8 7 6

Printed in the United States of America

CONTENTS

TO THE STUDENT vii
INTRODUCTION ix
UNIT ONE   TRAVEL CHINA 1

Section One   Introduction to Chinese Food 2
  Chapter 1   Chinese Food History 3
  Chapter 2   Exploring Chinese Recipes 8
  Chapter 3   Chinese Recipe Demonstrations 9

Section Two   Planning Your Chinese Meal 13
  Chapter 4   Selecting Your Chinese Menu 14
  Chapter 5   Chinese Recipes: Nutrition,
                Convenience, and Cost 16
  Chapter 6   Table Settings and Table
                Manners 26
  Chapter 7   Your Chinese Meal Planning
                Form 30

Section Three   Evaluating Your Chinese Meal 34
  Chapter 8   Chinese Product Evaluation 35

Activities for Unit One 39
Recipes for Unit One 53

UNIT TWO   TRAVEL ITALY 81

Section Four   Introduction to Italian Food 82
  Chapter 9   Italian Food History 83
  Chapter 10   Exploring Italian Recipes 89
  Chapter 11   Italian Recipe Demonstrations 90

Section Five   Planning Your Italian Meal 94
  Chapter 12   Selecting Your Italian Menu 95
  Chapter 13   Italian Recipes: Nutrition,
                Convenience, and Cost 97
  Chapter 14   Table Settings and Table
                Manners 108
  Chapter 15   Your Italian Meal Planning
                Form 112

Section Six   Evaluating Your Italian Meal 116
  Chapter 16   Italian Product Evaluation 117

Activities for Unit Two 121
Recipes for Unit Two 135

v

UNIT THREE	**TRAVEL MEXICO** 161	
Section Seven	**Introduction to Mexican Food** 162	
Chapter 17	Mexican Food History 163	
Chapter 18	Exploring Mexican Recipes 171	
Chapter 19	Mexican Recipe Demonstrations . 173	
Section Eight	**Planning Your Mexican Meal** 177	
Chapter 20	Selecting Your Mexican Menu 178	
Chapter 21	Mexican Recipes: Nutrition, Convenience, and Cost 180	
Chapter 22	Table Settings and Table Manners 190	
Chapter 23	Your Mexican Meal Planning Form 194	
Section Nine	**Evaluating Your Mexican Meal** ... 198	
Chapter 24	Mexican Product Evaluation 199	

Activities for Unit Three 203
Recipes for Unit Three 217

GLOSSARY 241
INDEX 247

TO THE STUDENT

Americans have developed a high level of food awareness. Eating the food of different countries is popular, entertaining, and educational. Preparing and serving these foods can be an adventure.

This workbook provides opportunities to plan, prepare, and evaluate international foods for your personal meals or for future occupational objectives. You will also learn how to work cooperatively in a team; be a competent host or hostess; and comprehend and appreciate the differences in international cuisines and the historical and geographical reasons for these differences.

These experiences may increase your desire to prepare international recipes at home. Many grocery stores now stock the necessary ingredients, so that cooking foreign foods at home is easy and enjoyable.

In this workbook, you will explore the cooking styles of China, Italy, and Mexico. Each chapter is carefully designed to help you move through meal preparation and serving steps. The recipes are representative of the classic cooking styles of each country. You will also learn about the origin and background of the cooking traditions within these countries.

The workbook includes recipes to be used in the classroom, as well as other recipes for you to use at home. When you have completed the activities, the workbook and the individual recipes are yours to keep.

The large number of recipes from each country allows you to choose from a wide selection of dishes when planning foreign menus at home. You may specialize in dishes from one country for one meal, or you may choose an international theme and serve dishes from all three countries. Having the recipes from China, Italy, and Mexico should encourage you to continue to explore the world of international cooking. These experiences may lead you to international career choices, such as restaurant chef, hotel manager, or travel agent.

INTRODUCTION

WHY STUDY INTERNATIONAL COOKING?

Few cooks prepare dishes based exclusively on the cuisines of their own countries. Here in the United States, kitchens are filled with good foods prepared not only from native products, but also from tasty and exotic ingredients found in Europe, Asia, and neighboring American countires. In fact, many Americans have become international cooks. This workbook is designed to help students become familiar with Chinese, Italian, and Mexican cuisines.

In grocery stores now, we may choose from a variety of Chinese produce, Italian pastas, and Mexican sauces. Students will have the opportunity to become familiar with these products as they select and prepare recipes typical of the three cuisines being studied.

The international foods text workbook brings the regional cuisines of China, Italy, and Mexico to the classroom. Preparing and tasting these foods will give students much of the expertise necessary to prepare tasty recipes for their personal or professional use.

Also included are short food histories of China, Italy, and Mexico, especially concerning the dishes that students will make. Students will gain a greater understanding of the meal patterns of these countries and a greater appreciation of their people, becoming more conscious of the world outside the United States.

WHAT MAKES THIS INTERNATIONAL FOODS WORKBOOK UNIQUE?

Exploring International Foods is more than just an ordinary classroom cookery course. Each unit is divided into three sections that guide students through the basic steps of planning, cooking, and evaluation of meals. Each chapter has been designed to be clearly understood and used flexibly in the classroom. This comprehensive course also provides recipe demonstrations, nutrition guidelines, lessons in determining the cost of a recipe, table-setting directions, and etiquette suggestions.

There are seven self-directed activities in each unit; the workbook is action-oriented. It reinforces text material with appropriate activities that allow students to participate while they are being led systematically through the course.

A summary of each unit's activities is listed below:

Activity 1	Food History Review
Activity 2	Recipe Match
Activity 3	Map Review
Activity 4	Selecting Your Menu
Activity 5	Meal Cost Sheet
Activity 6	Meal Planning Form
Activity 7	Product Evaluation Form

There are eighteen classroom recipes from each country that give the student many choices. There are five *additional* recipes for the student to use at home, making a total of twenty-three recipes for each country. Students determine the class menu for each country by selecting one of three recipes in each of six food categories. Students may keep all recipes to use at home when their classroom experience is completed.

Some of the recipes are divided into steps that allow for two preparation days, if needed. Ingredients or substitutions for the recipes are readily available in most grocery stores. For further convenience, italicized terms are defined in the glossary.

CAN STUDENTS EASILY COMPLETE THIS WORKBOOK?

Exploring International Foods is a hands-on workbook that is easy for students to use. Because it is divided into eight, self-explanatory chapters for each country, it saves preparation time. Since the workbook is individualized, students can progress at their own pace.

The following is a general description of the eight chapters of each country's text:

Food History

The student learns how traditional foods originated and how that country has influenced cooking in the world. Completing Activity One reinforces the student's awareness of the country's history, people, and cuisine.

Exploring Recipes

In four steps, the student obtains a general idea of the nature of that country's cooking. Activities Two and Three increase the student's understanding of the recipes.

Recipe Demonstrations

Two of the additional recipes are demonstrated in the classroom. Notes taken during the two demonstrations and the student's own answers to questions about them remain in the workbook as a convenient reference.

Selecting Your Menu

In two steps, including Activity 4, students are carefully guided in their choice of one of three recipes from each food category. Students will select a total of six recipes for their class to prepare.

Recipes: Nutrition, Convenience, and Cost

Students complete the following in the workbook: A Food Group Menu Chart and Equipment Planning Form, which ensures efficiency on preparation day. Activity 5 helps them compute the cost of their kitchen group's recipe and the cost of the entire meal.

Table Setting and Table Manners

Students draw a correct placesetting in the workbook once they are familiar with the way to set a buffet and dining table. Seven suggestions help students ensure more pleasant mealtimes. Table manners are an important part of the student evaluation of the buffet meal.

Your Meal Planning Form

This sample form enables students to successfully complete Activity 6, their own Meal Planning Form. Students then review their kitchen assignments, duties, time schedule, equipment, and recipe before starting to prepare their recipes.

Product Evaluation

Students use the sample Product Evaluation Form as a guide to complete Activity 7. The food preparations are rated in appearance, texture, and flavor. Students explain what factors contributed to the product's success and what could have been done to improve it.

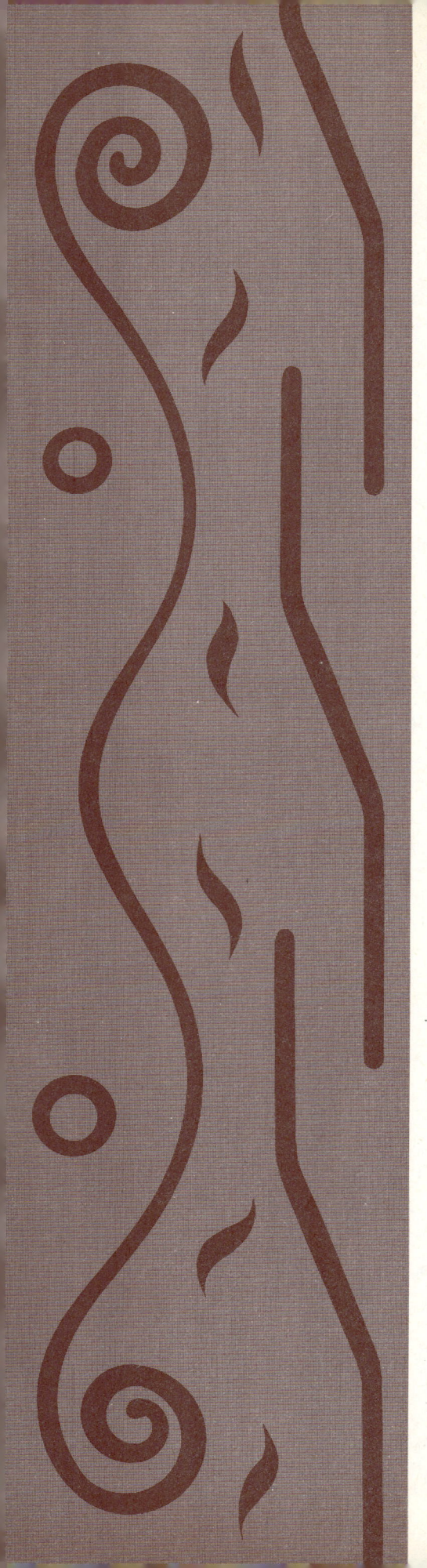

WHAT OTHER WAYS CAN THIS WORKBOOK BE USED?

This workbook is flexible in design and content. It was written to be easily adapted into a home economics/cooking curriculum. Flexible features of the workbook include:

- China, Italy, and Mexico can be taught in any sequence, in progression, or separately during the year.
- All activities are easily removed for student use and for collection and evaluation.
- All recipes are easily adapted to class-period lengths.
- The recipes can be removed for student use.

WHAT ARE THE FEATURES OF THE MANUAL?

The manual provides additional activities for China, Italy, and Mexico.

A seven-day lesson plan in the manual includes all workbook materials, saving preparation time.

WHAT ELSE IS AVAILABLE FOR THIS WORKBOOK?

A filmstrip, which provides much information about the Chinese, Italian, and Mexican foods relevent to this workbook, is available from South-Western. This filmstrip helps students learn about China's, Italy's, and Mexico's:

- Culinary regions
- Historical food traditions
- Lifestyles
- Variety of foods
- Cooking methods
- Nutrition
- Meal patterns
- Family meals

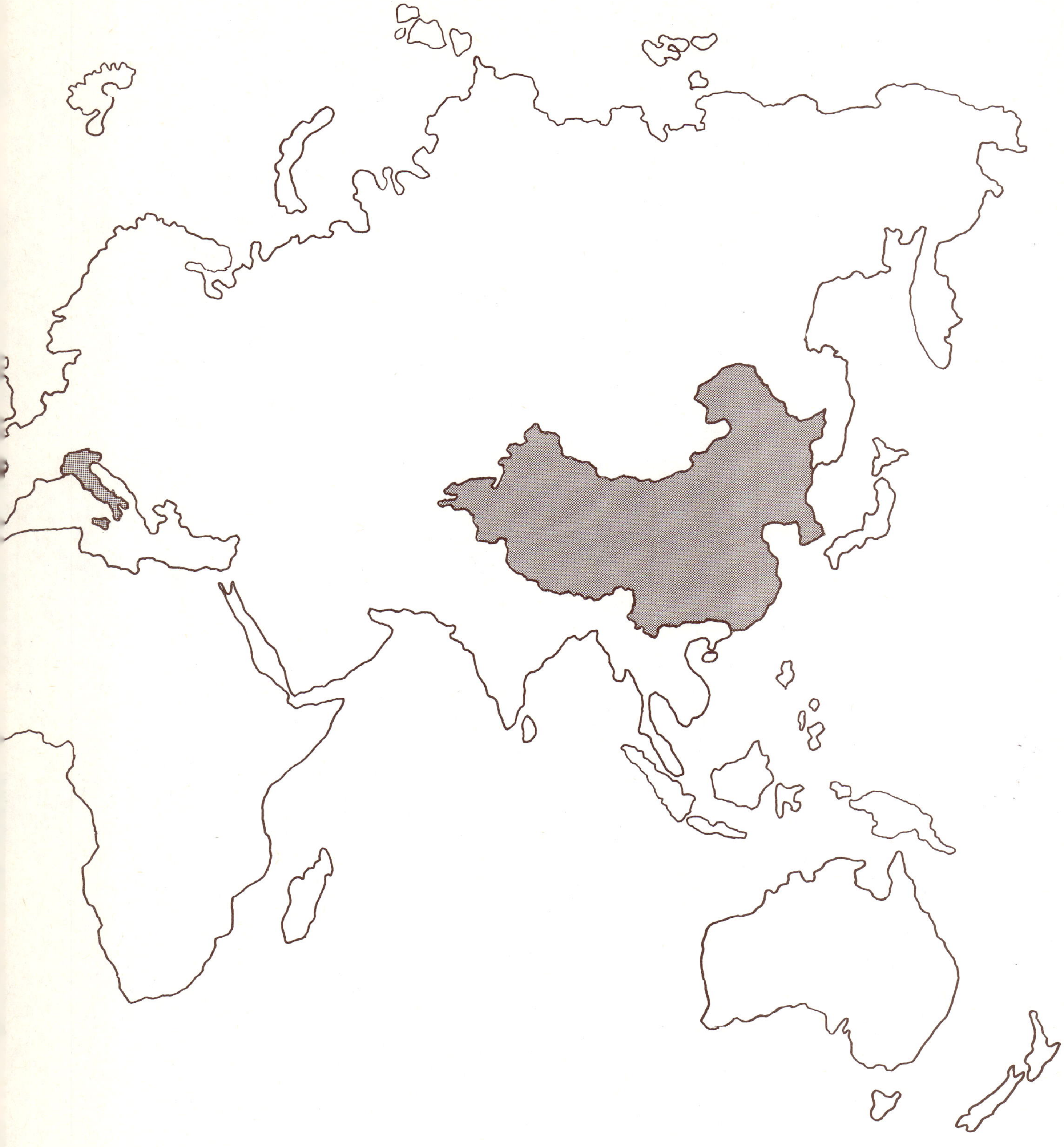

Exploring International Foods

Travel China

Section One

INTRODUCTION TO CHINESE FOODS

你吃過飯沒有？

"Have you eaten?" Instead of "hello," this is the greeting when friends meet in China. To the Chinese, this greeting is quite appropriate, especially when you consider China's enormous population. It has always been a major challenge to provide enough food for the people, and so your culinary tour of China begins with a look at the history of food in China. You will learn what has made every Chinese person a food expert and why Chinese food is thought to be one of the most exotic cuisines in the world.

Reading the recipes will give you a chef's tour through four of China's geographical regions. These regions may also be seen as culinary regions. The 23 recipes were selected from over 5,000 well-known dishes that have existed in China for centuries. The recipes include classic examples of Chinese soups, chicken dishes, pork dishes, vegetable dishes, doughs, and sweets.

As you read the recipes and learn the ingredients that are used in Chinese foods, you will begin to experience the flavor of Chinese cooking. After you identify on the map the region where each dish is prepared, you will feel you have traveled throughout China.

The highlight of your introduction to China will involve your observing the preparation of Fire Pot and Onion Cakes. Sampling these demonstration dishes will give you a taste of what you have to look forward to when you cook your own Chinese meal. In this section you will find

- a Chinese food history
- a map of China's regions
- 23 Chinese recipes

1

CHINESE FOOD HISTORY

The more you know about the history of Chinese food, the better you will understand the influence that food has had on Chinese culture. As you become aware of China's long history and the value that the Chinese place on food and eating, you will discover why cooking is an art and why dining is considered a ceremony in that country.

Much of what we know about the history of Chinese cooking comes from records kept by poets and philosophers and from the artifacts discovered in excavations of ancient Chinese villages and tombs. Chinese history is very old and very civilized. China has a recorded history of twenty-six centuries, while the United States has a history of only two centuries.

A recent village excavation unearthed a vessel for steaming food from the period 5,000–3,000 B.C. It is believed that such vessels were used for cooking *millet*, a grain. Millet bursts when steamed, and the eater then chews the millet to extract the soft starchy part and spits out the husks.

By 2000 B.C., the Chinese were farming, raising cattle and making fine pottery. They lived in mud houses that were clustered in small villages protected by pounded earth walls. The early Chinese were farmers and considered themselves more civilized than their neighboring nomadic herders and hunters.

Over the centuries, each ruling dynasty has improved Chinese cuisine. The ruling class was able to devote time to the culinary arts. Imperial palaces often controlled as many as 4,000 peasants. Of these, 2,400 were responsible for just food and wine! A further breakdown indicates that there were 128 chefs for the imperial family's food; 162 dietitians; 335 specialists in grains, vegetables, and fruit; 342 specialists in fish; 24 specialists in turtle and shellfish; 70 meat specialists; 62 specialists in game; and 62 pickle and sauce specialists.

Shang, the first dynasty, ruled northern China from about 1500 to 1066 B.C. The Emperor commanded armies from a central palace and supervised an elaborate court life. Artifacts—including bronze vessels, jade, ivory, and marble sculptures, daggers, axes, and elaborate harnesses and chariots—provide evidence of an advanced society. Relics from 1000 B.C. indicate that the Chinese were steaming, grilling, deep-frying, and roasting food. They used seasonings such as ginger root, *scallions* (similar to green onions), and garlic. These seasonings are still popular flavors in Chinese cooking.

One of the early proponents of eating as a ceremony was Confucius, who lived from 551 to 479 B.C. Confucius established rules for the "correct" preparation and presentation of foods. Meat had to be chopped finely. Vegetables had to be fresh and of good quality. Rice had to be polished white—though we now know that polishing eliminates protein and vitamins. The Taoists, a religious group, taught the value of eating young plants raw. Eating for health has been a part of the food philosophy of China for centuries.

Cooking became further sophisticated during the Han Dynasty (206 B.C.–A.D. 220). The technique of flour milling, first developed in India, became known in China, and the Chinese began to make noodles. Chopsticks were introduced at this time. Prior to this time, the Chinese had been using their fingers and a knife as their only utensils.

Chinese folk medicine has greatly influenced food preparation. During the Han dynasty the need for a balanced and complete diet was recorded. The correct blending of cereals, fruit, meat, and vegetables was considered important to the sound development of both the mind and the body.

Dining as a great ceremony in China reached its height more recently during the Ching Dynasty (A.D. 1644–1911). Manners, courtesy, and etiquette were strictly observed. There was much bowing of host and guest. The host would bow to the chair, to the chopsticks, and to the wine cup that the guest was to use, and the guest would bow in return. The table was usually round so conversation could flow easily and the food could be reached by everyone. The host sat opposite the guest of honor. There were rules dictating which subjects could be discussed at the table. Politics, religion, or anything that might interfere with the friendly mood of the guests was not permitted.

FACTORS AFFECTING CHINA'S FOOD TRADITIONS

Today, the influential dynasties have disappeared from China, and there is an entirely new form of government. However, food is still very important to the Chinese people.

Several factors have determined the course of cooking and eating in China. These include: China's terrain, its climate, its enormous population, its lack of natural sources of cooking fuel, and its geographical location.

Even though China is slightly larger than the United States, only about 11 percent of its land can be cultivated as compared to 80 percent in the U.S. This is because 60 percent of the land in China is mountainous, while much of the rest is too dry or has a climate that prohibits a lengthy growing season. As a result, the Chinese have developed a great respect for food.

China, in the 1983 census, had a population of over 1 billion people, about four times that of the United States. China has had a history of famines. Most people live in the fertile plains and deltas in the eastern part of the country, yet, eating has never been taken for granted by this large mass of people. Food, a major topic of conversation in China, is never wasted.

The Chinese also appreciate the artistic value of cooking and eating. Even the lowest forms of food, such as grubs, grasshoppers, or snakes, are presented with artistry, flavor, and flair. Great imagination has made possible the preparation and enjoyment of unusual foods, such as birds' nests, sharks' fins, sea cucumbers, ducks' webbed feet, bear paws, and tree fungus. The early Chinese were well aware that the people who ate these foods would not develop brittle bones.

To compensate for China's lack of sufficient natural sources for cooking fuel, food preparation techniques such as stir-frying and sautéeing have been developed because they require little fuel. Deep-frying is also common because it takes less heat to boil oil than it does to boil water. Steaming is another popular cooking method. Several steamers are placed on top of each other over one source of heat. Most Chinese homes do not have ovens, so some breads and pastries are cooked by steaming.

The way food is cut for cooking is also important to conserving fuel in China. Ingredients are cut into small, bite-sized pieces because they cook faster that way. When they are cut in the same size and in the same manner they are all done at the same time. Vegetables are cut on the diagonal; they cook faster because more of their surface is exposed to the heat. This carries out another basic principle of the Chinese cooking philosophy, which is to preserve food value when cooking.

Geography has always played an important role in the quality of food. China developed strong local food customs because the geographical barriers of the country kept people from migrating too far from their villages. These barriers also kept out people from other countries. Communication, therefore, was slow in so vast a country.

Today China has four major culinary regions. The cuisine of each bears the name of a city or province located in that region: northern (Beijing), southern (Canton), eastern (Shanghai), and western (Sichuan) (see Figure 1.1). In the United States, Cantonese cooking is the best known Chinese cuisine. This is because of the large number of immigrants who came from the southern coast of China to help construct the new railroads in the United States in the late 1800s.

CURRENT FOOD PRACTICES IN CHINA

Today, along with regional differences, there are many foods and dishes that are used and prepared in almost the same way all over China.

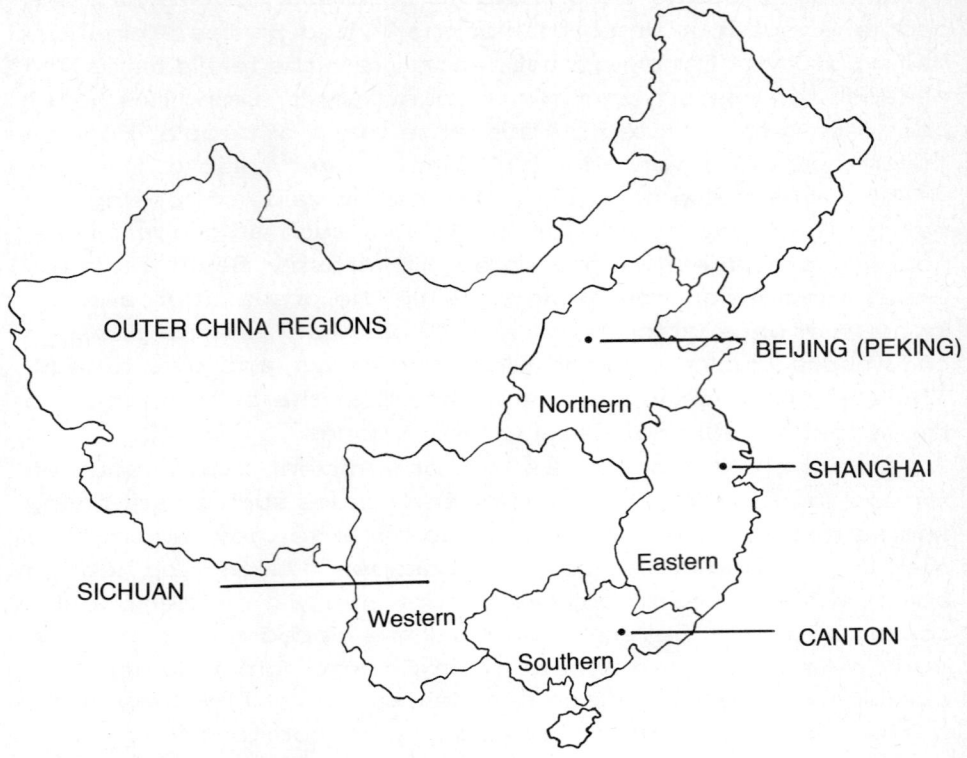

Figure 1.1. Culinary Regions of China

Meat and fowl in China consist largely of pork, duck, and chicken because these animals are easy to raise, and they require little effort and expense to feed.

Fish and shellfish also constitute a major part of the Chinese diet. One method of catching fish is quite ingenious. The Chinese use cormorants, fish-eating birds, to do the job for them. First, they train the birds to return to their owners. Then they put a ring around each cormorant's neck so that the bird is not able to swallow fish. Finally, the cormorants fly free, catching and returning fish to the boat. The birds know that they will be rewarded with fish to eat when the ring is removed at the end of the day.

Because refrigerated food loses some of its quality and freshness, Chinese cooks most often use fresh or preserved ingredients. They shop daily for fresh poultry, fish, and vegetables and decide what to eat only after seeing what is the freshest and best value at the market. The use of preserved foods such as vegetables, fish, seafood, and meat, probably stems from days when the Chinese experienced great famines. Preserving food by salting, pickling, and drying helped the Chinese prepare for such periods. Today, dried vegetables are routinely reconstituted and used with fresh vegetables to improve the flavor of soups and stews.

Many spices and seasoning agents are also used in Chinese cooking. The Chinese do not consider seasonings and food as being different, but think of food as a seasoning and seasoning

Table 1.1 Ingredients Common to Chinese Recipes

*bamboo shoots	*garlic	potatoes/sweet potatoes
*bean curd	*ginger root	radishes
*bean sprouts	*green beans	*rice
*celery	*green onions	*scallions
*cellophane noodles	*ham	*sesame oil
coriander	*litchi nuts	*shrimp
*cucumbers	*mandarin oranges	*soy sauce
*dates	*mushrooms	*Sichuan pepper
eggplant	noodles	*water chestnuts
*fowl	*oyster sauce	*wrappers/skins

*Foods used in one or more of the Chinese recipes.

as a food. The most common ingredients in Chinese cuisine are listed above in Table 1.1.

MEAL PATTERNS

In a Chinese home, there are usually three meals a day, plus snacks such as fresh fruit or pastries. Cookies and cakes may be eaten as snacks, but they are never eaten at the conclusion of a meal.

All foods, including the soup, are placed on the table at once. Soup may be eaten at any time during the meal because it might be the only liquid at the table. Tea is not usually served during a meal, only before or after (the Chinese people began drinking tea for hygiene, noticing that those who drank boiled water enjoyed better health).

Each person has a bowl of rice, but the other foods are communal. That is, each person simply reaches for what he or she wants from the other dishes on the table, a chopstickful at a time, followed by a chopstickful of rice. Children are taught to eat so that no one is ever aware of their favorite food; they are told to take equal amounts from each dish.

Traditionally, a meal consists of one part meat to three or four parts vegetable. In most cases, vegetables are fillers, and the rice or other grain food is considered the main dish. Rice is the most important element in a meal, and Chinese meals, morning, noon, and night, are based on a bowl of rice. Various dishes, such as vegetables with bits of pork, eggs, bean curd, relishes, and soups, merely accompany the rice.

When a guest is expected, the quantity of each dish is not increased—another dish is added to the meal. This custom probably originated during the time when there was so little of each different kind of food that a new dish would have to be created from another ingredient.

Turn to the Activities for the China unit and remove Activity 1, Chinese Food History Review. Complete the Chinese Food History Review and give it to your instructor for evaluation.

2

EXPLORING CHINESE RECIPES

In this chapter you will use the Chinese recipes provided at the end of the China unit. You will become familiar with Chinese cooking by reading each recipe and completing two related activities. The recipes are yours to keep.

Complete this chapter by following Steps 1 through 4:

Step 1: Remove the Chinese recipe sheets and cut them apart.

Step 2: Read the Chinese recipes and recipe descriptions. Note that the recipes are labeled in the following categories: Soups, Chicken Dishes, Pork Dishes, Vegetable Dishes, Doughs, and Sweets. For example, the Egg Drop Soup recipe is labeled, "Food Category: Soup."

The last five recipes are marked with an asterisk (*). You will read and use these recipes to complete some of the activities but *not* use them in your menu plans. These recipes are added for you to prepare at home.

Each recipe is rated low cost, moderate cost, or high cost. The cost is based on the prices of the ingredients. The cost of each ingredient may vary due to seasonal changes and location. On the back of each recipe is a brief history of each dish and information about the region where the dish is popular.

Step 3: Remove Activity 2, Chinese Recipe Match. Completing this activity will make you aware of recipe histories, names, food categories, and ingredients. Review both sides of each recipe in order to finish this activity. When finished, give your Chinese Recipe Match to your instructor for evaluation.

Step 4: Remove Activity 3, Chinese Map Review. Completing this activity will help you become familiar with the four culinary regions of China and the regions where the recipes are popular. Review the descriptions of the recipes as you do this activity. When finished, give your Chinese Map Review to your instructor for evaluation.

8 Section One • Introduction to Chinese Foods

3
CHINESE RECIPE DEMONSTRATIONS

In this chapter you will get to the heart of Chinese food by tasting classic Chinese cooking. Two Chinese recipes will be demonstrated, and you will learn how to prepare them. While the recipes are being demonstrated, be sure to take good notes. The information in your notes will help you prepare the dishes later. The answers to the questions below will add to your knowledge of the recipes. Having the answers explained during the demonstrations and in the recipes will ensure your success.

FIRE POT DEMONSTRATION

Notes: _____
_____
_____
_____
_____
_____
_____
_____
_____
_____
_____
_____

QUESTIONS ON THE FIRE POT DEMONSTRATION

1. What can you do to flank steak to make it easy to cut?

2. How should flank steak be cut?

3. How should mushrooms be cleaned, and why should they be cleaned this way?

4. In this recipe, what should be done to the cellophane noodles before frying?

5. What should you be careful to do when you are cooking pork?

6. What can you do to prevent the noodles from sticking during the cooking process?

_____
_____
_____

ONION CAKES DEMONSTRATION

Notes: _____
_____
_____
_____
_____
_____
_____
_____
_____
_____
_____
_____
_____
_____
_____
_____
_____
_____
_____

QUESTIONS ON THE ONION CAKES DEMONSTRATION

1. What happens to the dough during the 30-minute standing period?

   _____
   _____
   _____

2. What can you substitute for scallions?

   _____
   _____
   _____

3. Why should you sprinkle oil on the breadboard?

   _____
   _____
   _____

4. Why should you divide the dough in half before rolling it?

   _____
   _____
   _____

5. Why should you pinch the ends of the rolls?

   _____
   _____
   _____

6. Why should you oil the rolling pin?

   _____
   _____
   _____

Section Two

PLANNING YOUR CHINESE MEAL

You have already explored China by way of map, history, recipes, and sample tasting. Now your class will prepare a Chinese meal. This meal will have the same native Chinese flavor that you would find if you were actually in China.

The success of your Chinese meal depends upon the combined effort of all students in each kitchen group. The food should be well prepared and attractively displayed on the buffet. The dining table should be properly set, and the kitchen should be clean. Remember that good table manners enable you to have an enjoyable dining experience.

While working in your assigned kitchen group, you must have your duties clearly in mind to ensure that the Chinese meal is a success. Planning ahead for the cooking and evaluation days will give you the confidence necessary to carry out your duties smoothly. Each part of this section is designed to prepare you for both the cooking and evaluation days.

In this section you will find

- a guide to help you select your Chinese menu
- guides for Chinese recipe nutrition, convenience, and cost
- directions for setting a buffet and dining table
- seven ways to improve table manners
- a planning form for the cooking and evaluation days

4

SELECTING YOUR CHINESE MENU

An everyday meal in China normally consists of a large bowl of rice accompanied by a few strips of meat, several dried shrimp, or some well-seasoned vegetables. Your meal, however, will be similar to a meal served in a Chinese home for a special occasion; on special occasions the number and variety of dishes are increased. There is no main dish in a Chinese meal. Instead, there are a variety of dishes served at the same time.

You will select your menu from recipes in the following food categories: soups; chicken dishes with rice; pork dishes; vegetable dishes with bean curd; doughs; and sweets. Each food category has three recipes. You will choose one recipe from each category. Remember that the recipes marked with an asterisk are for home use only.

After selecting one recipe from each of the food categories, you will have a total of six recipes, one of which you and your kitchen group will prepare.

A brief description of the food categories from which you will choose follows:

Soup	Soup is always included with meals. There is seldom any other liquid refreshment served.
Chicken Pork	Small amounts of chicken or pork are combined with vegetables and served with a savory sauce.
Vegetables	Freshness is the most important quality the Chinese look for in vegetables. Freshness is preserved by a cooking technique called *stir-frying*. *Bean curd* is coagulated soy bean milk, and it provides the major source of protein in meatless dishes.
Doughs	The dough category includes dishes that are not usually served with a Chinese meal, but are eaten as snacks.
Sweets	Sweets are not normally served with everyday meals in a Chinese home. These recipes,

however, are examples of sweets that might be served at a special-occasion meal or for a between-meal treat.

The Chinese have created an art through the use of a variety of flavors, textures, and colors within each dish. They insist that each dish be pleasing to the eye. They are careful to select dishes that balance the artistry of the meal with its nutritional value.

As you read the Chinese recipes, decide which you think would make the most appealing combination of dishes for the buffet. First, consider the flavor. The Chinese recognize five flavors: sweet, sour, bitter, pungent, and salty. They try to include all of these in a meal and to balance the taste of each dish with one of a contrasting flavor. For example, a highly seasoned dish would be balanced by a mildly seasoned one. Second, consider texture. The Chinese contrast the crisp with the smooth, the tender with the firm. Different cooking techniques create a variety of textures. *Stir-frying*, *deep-fat-frying*, *steaming*, *cooking in water*, *braising*, and *baking* are techniques from which you may choose. Last, consider color and appearance. The Chinese expect the colors of the dishes to be pleasing and the ingredients to be of uniform size within each dish. What is pleasing to the eye should then be pleasing to the stomach.

When selecting a menu be adventurous. Choose recipes you have neither tasted nor prepared. Look for ingredients that you have not tried. New taste experiences contribute to the excitement of cooking recipes from other countries. You may be pleasantly surprised, and as a result, you will develop a broader taste palate. Don't be concerned with unfamiliar or complicated directions. Remember, your kitchen group will prepare only one recipe, so you will have ample time to study it and clear up anything that you do not understand.

Select your menu in these two easy steps:

Step 1: Read the Chinese recipes. After you are familiar with them, proceed to Step 2.

Step 2: Remove Activity 4, Selecting Your Chinese Menu. Complete the activity and give it to your instructor for evaluation. He or she will tell you how the class menu will be selected and how the kitchen group will determine which recipe it will prepare.

5

CHINESE RECIPES: NUTRITION, CONVENIENCE, AND COST

In this chapter you will consider the nutritional value of your menu. You will learn how to determine if your recipes are convenient to prepare and how much your meal will cost. The knowledge you gain from completing this chapter will give you a good background for selecting recipes and planning meals when you are cooking on your own.

NUTRITION

A variety of healthy food is essential to good nutrition. Because people eat not only to enjoy the taste of food but also to remain healthy, it is necessary to consider the nutritional value of your recipes. For example, rice is a grain product and a good source of carbohydrates for energy, but it would be poor nutrition to eat just plain rice all day.

Your body requires more than just energy foods: it needs the other nutrients that are found in the four major food groups.

- meat, poultry, fish, eggs, and *legumes* (dried beans and peas)
- milk products
- fruit and vegetable
- bread and cereal

Eating the recommended amount of food from each group provides the required nutrients needed in your daily diet.

Table 5.1 shows the necessary servings per day from each food group for your age:

Table 5.2 will help you determine the number of servings from these food groups provided by your Chinese meal. The completed chart will indicate which food group your meal has too

Table 5.1 Necessary Servings Per Day

Food Group	Servings
Meat/Poultry/Fish/Eggs/Legumes	2
Milk Products	4
Fruit/Vegetable	4
Bread/Cereal	4

much or too little of. If it is low in one group, you should simply include food from that group in another meal that day. If it is high in another group, you should decrease the amount of food in that group at another meal.

The Chinese, by virtue of their meal planning, maintain a well-balanced diet. For instance, it is common for a meal to include a food such as rice or noodles that is high in carbohydrates; in addition, several vegetables are served. The nutritional emphasis is on carbohydrates rather than protein. No Chinese cook would ever have a whole roast or entire chicken for just one family dinner. Proteins are made up of amino acids. Those proteins which contain the essential amino acids are called complete proteins; they are obtained in meat, poultry, eggs, fish, and shellfish. Those proteins which do not contain the essen-

Table 5.2 Food Group Menu Chart

Food Groups	Meat/Poultry Fish/Eggs/ Legumes	Milk Products	Fruit/ Vegetable	Bread/ Cereal
Daily Necessary Servings*	2	4	4	4
Soup:				
Chicken Dish:				
Pork Dish:				
Vegetable Dish:				
Dough:				
Sweet:				
Totals				
Servings Still Needed				

*for your age group

tial amino acids are called incomplete proteins; they are obtained in vegetables, dried beans, dried peas, and grains. A meal of two incomplete-protein foods, such as beans and rice, will provide a more complete protein. Although rice and noodles contain some plant protein, another important protein source is soybean products, such as bean curd. When soy products are combined with rice, the dish has an even higher protein value than when either rice or soy is eaten alone.

The Chinese do not use dairy products. However, they do use soybean products, which contain more digestible calcium than equivalent amounts of milk. Another plus for Chinese food is that it is low in fat because little meat is eaten. Chinese diets are also low in sugar because sweet desserts are not a normal part of Chinese meals.

Follow these directions for completing the Food Group Menu Chart.

1. List the recipes your class has selected in the Recipes column on the chart.
2. Read the ingredients of each recipe and check (√) the major food group into which each falls. A recipe may fall into more than one food group. When this occurs, only major ingredients are classified.
3. Total the number of servings in each food group column.
4. Using Table 5.2, write the number of servings needed to attain the necessary daily food group recommendations.

CONVENIENCE

You will know a recipe is convenient if

- you easily can obtain the ingredients
- you have the necessary equipment to make the dish
- you have adequate time to prepare it

Because some ingredients are too expensive or not available, other ingredients, which still assure the desired results, can be substituted. For example, the *sesame seed paste* in Pon Pon Chicken may not be available. However, peanut butter can be substituted without altering the flavor of the dish.

First, make a list of the equipment needed. Then check the kitchen to see if all the equipment is there. The correct equipment is essential for the smooth and efficient preparation of your recipe. Carefully read the recipe to determine how much time will be required, and make sure that the recipe fits into your time schedule. Preparing part of the recipe one day and completing it the next will be more convenient.

The decision to prepare Chinese food may result in some minor inconveniences. You might have to search the grocery store for certain ingredients, such as *litchi nuts*, that you are not accustomed to buying. You might have to purchase new equipment or figure out how to improvise with what you have in order to prepare a recipe at home. For example, the recipe for Pork Steamed Buns calls for a steamer, which you might not have. However, you can make your own by removing the tops and bottoms from two seven-ounce tuna cans and setting them in a large deep kettle with a lid. Place a cake rack or plate on the tuna cans. This will support the buns. You will find that the opportunity to try a new Chinese dish is worth your effort to figure out how to improvise a special piece of equipment.

Answer the following questions, to help your recipe preparation. Planning ahead will ensure efficiency on preparation day.

1. What recipe ingredients are not available? _____
_____

2. What major pieces of equipment (pans, bowls) will be necessary?
_____
_____

3. What utensils will be necessary? _____
_____

4. What necessary equipment is missing? _____
_____

5. How might you improvise this missing equipment?
_____
_____

6. How much time will your recipe take to prepare?

(Estimate) _____

7. How do you rate the convenience of your recipe?

Check (√) one:

____ quick and easy

____ somewhat involved

____ difficult but worth the effort

COST

In this activity, each kitchen group will compute the cost of its recipe. Afterwards, you will total the cost of all recipes and find out the cost of the entire meal.

Soon you will be responsible for your own food budget. You will want to keep your food costs within the amount of money you have budgeted. You must know if you can feed the desired number of people within your budget. Knowing the cost of individual servings will help you determine if you can.

If a recipe costs $10.00 to prepare and makes ten servings, it costs only $1.00 per serving; however, if that dish made only four servings, the cost would more than double to $2.50 per serving. The cost of the recipe per serving is the meaningful figure.

Study the example of the Chinese Meal Cost Sheet (Figure 5.1). The cost per serving of Fried Rice has been determined.

SECTION A — Name of Recipe: *Fried Rice*

(1) Recipe Ingredients	(2) Amount Required	(3) Price Per Item	(4) Amount of Store Container	(5) Cost Computation	(6) Total Ingredient Cost
rice	½ cup	.73	1 pound 12 ounces (28 oz.)	.73 ÷ 28 = .026 or .03 ½ C = 4 oz. 4 × .03 = .12	.12
oil	2 T.	1.81	1 quart	1.81 ÷ 64 = .028 or .03 2 × .03 = .06	.06
eggs	2	.85	1 dozen	.85 ÷ 12 = .071 or .07 2 × .07 = .14	.14
shrimp	½ cup	2.65	½ pound	2.65 ÷ 2 = 1.32½ or 1.33 amount required	1.33
green onions	½ cup	.29	1 bunch	exact amount required	.29

SECTION B ⟶ Total Recipe Cost: **$1.94**

SECTION C — Total Recipe Cost ÷ Number of Servings = Cost Per Serving
(**$1.94**) ÷ (**6**) = (**.32**)

Figure 5.1. Sample Filled-in Activity 5

Fried Rice

2 cups rice
4 cups water
2 tbsp. oil
2 eggs, slightly beaten
½ cup shrimp
½ tsp. salt
⅛ tsp. pepper
½ cup green onion, chopped fine
3 tbsp. soy sauce

Figure 5.2. Recipe for Fried Rice

By studying these steps, you will be able to follow the directions for completing your own Chinese Meal Cost Sheet. See how Mary Hughes determined the cost of Fried Rice.

Step 1: Mary read the recipe to determine what ingredients should be included in figuring the cost of the recipe (see Figure 5.2). Ingredients such as salt, pepper, cornstarch, baking soda, vinegar, and most seasonings were on hand in the kitchen, so it was not necessary to include small amounts of these items when figuring per serving cost. Mary decided the cost of the salt and pepper did not have to be included. She recorded the remaining ingredients for Fried Rice in Column 1 of the Chinese Meal Cost Sheet.

Step 2: Mary wrote the amount of each ingredient she needed in Column 2.

Step 3: Mary took the Chinese Meal Cost Sheet to the grocery store. She listed the price the store charged for each item in Column 3, and then she bought the quantity of each ingredient closest to the amount she needed.

Step 4: Mary listed the amount of the item's store container in Column 4. Stores sell items in different measurements, weights, and quantities, depending on the item itself. Pints, quarts, gallons, ounces, pounds, bunches, or "per each" are common quantity terms.

Table 5.3 Table of Weights and Measures

3 teaspoons	1 tablespoon
4 tablespoons	¼ cup
5⅓ tablespoons	⅓ cup
8 tablespoons	½ cup
16 tablespoons	1 cup or 8 ounces
2 cups	1 pint
2 pints	1 quart
4 cups	1 quart
4 quarts	1 gallon
16 ounces	1 pound

Step 5:   Mary computed the cost of each ingredient in Column 5. When necessary, she referred to the Table of Weights and Measures or to the Table of Equivalent Amounts (see Tables 5.3 and 5.4).

Tables 5.3 and 5.4 will help you figure the cost of the ingredients in a recipe. To use the tables, you need to know the amount of each ingredient required for your recipe. Here are two examples:

1. Suppose your recipe calls for 7 tablespoons of oil and you want to figure the cost. Table 5.3 shows that 16 tablespoons equal 1 cup, and 4 cups equal 1 quart. Multiply 4 ×

Table 5.4   Equivalent Amounts (Approximate)

Item	Common Weights or Units	Equivalence in Cups or Spoons
Apples	1 pound (3 medium)	2½ cups pared and sliced
Bamboo Shoots	15-ounce can	1½ cups
Bean Curd	1 pound (4½" × 5½" × 1½")	2 cups
Bean Sprouts	1 pound	6 cups
Brown Bean Paste	8-ounce can	¾ cup
Butter	1 pound (4 sticks)	2 cups
	1 stick	½ cup
Carrots	1 pound (6 medium)	2 cups sliced
Celery	10 stalks per bunch (average)	5 cups
	1 stalk	½ cup sliced
Chicken, uncooked	3½ pounds	3 cups cooked and boned
	1 large breast	2 cups cooked and diced
Chicken Bouillon Cubes (for broth)	3.33-ounce package (25 cubes)	25 cups with water
	1 cube	1 cup with water
Cornstarch	1 pound	2 cups
Dates, pitted	8-ounce package	1¼ cups chopped
Flour, wheat	1 pound	4 cups unsifted
Gelatin	4-ounce package (4 envelopes)	1 envelope will thicken 2 cups of liquid

22   Section Two ● Planning Your Chinese Meal

Table 5.4 (Continued)

Item	Common Weights or Units	Equivalence in Cups or Spoons
Ham, sliced	8-ounce package (8 slices)	1 cup chopped
Leeks	1 bunch (5 medium) 10 thin slices per leek	3 cups sliced
Mushrooms, uncooked	1 pound (24 small to medium)	4 to 5 cups sliced
Onions, dry	1 pound (3 large, 4 medium, 5 small)	3 cups
green	1 bunch with tops (5 onions)	½ cup sliced
Oranges	1 pound (2 large, 3 medium, 4 small)	2 cups sectioned
	1 medium	2 to 3 tablespoons per rind or ½ cup juice
Oyster Sauce	8-ounce bottle	1 cup
Peanut Butter	1-pound 4-ounce jar	17 tablespoons
Peas, green	1 pound	1 cup shelled
frozen	10 ounces	2 cups cooked
	¼ 10-ounce box	½ cup
snow	6 ounces	1 cup cooked
Pepper, (bell)	1 pound (3 to 6 small)	4 cups chopped
	¼ pound	1 cup chopped
Rice	½ pound raw	1 cup raw, 3 cups cooked
Sesame Seeds	2.6-ounce jar	½ cup
Sesame Seed Paste	8-ounce jar	1 cup
Shrimp, cooked and shelled	1 pound	2 cups
	¼ pound (8 to 10)	½ cup
Spinach	1 pound (3 cups) raw	1⅓ cups cooked
Sugar, granulated	1 pound	2 cups
Walnuts, shelled	1 pound	4 cups
Water Chestnuts, whole	8-ounce can	¾ cup sliced

16, which is 64—the number of tablespoons in 1 quart. Next, divide the current market price for 1 quart of oil by the number of tablespoons in 1 quart (64). This gives you

> 1. Rice
>   Store quantity .... 1 pound, 12 ounces
>   Store cost (in dollars) .... .73
>   Cost per ounce .... .73 divided by 28 = .026 or .03
>   Amount required (4 ounces) × cost for one (.03) = Cost for ingredient (.12)
>   In Table 5.4, Mary found that 8 ounces of rice = 1 cup. So ½ cup = 4 ounces.
> 2. Oil
>   Store quantity .... 1 quart
>   Store cost (in dollars) 1.81
>   Cost per tablespoon .... 1.81 divided by 64 = .028 or .03
>   Amount required (2 tablespoons) × cost for one (.03) = Cost for ingredient (.06)
>   In Table 5.3, Mary found that 16 tablespoons = 1 cup, and 4 cups = 1 quart. So 4 cups = 64 tablespoons.
> 3. Eggs
>   Store quantity .... 1 dozen
>   Store cost (in dollars) .... .85
>   Cost per egg .... .85 divided by 12 = .071 or .07
>   Amount required (2 eggs) × cost for one (.07) = Cost for ingredient (.14)
> 4. Shrimp
>   Store quantity .... ½ pound
>   Store cost (in dollars) 2.65
>   Cost per 1 cup (½ pound) 2.65
>   Amount required (½ cup) × cost for one (2.65) = Cost for ingredient (1.33)
>   In Table 5.4, Mary found that 2 cups = 1 pound of shrimp. So ½ pound = 1 cup.
> 5. Green Onions
>   Store quantity .... 1 bunch
>   Store cost (in dollars) .... .29
>   Cost per ½ cup (1 bunch) .... .29
>   Amount required (½ cup at .29) = Cost for ingredient (.29)
>   In Table 5.4, Mary found that 1 bunch of green onions with tops = ½ cup.

Note: All costs should be approximate. When a price per unit comes out unevenly, round up (as stores do) to the nearest cent.

Figure 5.3. Recipe Cost Analysis

the price per tablespoon: $1.84 ÷ 64 = $.028, which is approximately 3 cents per tablespoon. Finally, 7 × $.03 = $.21 which is 21 cents, the cost of 7 tablespoons of oil.

2. Your recipe calls for ½ cup of butter, and you want to figure the cost. Table 5.4 shows that 4 sticks equal 1 pound of butter, and 1 stick equals ½ cup of butter. Divide the current market price for one pound of butter by 4: $189 ÷ 4 = $.471, or 47 cents, the cost of ½ cup of butter.

Figure 5.3 shows an explanation of the computation Mary did in Column 5, using both tables.

Step 6: In Column 6, Mary recorded the answers she had computed in Column 5.

Now you are ready to figure the cost of your recipe. Remove Activity 5, Chinese Meal Cost Sheet. Follow the directions given here to complete this activity. Refer to the example of Mary Hughes if you need help. Remember, the recipe cost you compute should be *approximate*. Current market prices should be used to determine the cost of your recipes. You can read grocery store advertisements or go to the market to find out current prices.

First, fill in the name of the recipe your kitchen group will prepare in the space provided. Then do as follows:

Section A

Column 1: Determine what ingredients should be figured in the cost of the recipe. List each of these ingredients.
Column 2: List the amount of the ingredient your recipe requires.
Column 3: List the price of the item.
Column 4: List the amount of ingredient in store container.
Column 5: Show your computation of the cost per ingredient.
Column 6: List the cost of each ingredient.

Section B

Add the cost of each ingredient in Column 6 to get the total cost of the recipe. Write that figure in Section B.

Section C

Divide the total cost of the recipe by the number of persons it serves to determine the cost per serving. Write these figures in Section C.

Section D

Column 1: List the recipes prepared by other kitchen groups.
Column 2: List the total cost of each recipe.
Column 3: List the cost per serving of each recipe.

Section E

Add the cost of each recipe in Column 2 to get the cost of the total meal. Write that figure in Column 2. Add all of the recipe costs for each serving in Column 3 to determine the total cost of the meal per serving. Write that figure in Column 3.

Give your completed Chinese Meal Cost Sheet to your instructor for evaluation.

6
TABLE SETTINGS AND TABLE MANNERS

BUFFET SETTINGS

It is important to know how to set the buffet and dining tables properly when you serve your Chinese meal. If you are the host or hostess, setting the tables is one of your duties. You will place the dish your kitchen group prepares on the buffet table and set your kitchen group's dining table. Even if you are not the host or hostess, it is every kitchen group member's responsibility to make sure that the buffet and dining tables are set properly. A properly set table adds to the enjoyment of the meal.

Serving a meal buffet-style is extremely efficient for entertaining. A buffet enables a large group of people to serve themselves easily in a short period of time. This is particularly important at school.

Elaborate buffet table decorations are not a Chinese custom. The Chinese prefer the attention to be centered on the artistry of the food. However, Chinese collectibles or flowers in a Chinese vase will add to the beauty of the table and the spirit of the meal. You might use one or more of the following: bamboo matting as a table cover, a clear glass bowl with floating blossoms, lacquered boxes, or Chinese lanterns.

The correct placement of the food is important. Everything should be organized to assure ease in serving. The foods for each course are placed next to each other in the order you wish them to be selected. The foods for the Chinese meal designed for your class are placed on the buffet table and served in the following order:

- Rice
- Chicken Dish
- Pork Dish
- Vegetable Dish
- Doughs
- Soup
- Sweets

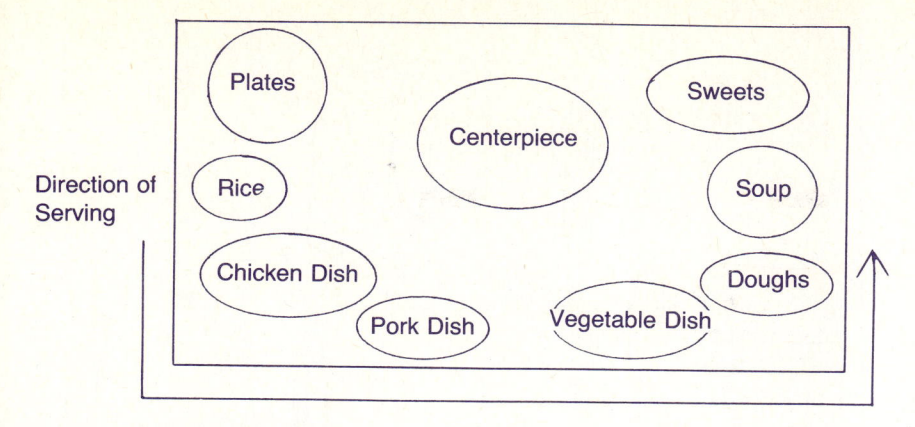

Figure 6.1. Buffet Table

Figure 6.1 illustrates a correctly set buffet table for your Chinese meal.

It is easier for you to carry and fill your plate if you pick up the soup near the end of the buffet. This way, the soup will be eaten soon after it is served and will still be warm.

DINING TABLE SETTINGS

How you set the dining table in your classroom depends on the equipment available. If you plan to use chopsticks, place them, instead of the knife, to the right of the plate and eliminate the fork. If you want to try chopsticks but still use flatware, follow the basic tablesetting plan below, and place the chopsticks above the plate. The following directions tell how a basic table should be set. Refer to Figure 6.2 as you read the instructions.

1. The napkin, plate, and flatware should be placed one inch from the edge of the placemat. If you have trouble judging an inch, use your thumb as a ruler. From the tip of your thumb to the first joint is approximately one inch.
2. If you are serving buffet style, the plates will be on the buffet table. The utensils must be correctly positioned on the dining table so that there will be room for the plate after it has been filled from the buffet. To set the table properly, use one plate as a guide to position the utensils correctly.
3. The knife is placed to the right of the plate, with the sharp edge facing the plate.
4. The spoon is placed next to the knife.
5. The waterglass is placed at the tip of the knife.
6. The fork is placed to the left of the plate, with the tines facing up.
7. The napkin is placed beside the fork and folded so that it opens like a book.

Now that you are familiar with the way to set a dining table, draw a place setting on the placemat in Figure 6.3. Include the

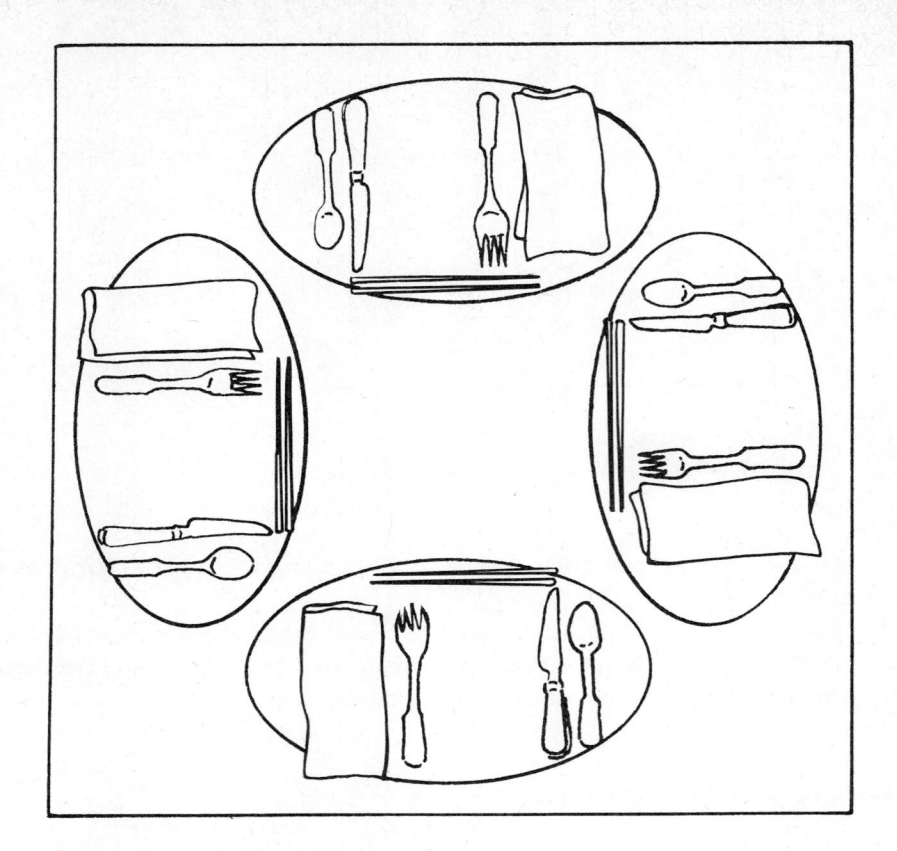

Figure 6.2. Dining Table

table equipment that you have available for your kitchen group. The completed drawing will remind you how the table should be set for your Chinese meal.

TABLE MANNERS

Good table manners allow you and your companions to have a pleasant mealtime experience. Your concern for the pleasure of others at the table is obvious from your good manners. Be aware of good table manners and practice them while eating at all times—not just in the classroom. Eventually good manners will become second nature.

The Chinese use chopsticks instead of knives and forks. Since

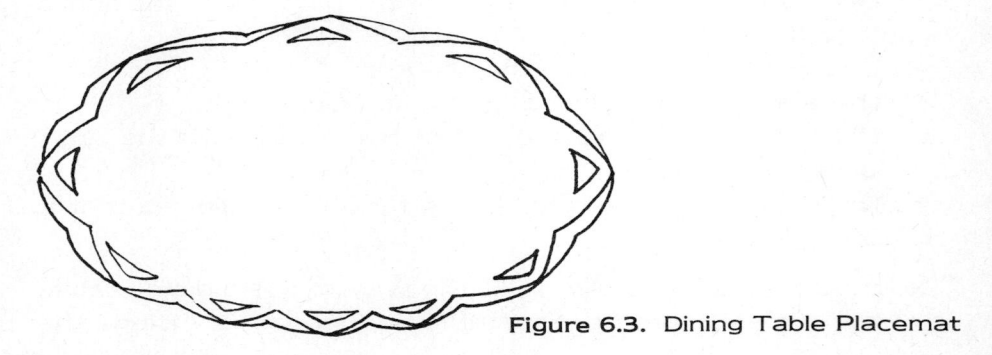

Figure 6.3. Dining Table Placemat

Section Two ● Planning Your Chinese Meal

Chinese food is chopped into bit-sized pieces or cooked until tender, it can easily be eaten without being cut with a knife. Chopsticks are made of silver, ivory, lacquer, plastic, or bamboo. Bamboo is used because it can withstand heat or cold and is not slippery. In Chinese homes, bamboo chopsticks are also used as cooking utensils.

After your meal is finished, you will evaluate the manners you observed during the meal with your kitchen group. Here are some suggestions for good table manners.

1. Make sure you are well-groomed before you serve yourself at the buffet table. Check that your hands and fingernails are clean and your hair and clothes are neat.
2. After you have served yourself, put your plate at your table setting, then sit down from the left side of your chair.
3. Unfold your napkin when the host or hostess at your table does. Do not shake it open. A small napkin may be opened completely, while a large dinner napkin may be left folded in half.
4. Begin eating when your host or hostess does. Eat slowly, one piece of food at a time. Do not talk with your mouth full; take small bites that can be easily swallowed, so that you will be able to talk. Chew your food quietly with your mouth closed.
5. Sit upright when you eat. Keep your arms off the table and your hands away from your face and hair. Do not play with anything on the table.
6. It is the responsibility of the host or hostess to keep the conversation moving while making sure that everyone is included. Each person, however, should contribute to the conversation. Listen to others and acknowledge what they say.
7. When you have finished eating, place your knife (carving end well in the center of the plate) and fork (tines up) across the center of your plate, parallel to each other. When everyone has finished eating, the host or hostess will put his or her napkin on the table. This signals that the meal is completed. Place your napkin on the table without refolding or crumpling it. Return it, loosely gathered, to its original place to the left of the plate. If you have to get up during the meal, put your napkin on your chair. If you put it on the table, it may get in the way of the person sitting next to you. Also, if your napkin is messy, it isn't an attractive sight for anyone to see while eating.

7

YOUR CHINESE MEAL PLANNING FORM

You will use your Chinese Meal Planning Form during the cooking and evaluation days. On the cooking day you will prepare as much of the recipe as possible. On evaluation day, you will finish preparing the recipe, set the dining table, arrange the food on the buffet, serve yourself, eat, and write an evaluation of your recipe. The planning form has a time schedule to follow, so you will easily be able to complete all your responsibilities on both days. If you do run behind, the time schedule on your planning form lets you know what still must be completed.

The success of both the cooking and evaluation days depends on the ability of the kitchen group members to work together to ensure that all the duties are completed correctly. You are expected to help other students in your kitchen group if you finish your job duties early. Your completed planning form will have the names and duties of the members of your kitchen group, so you will know how you can help each of them. For example, if you, as the host or hostess, finish your assigned duties early and see that the cook has not completed the recipe, you can offer to help. You will know how to help because you have read the recipe and are familiar with the ingredients. Carefully check to see that the place settings are correct on the dining table (refer to Chapter 6). Be aware of all of your kitchen group's duties, and if you see something has not been done right, alert the person who has that job responsibility and offer to help if you can.

HOW TO COMPLETE YOUR PLANNING FORM

Remove Activity 6, Chinese Meal Planning Form. Figure 7.1 shows a sample filled-in Chinese Meal Planning Form. Use this illustration as a guide for completing Activity 6. Use the front of

Activity 6 for a five-member kitchen group and the back for a four-member kitchen group.

Follow these directions when completing Activity 6.

Write your name, class period, kitchen number, and date due.

Write the names of each recipe your class will prepare. List your kitchen group's recipe first.

Write the names of each kitchen group member next to the appropriate kitchen job.

List recipe ingredients not in the kitchen. Carefully read the recipe your kitchen group will prepare and determine what ingredients will have to be obtained from outside your assigned kitchen.

Once you have determined which ingredients are not in your kitchen, list those ingredients and the amounts you will need. This will enable your teacher to know what has to be purchased from the grocery store or obtained from another storage area.

Each kitchen will have some staples such as salt, pepper, flour, sugar, baking powder, and baking soda. Check to see what staples are available in your kitchen. List these staples below:

STAPLES IN THE KITCHEN

1. _____   4. _____   7. _____

2. _____   5. _____   8. _____

3. _____   6. _____   9. _____

List equipment not in the kitchen. Refer to Figure 7.1. The missing equipment will be placed in the supply area ready for your kitchen group's use at the beginning of your cooking day. Devise a time schedule for all duties assigned to you on *cooking day*.

- Write the time you allot to read the recipe on cooking day.
- Write the time you allot for preparation duties assigned to you for cooking day. Write a few notes that will help you perform these duties.
- Write the time you allot for cleanup duties. Write your cleanup duty assignments.

Devise a time schedule for all duties assigned to you on *evaluation day*.

- Write the time you allot to read the recipe on evaluation day.
- Write the time you allot for preparation duties assigned to you for evaluation day. Include the time for final food preparation and setting the buffet and dining table. Write a few notes that will help you perform these duties.

Class Menu (1) Fried Rice (2) Won Ton Soup (3) Egg Rolls
(Your Kitchen's Recipe)
(4) Sweet and Sour Pork (5) Green Beans + Bean Curd (6) Almond Float

Name	Kitchen Job	Preparation Duties	Cleanup Duties
Carlos Ramirez	Cook	Prepare the recipe; prepare food for serving	Check kitchen (canisters, cupboards, drawers, counters, etc.) for cleanliness and order
Mary Hughes	Assistant Cook	Assist cook	Wash equipment; scour sink
Diana Stoltz	Host or Hostess	Obtain supplies needed; set table/set buffet	Clear table; clean table and chairs
Bob Iversen	General Assistant 1	Assume duties of anyone absent; assist where needed	Dry dishes
Jennifer Chin	General Assistant 2	Do weekly duty (see instructor); turn in evaluations; assist where needed	Put dishes away; clean range

Recipe Ingredients not in the Kitchen: 2 cups rice, 2 eggs, ½ cup fried bacon, ½ cup green onion, 3 T. soy sauce

Equipment not in the Kitchen: none

| Cooking-Day Time Schedule || Evaluation-Day Time Schedule ||
Time	Duty	Time	Duty
8:00-8:05	Read Recipe	8:00-8:05	Read Recipe
8:05-8:20	cook rice, cool, chop green onions	8:05-8:20	fry bacon, crumble, cook eggs, rice & other ingredients, place on buffet
8:20-8:40	refrigerate rice and onions	8:20-8:35	Serve Yourself and Eat
		8:35-8:40	Cleanup: check kitchen
8:40-8:50	Cleanup: check kitchen	8:40-8:50	Written Evaluation: Refer to Chinese Sample Activity 7.

Figure 7.1. Sample Filled-in Activity 6

- Write the time you allot to serve yourself and eat.
- Write the time you allot for cleanup duties. Write your cleanup duty assignments.
- Write the time you allot for the written evaluation.

Give your completed Chinese Menu Planning Form to your instructor for evaluation.

ARE YOU READY?

The success of your dish depends on your following recipe directions exactly and on your ability to complete your duties on time. On cooking day, use your completed Chinese Meal Planning Form to guide you through your duties and time schedule. All the duties must be finished and as much of the recipe prepared as possible, so that everything can be completed on evaluation day.

Before you start your duties, a quick review is necessary. Read the following questions. If you answer no to any of these questions, check your notes or any other source of information you have for help.

1. Are you familiar with your kitchen group's recipe?
2. Do you know what the cooking terms mean in your recipe?
3. Do you know your kitchen job assignment?
4. Do you know your preparation duties?
5. Do you know your cleanup duties?
6. Are you aware of your time schedule?
7. Do you know your co-workers' duties?
8. Are you prepared to help your co-workers if you finish your duties early?
9. Do you know where the equipment is located in the kitchen so that preparation and cleanup will be efficient?

When you have answered yes to all the questions, you are ready to begin your cooking-day duties. Enjoy your experience with China's cuisine.

請盡情
享受

Section Three

EVALUATING YOUR CHINESE MEAL

Whether you are evaluating a trip you have taken, a movie you have seen, or a meal you have helped prepare, you should always be aware of what did not meet your expectations. Your judgments and observations are important.

Consider the following questions concerning your Chinese meal:

- Did your kitchen group prepare a dish of the quality and taste you expected? How did the dish vary from your expectations?
- After tasting the dish, what changes would you suggest in the ingredients for the next time?
- How would you rate the appearance, texture, and flavor of all the dishes?
- What one dish did you especially enjoy? Give your reasons for this choice.

Answers to these questions will help in your evaluation of the foods that were prepared by you and your class. Remember, constructive criticism is the key to becoming a better cook, and an honest evaluation will improve your cooking in the future. In this section you will find

- a sample Chinese Product Evaluation Form
- a Chinese Product Evaluation Form for you to complete

8

CHINESE PRODUCT EVALUATION

Three criteria will be used to evaluate the food your class has prepared. These are appearance, texture, and flavor.

Appearance

Appearance is the color, size, and shape of the product. For example, Sweet and Sour Pork will have a good appearance if the pork is fried golden brown, and the pork, green peppers, and carrots are all uniform in size. Chinese cooks insist that the food in the dish look appealing. The sauce that covers the pork and vegetables should be thick and clear. If a product looks so attractive to you that you can hardly wait to taste it, it should rate high in appearance.

Texture

The texture of a product is described as crisp, crunchy, flaky, moist, dry, tender, light, soft, or hard. A variety of contrasting textures in one dish is appealing. For example, Green Beans with Rice has a light, clear glaze over crisp, tender green beans, crunchy water chestnuts, and smooth bean curd. A dish with pleasing texture should earn a high rating.

Flavor

Flavor is a blend of taste and aroma. The aroma of food influences its flavor. Chinese cooks have mastered the art of combining many different flavors in one dish. For example, some of the flavor of Pon Pon Chicken comes from the aroma of its sauce ingredients. The *cayenne pepper* and *crushed red pepper* give the initial blast of heat; then the other flavors come through: the pungent aroma of *peppercorns*, the nippy taste of *ginger root*, the saltiness of *soy sauce*, the rich aromatic flavor of *sesame seed* paste, the tanginess of vinegar, the smoothness of peanut oil, the delicate taste of *green onions*, and the pungency of garlic. This spicy, flavorful sauce is in sharp contrast, in typical Chinese fashion, to the fresh, uncomplicated, pure flavor of the chicken.

If the appearance, texture, or flavor of a particular dish is not what you think it should be, try to determine what caused the disappointment. Improper cooking techniques negatively affect a recipe. For example, for Fried Sweet Wonton, if the oil is not the right temperature, the *wontons* will not cook properly. Either they will be overdone, too crisp, and dried out, or they will be underdone, soggy, and oily.

Cutting is a very important Chinese cooking technique. In Broccoli with Rice, if you do not cut the broccoli into uniform pieces, it will not all be cooked properly at the same time. Some pieces may be overdone, and some may be underdone.

Chinese cooks are expert at timing their cooking. Good timing is a necessity when preparing foods that cook fast, have ingredients added at different times, and often require several cooking methods. Wontons for soup should be simmered until just done. *Egg rolls* should be *stir-fried* until *crisp-tender*. These cooking techniques—*simmering*, *deep-fat-frying*, and stir-frying—require you to watch the food while it is cooking. Get to know when food looks finished. The times called for in the recipes are approximate. Try to visualize the steps before you start, so you won't be preoccupied with exact minutes. If you don't have everything ready when you start one of the dishes, the food may cook too long, and the finished product may not taste or look the way it should.

Evaluating the Chinese dish you have made will help you improve it the next time you make it. By altering the ingredients, you can create a different, but just as pleasing, dish. Your sight, taste, and imagination will provide you with clues on what to add or eliminate. Figure 8.1 is an example of a recipe for Fried Rice (compare with Figure 5.2) that can be altered with the following variations.

By applying one or a combination of the following ideas, you change the flavor of Fried Rice:

1. Add ½ cup frozen peas, thawed.
2. Add ½ cup toasted cashew nuts.
3. Add 1 cup sliced mushrooms.
4. Add 1 clove garlic, crushed.
5. Substitute ½ cup barbecued pork for shrimp.
6. Substitute ½ cup diced ham for shrimp.
7. Substitute ½ cup cooked chicken for shrimp.

Fried Rice

2 cups rice
4 cups water
2 tbsp. oil
2 eggs, *slightly beaten*

½ tsp. salt
⅛ tsp. pepper
½ cup green onion, chopped fine
3 tbsp. soy sauce

Figure 8.1. Fried Rice Recipe

8. Substitute for shrimp, 12 oz. (1-inch-wide-by-⅛-inch-thick strips) stir-fried flank steak, seasoned with *oyster sauce* and sesame oil.

EVALUATION FORM

Evaluation forms are used to help improve your cooking. Study the example of a completed evaluation form for Mary Hughes (see Figure 8.2).

Note that Mary wrote the names of the Chinese recipes her class prepared. She evaluated the foods by indicating in the appropriate column her opinion of their appearance, texture, and flavor. Mary then suggested a change in the ingredients for the dish she helped prepare. Next, she discussed her questions concerning the preparation of the recipe with her kitchen group and checked the appropriate spaces for the answers. After doing this, Mary found why her dish did not turn out as well as she had expected. She then wrote a paragraph telling what was

Write the names of the products that will be evaluated, and check (√) the space that best describes the product: E = Excellent, G = Good, P = Poor.

	Appearance			Texture			Flavor		
	E	G	P	E	G	P	E	G	P
1. Fried Rice			√	√			√		
2. Won Ton Soup	√			√			√		
3. Egg Rolls			√			√		√	
4. Sweet & Sour Pork	√			√				√	
5. Green Bean & Bean Curd	√			√			√		
6. Almond Float		√			√		√		
7.									
8.									

Write the name of the recipe your kitchen group prepared: *Fried Rice*
Describe how you would change the ingredients of your recipe to make a different product:
I would stir-fry 12 oz. flank steak (sliced 1" wide by ⅛" thick strips) seasoned in 1 tbsp. oyster sauce, 1 tsp. oil, and substitute this for shrimp.

Figure 8.2. Sample Filled-in Activity 7 (Continued)

Figure 8.2. (Continued)

Answer these questions about your recipe preparation. Check (√) the appropriate space.

	Yes	No
1. Were the ingredient amounts measured correctly?	√	
2. Were the proper utensils used for the measuring?	√	
3. Were the correct techniques used to prepare the ingredients?	√	
4. Were the ingredients added in the right order?		√
5. Was the correct size cookware used?	√	
6. Was the cookware prepared correctly?	√	
7. If the oven was used, was it preheated?		

Write a paragraph that explains what contributed to the product's success and what could have been done to improve the product:

We liked the delicate flavor produced by combining shrimp, onions, soy sauce, eggs and rice. We didn't realize how important it was to add the ingredients in order. We added the soy sauce before we put in the rice and the eggs turned brown. Next time, we will add the rice before the soy sauce and the rice will absorb the color more than the eggs.

Describe the good table manners that made the Chinese meal more enjoyable for your kitchen group: *I was glad we remembered to sit down from the left side of our chairs. That made it easier for everyone. We watched our hostess Diana, to know when to place our napkins in our laps and begin to eat.*

successful about the dish and how it should be prepared the next time to ensure the best results. Finally, after a discussion with her kitchen group, Mary described the good table manners that made the Chinese meal with her group members enjoyable.

Remove Activity 7, the Chinese Product Evaluation Form. Use the sample Figure 8.2 to complete Activity 7 and give it to your instructor for evaluation.

Name _____ Class Period _____ Kitchen Number _____ Date Due _____

Activity 1 CHINESE FOOD HISTORY REVIEW

Test your knowledge of Chinese Food History by completing the following sentences with the proper word or words. Place your answer in the answer column at the right.

Answers

1. It is believed that the Chinese cooked millet in vessels by __?__ as early as 5,000 to 3,000 B.C.

   1. _____

2. The ancient Chinese, unlike their neighboring herdsmen and hunters, relied on __?__ for their food.

   2. _____

3. As early as 1000 B.C., the Chinese culture, including the refinement of food, was highly developed. __?__, __?__, and __?__ were used for seasoning and are still an important part of Chinese cooking today.

   3. _____
   _____
   _____

4. __?__ was an early influence on the rules for "correct" food preparation and presentation.

   4. _____

5. A Chinese dining table is usually __?__ so that conversation can flow easily and food can be reached by everyone.

   5. _____

6. Even though China is slightly larger than the United States, only __?__ of China can be cultivated as opposed to 80 percent of the land in the United States.

   6. _____

7. The population of China, more than 1 billion, is __?__ times that of the United States.

   7. _____

8. Fast food preparation techniques such as stir-frying developed because China has little __?__ to use for cooking.

   8. _____

9. Ingredients are cut into small pieces because they cook __?__ and, as a result, use less fuel.

   9. _____

10. China's four major cuisines are named after the city of __?__ in the north, the city of __?__ in the east, the province of __?__ in the west, and the city of __?__ in the south.

    10. _____
    _____
    _____
    _____

11. Cantonese is the best known Chinese cooking in America because the people from Canton were the first to __?__ to America.

    11. _____

12. The most widely produced meat and poultry in China are __?__, __?__ and __?__ because they are inexpensive and easy to raise.

    12. _____
    _____
    _____

13. The use of __?__ food in Chinese cooking may stem from the days when the Chinese prepared for famines.

    13. _____

14. The main dish in the Chinese meal is __?__ or another __?__ food.

    14. _____
    _____

Name _____ Class Period _____ Kitchen Number _____ Date Due _____

Activity 2 CHINESE RECIPE MATCH

This activity will test your knowledge of popular and classic Chinese cooking. In the space provided in the answer column at the right of each definition in Column 2, print the letter of the phrase in Column 1 that matches the definition.

	Column 1		Column 2	Answers
a.	Egg Drop	1.	The egg cooks into long threads	1. ____
b.	Bean Curd	2.	The basic starch in northern China	2. ____
c.	Paper Wrapped	3.	Known in China as "meat without bones"	3. ____
d.	Ginger Root	4.	Most widely used meat in China	4. ____
e.	Sizzling Rice	5.	A crispy sweet eaten between meals	5. ____
f.	Broccoli	6.	This is hard, soft, cold, and warm at the same time	6. ____
g.	Chicken	7.	Served in the middle of a multi-course Chinese meal	7. ____
h.	Pork			
i.	Water Chestnuts	8.	A hot seasoning from Western China	8. ____
j.	Sichuan Pepper	9.	The way to seal in a food's flavor and juice	9. ____
k.	Wonton	10.	A gnarled tuber used for seasoning	10. ____
l.	Noodles	11.	A soup with dumplings of the same name	11. ____
m.	Steamed Buns	12.	A Chinese omelet	12. ____
n.	Almond Cookies	13.	A soup introduced by nomadic Mongols	13. ____
o.	Onion Cakes	14.	A dough food popular as dim sum	14. ____
p.	Egg Foo Yung	15.	A dough cooked in oil	15. ____
q.	Spun Apples	16.	The symbol of life	16. ____
r.	Fire Pot	17.	One of the few Chinese dishes which requires baking	17. ____
s.	Pot Stickers			
t.	Fried Sweet Wontons	18.	A pan-fried dumpling	18. ____
u.	Egg Rolls	19.	Not a nut, but the tuber of a water plant	19. ____
v.	Almond Float	20.	Stir-frying retains its color and flavor	20. ____
w.	Rice	21.	Favored over pork or beef in China	21. ____
		22.	A symbolic dish for New Year's Day	22. ____
		23.	A soup to delight the senses	23. ____

Activity 2 ● Chinese Recipe Match   41

Name _____ Class Period _____ Kitchen Number _____ Date Due _____

Activity 3 CHINESE MAP REVIEW

To complete this activity, match the recipe with the culinary region for which it is known. Write the letter of the recipe on the lines provided within each region of the map. For example, the first recipe is Egg Drop Soup. After reading the recipe for Egg Drop Soup, you know it is identified with the northern region. The letter "a" is written on the line in the northern region as an example.

Recipe

a. Egg Drop Soup
b. Sizzling Rice Soup
c. Wonton Soup
d. Chicken with Bean Sprouts
e. Paper-Wrapped Chicken
f. Pon Pon Chicken
g. Noodles in Meat Sauce
h. Shredded Pork
i. Sweet and Sour Pork
j. Bean Curd with Rice
k. Broccoli with Rice
l. Green Beans with Rice
m. Egg Rolls
n. Pork Steamed Buns
o. Pot Stickers
p. Almond Float
q. Fried Sweet Wonton
r. Spun Apples
s. Almond Cookies
t. Egg Foo Yung
u. Fire Pot
v. Fried Rice
w. Onion Cakes

Culinary Regions of China

Activity 3 ● Chinese Map Review   43

Name _____ Class Period _____ Kitchen Number _____ Date Due _____

Activity 4 SELECTING YOUR CHINESE MENU

By completing this activity, you will have a better understanding of the Chinese recipes. This will make choosing your menu easier.

Place a check mark (√) in the appropriate column(s) to complete the following activity.	SOUPS			CHICKEN			PORK			VEGE-TABLES			DOUGHS			SWEETS		
	Egg Drop Soup	Sizzling Rice Soup	Wonton Soup	Chicken with Bean Sprouts	Paper-Wrapped Chicken	Pon Pon Chicken	Noodles in Meat Sauce	Shredded Pork	Sweet and Sour Pork	Bean Curd with Rice	Broccoli with Rice	Green Beans with Rice	Egg Rolls	Pork Steamed Buns	Pot Stickers	Almond Float	Fried Sweet Wonton	Spun Apples
1. The recipes that use cooking techniques you have not tried.																		
2. The recipes that have unfamiliar ingredients.																		
3. The recipes that you have tasted before.																		
4. The recipes that you have tasted and would like to taste again.																		
5. The recipes that you have not tasted but would like to taste.																		
6. The soup recipe that would be your first choice to taste.																		
7. The chicken recipe that would be your first choice to taste.																		
8. The pork recipe that would be your first choice to taste.																		
9. The vegetable recipe that would be your first choice to taste.																		
10. The dough recipe that would be your first choice to taste.																		
11. The sweets recipe that would be your first choice to taste.																		

(Continued)

Activity 4 (Continued)

You have now selected the dishes you would like to taste. Will your choices provide a variety in color, shape, texture, and flavor? After carefully considering this question and making any changes, write your recipe selections for the menu you would like your class to prepare.

Soup _____   Vegetable Dish _____

Chicken Dish _____   Dough _____

Pork Dish _____   Sweets _____

Name _____ Class Period _____ Kitchen Number _____ Date Due _____

Activity 5 CHINESE MEAL COST SHEET

SECTION A Name of Recipe:

(1) Recipe Ingredients	(2) Amount Required	(3) Price Per Item	(4) Amount of Store Container	(5) Cost Computation	(6) Total Ingredient Cost

SECTION B ──────────────────────→ Total Recipe Cost: _____

Total Recipe Cost ÷ Number of Servings = Cost Per Serving

SECTION C ──→ (_____) ÷ (_____) = (_____)

SECTION D

Final Class Meal Cost		
(1) Recipe	(2) Recipe Cost	(3) Cost Per Serving
Soup:		
Chicken Dish:		
Pork Dish:		
Vegetable Dish:		
Dough:		
Sweets:		

SECTION E TOTALS: Meal Costs: | Meal Cost Per Serving:

Name _____ Class Period _____ Kitchen Number _____ Date Due _____

Activity 6 CHINESE MEAL PLANNING FORM (FOUR-MEMBER KITCHEN)

Class Menu (1) _____ (2) _____ (3) _____
(Your Kitchen's Recipe)
(4) _____ (5) _____ (6) _____

Kitchen Jobs and Duties

Name	Kitchen Job	Preparation Duties	Cleanup Duties
	Cook	Prepare the recipe; prepare food for serving	Check kitchen (canisters, cupboards, drawers, counters, etc.) for cleanliness and order
	Assistant Cook	Assist cook	Wash dishes; scour sink
	Host or Hostess	Obtain supplies needed; set table/set buffet; do weekly duty (see instructor)	Clear table; clean table and chairs
	General Assistant	Assume duties of anyone absent; turn in evaluation; assist where needed	Dry dishes; put dishes away

Recipe Ingredients not in the Kitchen: _____

_____

Equipment not in the Kitchen: _____

Cooking-Day Time Schedule		Evaluation-Day Time Schedule	
Time	Duty	Time	Duty
_____	Read Recipe	_____	Read Recipe
_____	_____	_____	_____
_____	_____	_____	_____
_____	_____	_____	_____
_____	_____	_____	Serve Yourself and Eat
_____	_____	_____	Cleanup: _____
_____	Cleanup: _____		Written Evaluation: Refer to Activity 7.

Activity 6 ● Chinese Meal Planning Form (Four-Member Kitchen)   49

Name _____ Class Period _____ Kitchen Number _____ Date Due _____

Activity 6   CHINESE MEAL PLANNING FORM (FIVE-MEMBER KITCHEN)

Class Menu   (1) _____ (2) _____ (3) _____
        (Your Kitchen's Recipe)
                (4) _____ (5) _____ (6) _____

Kitchen Jobs and Duties			
Name	**Kitchen Job**	**Preparation Duties**	**Cleanup Duties**
	Cook	Prepare the recipe; prepare food for serving	Check kitchen (canisters, cupboards, drawers, counters, etc.) for cleanliness and order
	Assistant Cook	Assist cook	Wash equipment; scour sink
	Host or Hostess	Obtain supplies needed; set table/set buffet	Clear table; clean table and chairs
	General Assistant 1	Assume duties of anyone absent; assist where needed	Dry dishes
	General Assistant 2	Do weekly duty (see instructor); turn in evaluations; assist where needed	Put dishes away; clean range

Recipe Ingredients not in the Kitchen: _____
_____
_____

Equipment not in the Kitchen: _____

Cooking-Day Time Schedule		Evaluation-Day Time Schedule	
Time	**Duty**	**Time**	**Duty**
_____	Read Recipe	_____	Read Recipe
_____	_____	_____	_____
	_____		_____
	_____		_____
	_____		Serve Yourself and Eat
	_____		Cleanup: _____
	Cleanup: _____		Written Evaluation: Refer to Activity 7.

50   Activity 6 ● Chinese Meal Planning Form (Five-Member Kitchen)

Name _____ Class Period _____ Kitchen Number _____ Date Due _____

Activity 7 CHINESE PRODUCT EVALUATION FORM

Write the names of the products that will be evaluated, and check (✓) the space that best describes the product: E = Excellent, G = Good, P = Poor.

	Appearance			Texture			Flavor		
	E	G	P	E	G	P	E	G	P
1.									
2.									
3.									
4.									
5.									
6.									
7.									
8.									

Write the name of the recipe your kitchen prepared: _____

Describe how you would change the ingredients of your recipe to make a different product:

_____
_____
_____
_____
_____

Answer these questions about your recipe preparation. Check (✓) the appropriate space.

		Yes	No
1.	Were the ingredient amounts measured correctly?		
2.	Were the proper utensils used for measuring?		
3.	Were the correct techniques used to prepare the ingredients?		
4.	Were the ingredients added in the right order?		
5.	Was the correct size cookware used?		
6.	Was the cookware prepared correctly?		
7.	If the oven was used, was it preheated?		

Activity 7 (Continued)

Write a paragraph that explains:
1. What contributed to the product's success?
2. What could have been done to improve the product?

_____
_____
_____
_____
_____
_____

Describe the good table manners that made the meal more enjoyable for your kitchen group:

_____
_____
_____
_____
_____
_____

EGG DROP SOUP

Food Category: Soup　　　　　　　　　　　　　　　　　　　　　　　　　　　*Low Cost*

6 cups chicken broth
4 oz. spinach

1 green onion
2 eggs

1 tsp. salt
2 tbsp. cornstarch dissolved in 2 tbsp. cold water

1. Wash and separate spinach leaves. Break into 4-inch sections.
2. Beat eggs.
3. Bring chicken stock to boil. Add salt and spinach.
4. Add cornstarch paste. Stir a few seconds until stock thickens.
5. Slowly add eggs. Stir gently in one direction so threads form. Turn off heat immediately. Taste. Add salt if necessary.
6. Pour soup into warm bowl. Garnish with chopped green onion. Serve at once. Serves 6.

Recipe Tips

- *If pressed for time, use bouillon cubes (one cube per cup of water) to make broth.*
- *Warm bowl by placing it in hot water.*

SIZZLING RICE SOUP

Food Category: Soup　　　　　　　　　　　　　　　　　　　　　　　　*Moderate Cost*

Rice Crusts

2 cups water
1 cup long-grain rice
½ tsp. salt

Soup

1 qt. chicken broth
½ tsp. salt
½ tsp. light soy sauce
½ tsp. sugar
dash of pepper
1 tbsp. cornstarch mixed with ¼ cup water
¼ cup shelled shrimp
½ cup cooked chicken, diced
½ cup peas
½ cup small mushrooms
3 tbsp. minced green onions
oil for deep-frying

1. To prepare rice crusts, bring water to boil in heavy pan. Add salt and rice. Stir and cover tightly. *Do not peek.*
2. Turn heat to medium. Cook for 5 minutes. Turn heat to medium low. Cook for 30 minutes.
3. Lift out soft white rice and use golden crusts on bottom of pan.
4. Bring chicken broth to boil. Add salt, soy sauce, sugar, and pepper.
5. Stir in cornstarch mixture until soup thickens and becomes smooth.
6. Add shrimp, chicken, peas, and mushrooms. Simmer for 5 minutes.
7. Heat oil in heavy skillet to 375 degrees and deep-fry rice crusts. Drain on paper towel, place in warm bowl.
8. Pour soup into warm bowl. Sprinkle with green onions. Serve immediately.
9. Drop rice crusts into hot soup at table. Serves 6.

Recipe Tips

- *Smell steam from rice pot frequently during 5-minute cooking time. Should it begin to smell burnt, immediately reduce temperature.*
- *Leftover rice may be used for making fried rice.*
- *Correct oil temperature is essential. If oil is too cool, foods will absorb it and become greasy; if too hot, foods will burn before they are cooked. Use a deep-fat-frying thermometer to check the oil tem-*

Egg Drop Soup is prepared all over China, but this version is most typical of northern China because it uses spinach as one of its ingredients. Spinach grows well in northern China, where winters are cold, summers are hot, and growing seasons are short.

This recipe for Egg Drop Soup is very much like everyday meatless Chinese soup. When the egg is added to the hot soup, it forms long egg threads.

The Chinese place a tureen of soup in the center of the table, along with the other dishes of food. At a banquet there may be several soups served throughout the meal. The Chinese think of soups as a means of cleansing the palate; thus they take the place of water, which is not served with meals.

---

perature. If you don't have a thermometer, drop a 1-inch cube of bread into hot fat. Time 1 minute. If bread is brown, oil temperature is correct.
- *Warm bowls by placing them in hot water.*

- To divide the preparation time of this recipe into two days, complete Steps 1 through 3, covering and refrigerating rice and cooked chicken overnight. Begin with Step 4 the next day.

Sizzling Rice Soup is popular all over China. This version is from eastern China, where sizzling rice dishes originated. Soy sauce and sugar are both common to the seasoning style of Shanghai in the east, and much of China's rice grows around the hundreds of shallow lakes formed by the Yangtze River.

Some say an enterprising cook created this dish centuries ago. A traveling emperor stopped at an inn late one night to eat. The only food left was an overcooked crust of rice at the bottom of a pot and a bowl of soup. The cook heated the rice until it was very hot, put it into the best bowl available, then poured the hot soup on top. To everyone's surprise the rice made a singing, sizzling sound! Thus sizzling rice was born, and the cook was praised for the discovery.

Sizzling Rice Soup appeals to three of our senses: those of the ears, the nose, and the palate.

WONTON SOUP

Food Category: Soup *Moderate Cost*

- ¾ lb. whole fresh spinach
- ¾ lb. lean boneless pork, ground fine
- 4 tsp. soy sauce
- ¾ tsp. finely chopped fresh ginger root
- ¾ tsp. salt
- 1 recipe wonton wrappers, prepared according to directions or
- 1 lb. egg roll wrappers cut into 3½-inch squares
- 6 cups chicken broth
- 1 cup fresh spinach leaves, torn into small pieces

Wonton Wrappers
- 3¾ cups flour
- 1 tsp. salt
- 2 eggs
- 1 cup cold water

1. Wash whole spinach leaves. Cook in small amount of boiling water until tender. Drain, squeeze dry, and chop.
2. Combine pork, soy sauce, ginger root, and salt. Mix thoroughly. Add cooked spinach. Stir.

Prepare Wonton Wrappers:

3. Beat eggs lightly. Sift salt and flour into bowl. Make a *well* in center of flour. Pour in eggs and cold water. With your fingers, mix ingredients until they can be gathered into soft ball. *Knead* dough in bowl for 4 or 5 minutes or until dough is smooth but still soft.
4. Divide dough into 4 equal balls. With a rolling pin, on a lightly floured surface, roll each ball into a 14-inch square, about 1/16 inch thick. For soup wontons or deep fried wontons, cut dough into 3½-inch squares with sharp knife or pastry wheel. *Makes about 4 dozen.*
5. To wrap filling, follow the steps below and refer to the illustrations (on back):
   (1) Place 1 tsp. of filling just below center of wrapper. Fold one corner over filling. Tuck edge under filling.
   (2) Dip finger in water and moisten exposed sides of wrapper. Roll up filled cylinder, leaving ½ inch of wrapper unrolled at top.
   (3) Beneath the roll, join ends and overlap

CHICKEN WITH BEAN SPROUTS

Food Category: Chicken *High Cost*

- 2 whole chicken breasts
- ½ egg white
- ¼ tsp. salt
- 2 tsp. cornstarch
- 1 tbsp. cold water
- 2 cups fresh bean sprouts
- ¼ cup cooked ham
- 2 tbsp. snow pea pods or green pepper
- 1 cup oil
- ½ tsp. sugar
- 1 tsp. cornstarch combined with 2 tbsp. water

1. Skin and bone chicken. Slice chicken along the grain into strips ⅛ inch thick. Cut again into 2-inch-long *julienne* strips. Mix chicken with egg white, salt, cornstarch, and cold water. Refrigerate for 30 minutes.
2. Soak bean sprouts in cold water for 10 minutes. Drain well.
3. Cut ham into julienne strips. *Shred* snow pea pods. Set aside.
4. Place a strainer over pot near cooking area. Heat *wok* or skillet to very hot over medium heat. Add oil and heat to about 280 degrees. Add chicken and stir quickly. Chicken shreds should separate within a minute. Pour oil and chicken mixture into strainer. After oil drains away, transfer chicken to a dish. Reserve oil.
5. Heat the same wok over high heat with 2 tbsp. reserved oil. Add bean sprouts and snow pea pods. *Stir-fry* for 1 minute. Add ham and cooked chicken. Stir-fry, mixing well. Add cornstarch and water mixture to chicken. Stir over high heat until liquid thickens and chicken is coated with a clear glaze. Serve hot.

Serves 6.

Recipe Tip

- *To get ½ egg white, gently beat whole egg white. Measure. Use ½ total amount.*

Step 1
Step 2
Step 3

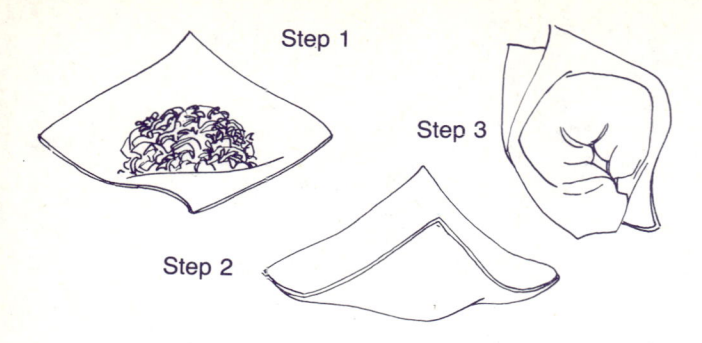

Wrapping Wontons

slightly. Pinch the ends firmly together. Place finished wontons on plate and cover with dry towel.

6. Bring 2 quarts water to boil. Drop in wontons. Return to boil, reduce heat, and cook uncovered for 5 minutes or until tender and a bit resistant to the bite. Drain.
7. Wash 1 cup torn spinach leaves. Bring broth to boil in pan. Add spinach and wontons. Return to boil. Pour into warm bowl.
Serves 6.

Recipe Tips

- *Do not overknead or dough will become too stiff.*
- *If wrappers will not be used immediately, cover them with lightly dampened towel.*
- *To freeze wrappers, wrap them tightly in plastic wrap.*

Wheat is the main ingredient in the wrappers for small dumplings called wontons, which were introduced to the U.S. from Canton. Wonton skins are filled with a variety of ingredients such as meat, seafood, or vegetables and can be cooked in several ways: deep-fried, pan-fried, steamed, braised, or boiled and added to soup broth, as they are in this recipe.

In China, Wonton Soup is eaten as a light meal or a snack. It is sold by street vendors, in wonton shops, or in "fast food" restaurants. The steaming dumplings are ladled into bowls of broth with a dash of soy sauce and sesame oil and, perhaps, a sprinkling of minced vegetables.

No matter how poor the farmers are in Chinese villages, they always keep chickens for special occasions such as birthdays and the new year. This is possible because chickens require little upkeep. Chickens scratch in the dirt, eat worms and grubs, and scavenge the grain that is accidentally dropped in the yard. Chicken is favored over pork and beef in China, and constant demand for it makes it relatively expensive.

This recipe is typical of eastern Chinese cooking. It makes use of the region's excellent ham, salt, and sugar to enhance the flavors. Vegetables also are abundant in the mild climate. Crunchy *bean sprouts,* which are two to three inches long, come from the mung bean. In fact, bean sprouts are one of the most popular fresh Chinese vegetables found in the United States. Snow peas are eaten while still in their pods. They are crisp, flat, and tender. They are also readily available in the U.S.

PAPER-WRAPPED CHICKEN

Food Category: Chicken *High Cost*

- 1 lb. chicken breasts
- 1 tsp. sugar
- dash white pepper
- 2 tbsp. oil
- 1 tbsp. dark soy sauce
- waxed paper or foil
- 20 very thin slices of bamboo shoots
- 20 very thin slices of cooked ham
- 20 very thin slices of leek
- oil for deep-frying

1. Bone and skin chicken. Thinly slice into 1½- × ¾-inch pieces.
2. Combine sugar, pepper, oil, and soy sauce.
3. Cut waxed paper or foil into twenty 4-inch squares.
4. Grease squares of waxed paper or foil.
5. To wrap filling, follow the steps below and refer to the illustrations:
   (1) Dip each piece of chicken in soy sauce mixture and place diagonally in middle of square. Top with slice of bamboo shoot, ham, leek, and another piece of chicken dipped in the soy sauce mixture. Take bottom corner of waxed paper. Fold over chicken until it almost meets top corner.
   (2) Fold sides inward to form an envelope.
   (3) Fold top down.
   (4) Tuck flap under to secure package.

Repeat process until all papers and foods are used.

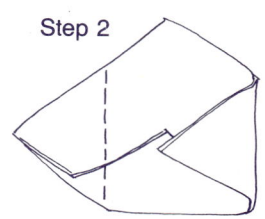

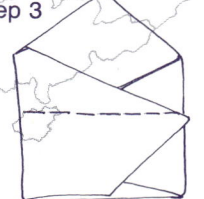

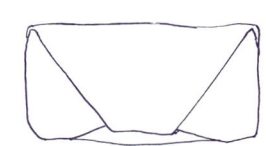

Step 1 Step 2 Step 3 Step 4

Wrapping Paper-wrapped Chicken

PON PON CHICKEN

Food Category: Chicken *Low Cost*

- 2 chicken breasts
- 3 tbsp. sesame seed paste thinned with 2 tbsp. chicken broth
  or
- 3 tbsp. smooth peanut butter thinned with 2 tbsp. sesame oil
- 2 tsp. light soy sauce
- 1 tbsp. red wine vinegar
- 2 tbsp. peanut oil
- 2 tsp. crushed red pepper
- 2 tsp. minced ginger root
- 1 tbsp. chopped scallions
- 1 tbsp. chopped garlic
- 1 tbsp. chicken broth
- ½ tsp. cayenne pepper
- 1 tbsp. toasted, ground Sichuan peppercorns
- 1 head lettuce

1. Wash lettuce. Pat dry with paper towels.
2. Place chicken breasts in simmering water for 10 minutes or until done. Strain, allow to cool, then bone and remove skin. Cut into thin strips.
3. Place sesame seed paste mixture (or peanut butter mixture) in small mixing bowl. Add soy sauce and vinegar, stirring well. Blend in oil, red pepper, ginger root, scallions, garlic, chicken broth, cayenne pepper, and ground peppercorns.
4. Mix sauce with chicken. Let stand until mixture reaches room temperature. Line bowl with lettuce torn into small pieces. Place chicken mixture over lettuce.

Serves 6.

Recipe Tips

- *To be authentic, use sesame seed paste instead of peanut butter, although the substitution works well and will not turn rancid as easily.*
- *To store fresh ginger root, wrap loosely in a paper towel and place in a sealed plastic bag in the refrigerator. It will keep up to one month.*

6. Heat oil in heavy skillet to 375 degrees. *Deep-fry* packages (a few at a time) for ½ minute.

7. Drain packages on paper towel and serve immediately.
   Serves 6.

Recipe Tip
- The correct oil temperature is essential. If oil is too cool, foods will absorb it and become greasy; If too hot, foods will burn before they are cooked. Use a deep-fat-frying thermometer to check the oil temperature. If you don't have a thermometer, drop a 1-inch cube of bread into the hot fat. Time 1 minute. If bread is brown, oil temperature is correct.

Shanghai and eastern China are well known for paper-wrapped dishes. Chicken cooked in paper retains its natural juice and flavor. The miniature paper envelopes insulate the food, keeping it warm until it is opened with chopsticks by the diner.

Vegetables are abundant in the lush countryside and waterways of the Lower Yangtze River. It is in this region that the *leeks* and fresh *bamboo shoots* for this recipe are grown. Leeks belong to the same family as the onion, but they differ in appearance. Leeks are large, with long, dark green leaves. They are sold only fresh (not canned) in stores.

Cone-shaped young bamboo shoots, which resemble asparagus, are delicately flavored and have a crunchy texture. In the United States, bamboo shoots are available in cans and do, fortunately, retain the crispy texture of fresh bamboo.

This recipe comes from the Sichuan province of western China, which is known for its hot, spicy food. The use of highly seasoned condiments in nearby Burma, Pakistan, and India has greatly influenced the food of western China. Also, because tall mountain ranges protect the plains, valleys, and deltas of the Yangtze River from winter cold and summer typhoons, the climate is semi-tropical, which is ideal for growing chilies and other spices. Spicy food is eaten in tropical climates because it aids perspiration, which has a cooling effect, and because it stimulates the appetite.

The Sichuan *peppercorns* that season this recipe produce a delayed reaction. At first, the peppercorns seem to have no taste at all, and then suddenly the flavor becomes strong and hot enough to make your tongue numb. Be careful, though—the more water you drink, the hotter the taste gets.

NOODLES IN MEAT SAUCE

Food Category: Pork *Moderate Cost*

4 scallions
¼ cup oil
1 lb. lean ground pork
½ cup brown bean paste
1 cup chicken broth
2 tbsp. granulated sugar
1 tsp. salt
1 tbsp. sesame oil
1 lb. Chinese noodles
1 cucumber
1 tbsp. garlic, chopped fine
1 cup small spinach leaves

1. Peel cucumber. Cut in half lengthwise and scoop out seeds. Cut lengthwise again in ⅛-inch-thick slices. Cut slices into strips ⅛ inch wide and 2 inches long.
2. Wash spinach leaves and pat dry.
3. Put cucumber, garlic, and spinach in individual dishes. Set aside.
4. Chop scallions fine. Set aside.
5. Set *wok* over high heat. When very hot, add 2 tbsp. oil. Add pork. Stir constantly until moisture has evaporated, about 4 minutes.
6. Add scallions and brown bean paste. Stir constantly. Cook until heated.
7. Add chicken broth, sugar and salt. When it boils, turn heat to low. Simmer, stirring occasionally, 10 minutes or until sauce is thickened. Pour into warmed bowl.
8. Stir in remaining 2 tbsp. oil. Simmer for 1 more minute.
9. Bring at least 2 quarts water to boil in large pot. Add noodles and bring water back to boil. Immediately add 1 cup cold water. Bring water to boil again.
10. Remove pot from heat, using strainer to transfer noodles to container. Run cold water over noodles to stop the cooking process. Drain excess water.
11. Return noodles to pot. Place over heat, stir once, and pour into *colander*. Shake colander to drain as much water as possible. Put noodles in large, warmed bowl.
12. Each person puts a share of noodles in individual bowl, pours meat sauce on top, and garnishes with cucumber, garlic, and spinach.

Serves 6 as a side dish.

SHREDDED PORK

Food Category: Pork *High Cost*

1 lb. boneless pork
1 tbsp. minced garlic
2 tsp. minced ginger root
2 scallions (white and green parts), shredded
¾ cup water chestnuts
2 cups peanut oil
1 tbsp. sesame oil

Marinade

1 egg white
1 tbsp. water chestnut flour or cornstarch
2 tsp. water

Seasoning Sauce

1 tsp. water chestnut flour or cornstarch dissolved in 2 tbsp. water
1 tbsp. dark soy sauce
1 tbsp. light soy sauce
2 tsp. wine vinegar
2 tsp. sugar
2 tsp. Chinese hot sauce
2 tbsp. chicken stock

1. Partially freeze pork. Slice pork thin, then *shred* very fine. Place shreds and ingredients for *marinade* in bowl and mix well. Refrigerate for at least 1 hour, or overnight.
2. Combine ingredients for seasoning sauce.
3. Place *wok* over high heat about 1 minute. Pour in peanut oil. Turn heat to medium until oil reaches 375 degrees. Restir pork in marinade. Turn heat to high. Add pork and marinade to wok, separating pork shreds, about 1 minute, until pork turns white.
4. Turn off heat. Pour oil and pork into *colander*. Set over bowl. Shake the colander gently to aid draining. Then place over clean bowl.
5. Return wok to high heat. *Stir-fry* garlic, ginger root, and scallions for 30 seconds. Add water chestnuts.
6. Restir seasoning sauce and add it all at once to wok. Stir-fry for 5 seconds.
7. Add the pork. Stir-fry for 15 seconds, or until sauce has evenly coated pork shreds. Add

Recipe Tips
- *Green onions may be substituted for scallions.*
- *Fettucini or linguini may be substituted for Chinese noodles.*
- *Warm bowls by placing them in hot water.*

Noodles have been eaten in China since the Han dynasty, over 2,000 years ago. Egg noodles are made from wheat and form the basic starch in northern China. Wheat is a staple crop of the north because, unlike rice, it grows well in the cold climate. Noodles in Meat Sauce with brown bean (soybean) paste is as popular in Beijing as spaghetti with meat sauce is in the United States. In the Chinese tradition, each person puts his or her own share of noodles in an individual bowl and pours meat sauce on top.

Normally, wheat products are eaten as the daily starch in northern China and as snacks in the rest of the country. Noodles, though, are an exception. They are the main dish all over China—especially at birthday meals, for noodles are also the symbol of longevity.

---

sesame oil. Turn off heat. Mix briefly, serve immediately in heated dish with rice. Serves 6.

Recipe Tips
- *You may substitute skinned, boned chicken for pork.*
- *The correct oil temperature is essential. If oil is too cool, foods will absorb it and become greasy; If too hot, foods will burn before they are cooked. Use a deep-fat-frying thermometer to check the temperature. If you don't have a thermometer, drop a 1-inch cube of bread into the hot fat. Time 1 minute. If bread is brown, oil temperature is correct.*

The fine, smooth texture and flavor of pork has been enjoyed for thousands of years in China. The Chinese find pork a very versatile meat. It is broiled, braised, barbecued, fried, stewed, and steamed. The flavor goes well with most vegetables and seasonings.

This recipe calls for deep-frying the pork in a large amount of oil and finishing the vegetables in a small amount of oil. This cooking style is unique to the Sichuan province. *Ginger root* is characteristic of the pungent flavors of Sichuan cooking. It is hot and spicy. These gnarled, whitish-brown tubers are sold fresh in American stores.

SWEET AND SOUR PORK

Food Category: Pork *High Cost*

- 1 lb. lean boneless pork
- 1 egg, slightly beaten
- 1 tsp. salt
- ¼ cup cornstarch
- ¼ cup flour
- ¼ cup chicken broth
- 3 cups oil

Sauce

- 1 tbsp. oil
- 1 tsp. finely chopped garlic
- 1 large green pepper
- 1 medium carrot
- ½ cup chicken broth
- 4 tbsp. sugar
- 4 tbsp. red wine vinegar
- 1 tsp. soy sauce
- 1 tbsp. cornstarch dissolved in 2 tbsp cold water

1. Seed and cut pepper into ½-inch squares.
2. Scrape carrot. Slice into 2-inch strips ¼-inch wide and ¼-inch thick.
3. Trim pork and cube into 1-inch pieces.
4. Mix egg, ¼ cup cornstarch, ¼ cup flour, ¼ cup chicken broth, and salt.
5. Add pork cubes to flour mixture. Stir, coating each piece of meat. Preheat oven to 250 degrees.
6. Pour 3 cups oil into wok and place over high heat. When oil reaches 375 degrees, drop in half of coated pork cubes. Fry for 5 or 6 minutes until pork turns crisp and golden brown. Remove pork with slotted spoon to casserole and keep warm in oven. Fry remainder of cubes and add to first batch.
7. To make sauce, pour off remaining oil in wok. Set pan over high heat for 30 seconds. Pour in 1 tbsp. oil and swirl around pan. Add garlic, green pepper, and carrot. Stir-fry for 2 to 3 minutes, until pepper and carrot darken slightly in color. Add ½ cup chicken broth, sugar, vinegar, and soy sauce. Bring to boil. Boil for 1 minute or until sugar has dissolved. Stir cornstarch mixture and add to pan. Stirring constantly, cook until sauce is thick and clear. Pour entire contents of pan over fried pork and serve at once with rice.

Serves 6 as side dish.

BEAN CURD WITH RICE

Food Category: Vegetables *Low Cost*

- 1 cup rice
- 2¼ cups water
- 1½ cups mushrooms
- ½ cup sliced bamboo shoots
- 2 tbsp. finely shredded ginger root
- ½ tsp. crushed dried hot chili pepper
- 2 cloves garlic, thinly sliced
- 1 green onion, cut into 2-inch sections
- Four 3- by 3-inch bean curd squares
- ½ tsp. salt
- 1 to 2 tbsp. oil
- 1 tsp. sugar
- 2½ tbsp. soy sauce

1. Bring 2 cups water to boil.
2. Add rice. Stir to moisten each grain of rice. Cover tightly. Without lifting lid, cook for 25 minutes. Let stand for 10 minutes.
3. Clean mushrooms. Cut mushrooms in half. Place on large plate.
4. Put bamboo shoots, ginger root, chili pepper, and green onions on plate with mushrooms.
5. Cut each bean curd piece into 8 pieces and sprinkle with salt. Set aside 10 minutes. Drain bean curd.
6. Heat wok to very hot and add oil. Fry bean curd over medium-high until light brown on one side, about 2 minutes. Then turn and fry curd cubes until light brown on all sides. Remove and set aside. Leave oil in wok.
7. Heat wok with remaining oil. Stir-fry ginger root, garlic, chili pepper, and green onions for 1 minute. Add bamboo shoots and mushrooms. Stir-fry for 2 minutes. Add fried bean curd, sugar, soy sauce, and water. Cover and bring to boil. Cook for 10 minutes over medium heat, stirring once. When sauce is reduced, serve in warmed bowls with rice. Serves 6 as a side dish.

Recipe Tips

- Clean mushrooms with a soft, wet brush. Do not immerse mushrooms in water; they absorb water and become spongy.
- Warm dish by placing it in hot water.

Recipe Tip

- The correct oil temperature is essential. If oil is too cool, foods will absorb it and become greasy. If oil is too hot, foods will burn before they are cooked. Use a deep-fat-frying thermometer to check the temperature. If you don't have a thermometer, drop a 1-inch cube of bread into the hot fat. Time 1 minute. If bread is brown, oil temperature is correct.

Pork is the most widely used meat in China, and for good reason. A pig fattens quickly on almost anything and does not require a large pasture. Also, pork mixes well with other foods, such as in this popular dish from Beijing. Here, pork is combined with green peppers and carrots.

Northern China is well known for having the best sweet and sour sauce in China. This version of Sweet and Sour Pork from Beijing may seem unusual to Americans because we are more familiar with the southern Chinese sauce with fruit or tomato sauce.

This hot, spicy dish is an example of western Chinese cooking. Many seasonings (ginger, garlic, chili pepper, and green onions) give it its multiple flavors, and the hot peppers, used in many western Chinese dishes, are said to stimulate the palate. While first you feel a sudden hot sensation (you may even perspire!), you then become clearly aware of the other flavors in the dish.

This recipe calls for crushed, dried, hot chili pepper. If you cannot buy dried chili pepper, substitute crushed, dried red pepper flakes found on the spice shelf in most supermarkets.

Fresh ginger, a root vegetable, is absolutely necessary to Sichuan food. Ginger adds a pungent flavor to complete the crisp spiciness of Sichuan cuisine.

A food in China for thousands of years, *bean curd* is known as "meat without bones." It is made from the milk extracted from soybean paste and is high in protein and calcium and low in fat. The texture and bland flavor of bean curd complement western Sichuan food by absorbing all the hot and spicy seasonings.

BROCCOLI WITH RICE

Food Category: Vegetable · Low Cost

1 cup rice
2 cups water
1 large bunch broccoli
3 dried red peppers
½-inch piece fresh ginger root
1 tbsp. cornstarch
¼ cup water
1 to 2 tbsp. oil
1 tsp. salt
⅔ cup water
Four 3- by 3-inch bean curd squares

1. Bring water to boil.
2. Add rice. Stir to moisten each grain of rice. Cover tightly. *Do not peek*. Cook for 25 minutes. Let stand for 10 minutes.
3. Wash brocolli. Cut *florets* off main stems of good-sized pieces. Cut off tough bottom part of stems. Slice stems in half lengthwise and then cut into pieces about 2 inches long.
4. Cut each pepper into 4 pieces.
5. Peel ginger, then *shred* into pieces about ⅛ inch wide.
6. Mix cornstarch and water in small bowl. Set aside.
7. Drain and *cube* bean curd.
8. Heat *wok* or skillet over high heat for 15 seconds. Add oil. Oil is ready when first bubbles appear. Add ginger root and red peppers. Stir for 5 seconds. Add broccoli and *stir-fry* for 1½ minutes. Make sure every piece is exposed to hot oil. Add salt and stir-fry broccoli for 1 minute longer. Add bean curd. Pour in water. Bring to a boil, then cover pan and cook for 8 minutes.
9. Mix cornstarch and water well. Just before broccoli is served, pour mixture into pan. Stir-fry broccoli a few seconds over high heat until sauce turns thick and clear. Serve in warmed bowls with rice.

Serves 6.

Recipe Tips

- *To store fresh ginger root, wrap loosely in a paper towel and place in a sealed plastic bag in the refrigerator. It will keep up to one month.*

GREEN BEANS WITH RICE

Food Category: Vegetables · Low Cost

1 cup rice
2 cups water
1 lb. fresh green beans
2 tbsp. oil
1 can water chestnuts
1 tsp. sugar
1½ tsp. salt
¼ cup chicken broth
1 tsp. cornstarch combined with 2 tbsp. water
Four 3- by 3-inch bean curd squares

1. Bring water to boil.
2. Add rice. Stir to moisten each grain of rice. Cover tightly. Without lifting lid, cook for 25 minutes. Remove from heat. Let stand for 10 minutes.
3. Cut off ends of green beans. Cut into 2-inch-long pieces. Wash and drain.
4. Heat *wok* or skillet over high heat until hot. Add oil. *Stir-fry* green beans and water chestnuts for 3 to 4 minutes. Reduce heat after 2 minutes. Add sugar and salt. Mix well. Add chicken broth. Cover wok and cook 2 minutes.
5. Drain and *cube* bean curd. Add to wok. Cover and cook for 1 to 2 minutes more until beans are tender.
6. Mix cornstarch and water thoroughly, and slowly add to wok. Stir until liquid thickens and beans and water chestnuts are coated with a light, clear glaze. Serve with rice in heated serving bowls.

Serves 6.

Recipe Tips

- *When spaces appear between the grains of rice, it is done.*
- *Warm bowl by placing it in hot water.*

Broccoli grows well in southern China; it is used more in cooking there than in any other part of China. This recipe is a good example of the emphasis that the Cantonese place on the flavor and quality of the main ingredient of a dish. The pepper and ginger highlight the broccoli flavor; they do not mask it.

Cantonese cooking also requires the addition of ingredients in a specific order, as in this recipe. First the broccoli, ginger, and red pepper are stir-fried in oil for a short time to seal in the fresh flavors. Then everything is simmered so that the broccoli cooks and all the flavors blend into the bean curd.

There are many types of bean curd—fresh, dry, fried, and pickled. Cakes of fresh bean curd are commonly found in American grocery stores. Bean curd has the consistency of firm custard. Children, with less developed palates, especially like its soft texture and clear, fresh taste.

This is a basic dish from eastern China, where fresh, natural flavors and ingredients are emphasized. Water chestnuts, used in this recipe, are found in the many ponds, streams, and lakes that irrigate eastern China. They are not part of the chestnut family at all. Water chestnuts are actually starchy, sweet tubers of water plants. They do not lose their crunchiness even when cooked. In fact, the canned variety retains as crisp a texture as the fresh. Combining bean curd, which is used extensively in eastern Chinese vegetable cooking, and rice, ensures a highly nutritional protein dish.

EGG ROLLS

Food Category: Dough *High Cost*

Wrapper Recipe
Purchased wrappers may be substituted

3 eggs
1 cup flour
2 tbsp. cornstarch
1 cup water

Filling Recipe

½ tsp. salt
1 cup shrimp, broken into pieces
½ cup finely chopped celery
¼ cup cooked and minced ham
¼ cup finely chopped water chestnuts
¼ cup finely chopped bamboo shoots
1 tbsp. soy sauce
2 tbsp. minced green onion
Fat for frying

1. Beat 2 eggs slightly. Beat in flour, cornstarch, water, and salt.
2. Heat greased skillet. Add 1 tbsp. batter. Tilt pan so batter runs evenly over the bottom. A round pancake will form. Fry one side only. Remove from pan. Repeat until all batter is gone.
3. Mix 1 egg with all remaining ingredients except fat.
4. To wrap filling, follow the steps below and refer to the illustrations (on back):
   (1) Place 1 tbsp. filling in center of fried side of pancake.
   (2) Fold sides of pancake inward until they meet.
   (3) Roll from bottom to top into rolls.
5. Heat greased skillet. Place rolls in hot pan, with exposed edge down. Brown all sides, adding fat to skillet as necessary.

Serves 6.

Recipe Tips

- *If pancakes are too thin to handle, add a bit more flour.*
- *If pancakes are too thick, add water drop by drop.*

PORK STEAMED BUNS

Food Category: Dough *Moderate Cost*

Dough

½ cake fresh yeast
¼ cup lukewarm water (105°–115°F.)
3 tbsp. butter
¾ cup milk, room temperature
¼ tsp. salt
½ cup sugar
1 egg, beaten
4 to 4½ cups flour

Seasoning Sauce

1½ tbsp. oyster sauce
1 tbsp. sugar
1½ tbsp. light soy sauce

Binder

1 tsp. flour
2 tsp. cornstarch
⅓ cup chicken stock

Filling

½ lb. roast pork
1½ cups chopped white onion
2 cloves garlic, minced
2 tbsp. oil
1 egg, beaten

1. For dough, *dissolve* yeast in water.
2. Melt butter. Allow to cool. Combine butter, milk, salt, and sugar in large bowl. Stir in dissolved yeast and beaten egg.
3. Gradually add enough flour to make soft dough. On lightly floured board, *knead* dough for 15 minutes. Place in greased bowl. Cover with greased wax paper and a damp towel. Let dough rise until double, about 1 hour.
4. Knead dough again for 5 minutes. Allow to rise, covered, for ½ hour.
5. Knead dough again for 5 minutes. Divide into 2 equal parts. On lightly floured surface, roll each part into cylinder shape, 12 to 14 inches long. Cut each into 9 pieces. Lightly flour both sides of cut pieces. Flatten slightly with heel of your hand.
6. Combine ingredients for seasoning sauce. Mix *binder*.
7. Dice pork into ½ inch cubes. Remove any fat.
8. Place *wok* or skillet over high heat 1 minute. Add oil. Heat until hot. Add onions and garlic. *Stir-fry* 1 minute. Add pork and mix briefly.

Step 1

Step 2

Step 3

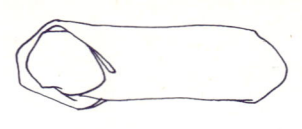

Wrapping Egg Rolls

This is an American adaptation of what are called spring rolls in eastern and southern China. We are most familiar with the version that is made in Canton. This version uses a batter of eggs and flour as the wrapper, while most Chinese versions call for a pastry dough.

In China, Egg Rolls are eaten on Chinese New Year because the rolls are symbols of prosperity. They are rarely included in a regular meal but are sometimes served as the final course at a banquet or eaten as snacks. Egg Rolls are great for parties, as they can be eaten with the fingers.

---

9. Restir seasoning sauce. Add to wok. Stir-fry for 1 minute.
10. Restir binder. Add to wok. Stir-fry for 30 seconds until sauce has thickened.
11. To fill buns, follow the steps below and refer to the illustrations:
    (1) Hold circle of dough in one hand; place 1 tbsp. filling in center of dough round.
    (2) Gently gather up sides of dough. Wrap sides over filling. Twist to seal.
    (3) Turn bun over. Pat into round shape.
12. Place each bun on a 2-inch square of waxed paper. Set aside and allow to rise for ½ hour. Steam for 15 to 20 minutes over rapidly boiling water. Do not crowd steamer because the buns will expand slightly. (If you do not have a steamer see Chapter 5 for instructions for improvising one.)
    Serves 6

Step 1

Step 2

Step 3

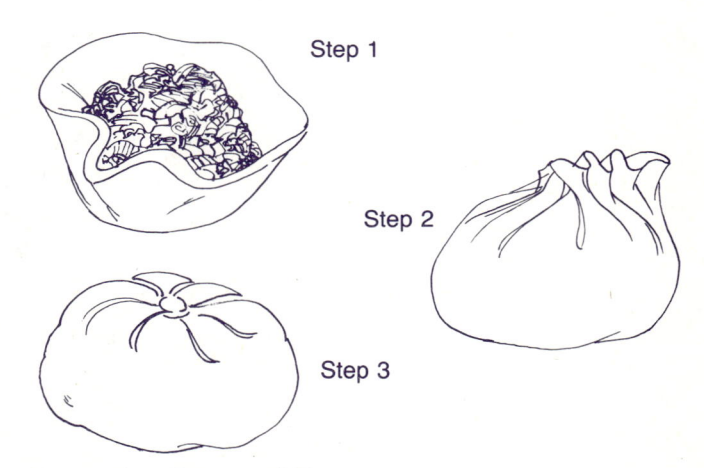

Wrapping Steamed Buns

Recipe Tips
- If you do not want to steam the buns, they may be baked at 375 degrees. Brush with beaten egg. Bake for 15 to 20 minutes or until golden.
- To divide preparation into two days, complete Steps 1 through 4. Cover dough with greased waxed paper and a damp towel. Place in refrigerator overnight. Begin with Step 5 the next day.

Also made in northern and eastern China, this recipe is typical of southern China, where steaming is a common cooking technique. Served as *dim sum*, which means "dot hearts" or "heart delights" in Cantonese, these small treats are enjoyed in tea houses from mid-morning to mid-afternoon. At the end of the meal, the waiter adds up the number of dishes on your table and calculates the cost of the meal. Seafood flavors are incorporated into this recipe by the use of *oyster sauce*.

POT STICKERS

Food Category: Dough *High Cost*

Filling

1 lb. lean ground roast pork
2 slices fresh ginger root, minced
2 green onions, minced
1 cup spinach
1 tbsp. soy sauce
2 tbsp. water
1 tbsp. cornstarch

Dough

2 cups flour
½ tsp. salt
¾ cup hot water

Additional Ingredients

4 tbsp. oil
⅔ cup stock or water

For Dipping

½ tsp. sesame oil
rice vinegar
chili oil
soy sauce

1. Combine filling ingredients. Let stand 20 minutes to blend flavors.
2. To prepare dough, combine flour and salt. Stirring constantly, gradually add hot water. On floured board, *knead* for 5 minutes.
3. Cover with damp towel and let rise 20 minutes. Knead again for 5 minutes and roll into ropes, 1 inch in diameter. Cut into forty 1-inch pieces.
4. Roll each piece into a 3-inch circle. Keep remaining pieces covered with towel.
5. To wrap filling, follow the steps and refer to the illustrations (on back):
   (1) Make 4 pleats on one half of skin. Bring other half up to form pocket. Insert 1 tbsp. filling.
   (2) Bring flap up and over to enclose filling. Pinch edges together. Repeat until all dumplings are filled.
6. Heat 2 skillets until very hot. Add 2 tbsp. oil to each skillet. Place one layer of pot stickers in skillets and cover. Lower heat for 5 minutes or until browned.
7. Add ⅓ cup stock or water to each skillet.

ALMOND FLOAT

Food Category: Sweets *Moderate Cost*

2 pkg. unflavored gelatin
1¾ cups cold water
1½ cups milk
1 tbsp. almond extract

Syrup

2 cups cold water
1½ cups sugar

Garnish

6½-oz. can mandarin orange sections
1-lb can litchi nuts

1. In large, ovenproof bowl, sprinkle gelatin over ½ cup cold water. Let soften 5 minutes.
2. Bring remaining 1¼ cups water to boil in small saucepan. Add to softened gelatin. Stir until gelatin has thoroughly dissolved and becomes clear. Stir in milk and almond extract. Pour mixture into flat 7½-×-12-inch dish. Custard should be about 1½ inches thick. Refrigerate for at least 3 hours, or until custard is firmly set.
3. Make syrup by dissolving ½ cup sugar in 2 cups cold water in small saucepan. Bring to boil. Cook, then chill in refrigerator. Syrup should be thin.
4. Make diagonal cuts 1 inch apart in the almond float. Make cuts in opposite direction to form diamond-shaped pieces. Carefully lift diamonds out of dish with small spatula. Arrange them with mandarin orange sections and litchi nuts in several layers in deep serving bowl. Pour on chilled syrup and serve. Serves 6.

Recipe Tip

- Litchi nuts are usually available in the foreign foods section of large grocery stores. If you cannot buy them, there is no substitute. Use additional mandarin orange sections.

Cover and cook until liquid has evaporated.
8. Place on warm platter, browned side up, and serve with dipping ingredients. *Makes 40.*

Recipe Tips
- Commercial round wonton skins, available in some markets, may be substituted.
- To store fresh ginger root for up to one month, wrap loosely in a paper towel and place in a plastic bag in the refrigerator.
- Warm platter by putting it in an oven preheated to lowest temperature.

Step 1

Step 2

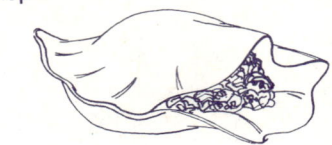

Wrapping Pot Stickers

Pot stickers are northern Chinese snacks. Wheat instead of rice is the main staple in northern China, and the heavy dough buns are meant to give the eater energy to provide warmth against severe northern winters.

These savory dumplings are filled with meat and vegetables. Because the pockets of dough look like they have stuck to the pan, they are called Pot Stickers. As you can see, the Chinese love poetic and whimsical names for food.

Chili oil is added for an extra-spicy taste. It is made by frying pungent chili peppers in oil until the *capsaicin* is extracted from the peppers, making the oil itself hot enough to pep up other dishes.

This light pudding is popular in southern China, where many fruits, including litchis, grow in abundance in the mild climate. Litchis are walnut-sized, but they are not really nuts. *Litchis* are sweet, fragrant fruits sold fresh, dried, or canned. They originally were brought to China from India. The Chinese like litchis for their exotic aroma and fruity flavor. Dried litchis taste like raisins and make a good snack. Canned litchis are shelled, pitted, juicy, and ready to use. Their distinctive flavor enhances many dessert sauces. At Chinese banquets, a light pudding such as Almond Float is often served as a change-of-pace in the middle of the multi-course meal. It is also served at the end of a family meal.

FRIED SWEET WONTONS

Food Category: Sweets   *High Cost*

- 1 pkg. egg roll wrappers
- 2 lb. pitted dates
- 2 cups walnuts, finely chopped
- 3 tbsp. freshly grated orange rind
- 3 to 5 tbsp. orange juice (or cold water) if needed
- 3 cups oil confectioners' sugar

1. Finely chop dates. Add a teaspoon or so of orange juice or water if dates are too sticky to cut.
2. Combine dates, walnuts, and *grated* rind in small bowl. *Knead* mixture with fingers until it can be gathered into a ball. If mixture is too dry, moisten with orange juice or water.
3. Roll 1 tbsp. filling between palms of hands to form cylinders 1 inch long and about ⅓ inch in diameter.
4. To fill wontons, follow the steps below and refer to the illustrations (on back):
   (1) Place cylinder of filling diagonally across each wrapper, just below center. Dip finger in water and moisten lower point of wrapper. Fold point over filling and tuck it underneath.
   (2) Roll up resulting tube.
   (3) Twist ends to seal.
5. Heat oil to 375. Use deep-frying thermometer. Deep-fry wontons 8 or 10 at a time, turning occasionally, for 2 or 3 minutes, or until they are golden brown and crisp. As they finish cooking, transfer wontons to paper towels to drain and cool. Just before serving, sprinkle wontons with confectioners' sugar. *Makes about 4 dozen.*

Recipe Tips

- *An easy way to clean the grater is to brush it with a pastry brush before washing.*
- *The correct oil temperature is essential. If oil is too cool, foods will absorb it and become greasy. If oil is too hot, foods will burn before they are cooked. Use deep-fat-frying thermometer to check the temperature. If you don't have a thermometer, drop a 1-inch cube of bread into hot oil. Time 1 minute. If bread is brown, oil temperature is correct.*

SPUN APPLES

Food Category: Sweets   *Low Cost*

- ¾ cup flour
- 1 egg
- ½ cup cold water
- 3 medium-size, firm Delicious apples
- 2 cups oil
- 1 cup sugar
- ¼ cup water
- 1 tbsp. sesame seeds

1. Put flour in mixing bowl. Beat egg with ½ cup cold water. Gradually add egg and water mixture to flour. Beat until batter forms.
2. Peel and core apples. Cut into 1-inch wedges. Add apples to batter.
3. Near cooking area set aside a large serving plate and a large bowl filled with 1 quart cold water and a dozen ice cubes.
4. Heat oil in heavy skillet to 350 degrees. Take coated apple pieces out of batter one by one. Fry in oil until light brown, about 2 minutes. Fry 7 or 8 pieces at a time. Put on tray to be fried again, later. Keep oil hot.
5. Add sugar and water to *wok*. Slowly bring to boil, stirring only until sugar has dissolved. Cook mixture without stirring until it reaches the *medium-hard crack* stage and its color changes to light brown. Reduce heat to lowest point.
6. Reheat apple pieces in hot oil. Immediately lift them out of the oil, place them in hot syrup, and sprinkle with sesame seeds. Turn heat to medium. Stir wedges to coat thoroughly with syrup. Take out one by one and drop into bowl of ice water. Syrup coating will harden instantly. Use strainer to transfer apples from ice water to serving plate. Serve immediately. Serves 6.

Recipe Tips

- *Bananas may be substituted for apples and prepared in the same manner.*
- *Steps 1 through 4 may be done ahead of time, but oil must be reheated.*

Step 1　　　　　Step 2　　　　　Step 3

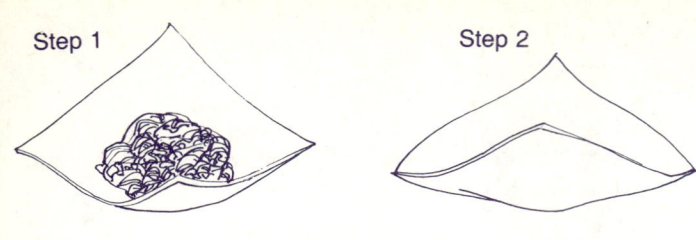

Wrapping Fried Sweet Wonton

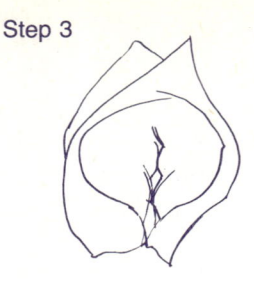

The Cantonese are noted for their crispy foods, and wonton is a familiar item in southern China. The region's mild climate provides an excellent range of ingredients, and the orange, used for flavoring, is one of the many fruits grown in the south. Although the Chinese do not often eat desserts, they do enjoy sweets between meals.

The Cantonese always are willing to try new recipes and foods, perhaps because Canton has been more exposed to the outside world than other culinary regions of China. Located at the Pearl River delta only a short distance from the sea, Canton has been a major trade center for more than 20 centuries.

- *The correct oil temperature is essential. If oil is too cool, foods will absorb it and become greasy. If oil is too hot, foods will burn before they are cooked. Use a deep-fat-frying thermometer to check the temperature. If you don't have a thermometer, drop a 1-inch cube of bread into hot fat. Time 1 minute. If bread is brown, oil temperature is correct.*

Spun Apples are one of the most famous Chinese dessert dishes. They are a specialty of Beijing. This recipe, in which hard candy glaze covers a warm, soft apple slice, most likely originated in the warmer, northern Chinese province of Shantung. Here, many apple orchards flourish in the mild climate.

Cooking this unusual dessert is dramatic, and it is worth having an audience in the kitchen. It is even more fun when guests use chopsticks and ice water to harden their own hot candied-apple wedges at the table.

FIRE POT*

Food Category: Soup   *High Cost*

- 1 pkg. cellophane noodles
- 6 fresh mushrooms
- 1 lb. Chinese cabbage or spinach
- 1 large bean cake cut into 1½ × 2 × ⅓ inch slices
- 8 to 10 shrimp mixed in ½ tsp. cornstarch
- 5 oz. flank steak, slightly frozen for easy slicing
- 5 oz. chicken breast
- 5 oz. lean pork
- 6 cups soup stock
- ½ green onion
- 1 slice ginger root
- 1 tsp. salt

For Dipping
- soy sauce
- hot sauce
- vinegar

1. Soften noodles in hot water. When they are soft, drain and arrange on plate (cut in half if too long).
2. Cut cabbage or spinach into large pieces. To prevent sponginess, clean mushrooms with a soft brush dipped in cold water. Slice mushrooms. Cut flank steak, pork, and chicken into thin, bite-size slices. Arrange on separate plates with bean cake and shrimp around fire pot on dining table.
3. Light pot with liquid fuel or turn on electric pot (350°F.). Add soup stock, green onion, ginger root, 1 teaspoon salt, about half of the cabbage and noodles. The remaining cabbage and noodles can be set on a plate and added by anyone during the meal.
4. Choose your desired ingredient. Put it in your small strainer and dip into boiling soup. The food is cooked in 2 or 3 seconds. Be sure the pork is well done, to prevent trichinosis. Have soy sauce, vinegar, and hot sauce available in separate bowls so each person can put the desired amount into his or her bowl.ND boiled ingredients into desired sauce.
5. A person can get soup from the pot any time with a serving spoon. The remaining soup is shared at the end of the meal. Water should be added occasionally to prevent sticking. Serves 6.

FRIED RICE*

Food Category: Rice   *Low Cost*

- 2 cups rice
- 4 cups water
- 2 tbsp. oil
- 2 eggs, slightly beaten
- ½ cup shrimp
- ½ tsp. salt
- ⅛ tsp. pepper
- ½ cup finely chopped green onion
- 3 tbsp. soy sauce

1. Bring water to boil.
2. Add rice. Stir and cover tightly. *Do not peek.* Simmer for 20 to 25 minutes. Let stand for 10 minutes. Chill overnight.
3. Heat 2 tbsp. oil. Add eggs and cook for 1 to 2 minutes, breaking into small pieces as they cook.
4. Add shrimp, salt, pepper, rice, and soy sauce in order listed.
5. Blend and cook over moderate heat for about 5 to 7 minutes until heated through.
6. Add green onions and stir gently. Serve in heated bowl.
Serves 6.

Recipe Tip

- When spaces appear between the grains of rice, it is done.

Recipe Tips

- *Substitute 6 chicken or beef bouillon cubes and 6 cups of water for soup stock.*
- *An excellent sauce can be made by mixing 3 tbsp. peanut butter with about 5 tbsp. water and ½ tsp. salt.*

The fire-pot method of cooking was introduced to China when the Mongolians invaded northern China in the 13th century. These nomadic tribes took goats and sheep with them on their wanderings for food; thus lamb was the meat originally used in this recipe, which is also called Fire Pot.

A Mongolian fire pot is a large brass pot that has a funnel and charcoal burner in the center. Around the burner is a moat filled with soup stock in which to cook the food. The pot was designed to cook meat and vegetables conveniently in boiling broth. In the 18th century, a prince gave a feast for his court that required the use of 1,500 Mongolian fire pots.

A fire pot is the preferred cooking method in the winter, especially in the subarctic north. Each person cooks his or her food in the pot at the table. The heat from the pots warms the diners. A deep electric skillet, a chafing dish, or a kettle over a hot plate may be substituted for the hot pot.

The cellophane noodles used with this dish are made from mung beans that are soaked, ground, strained into a fairly clear liquid and dried. Cellophane noodles are so named because they look like a tangle of transparent strands as they dry in the sun.

In China, rice is the symbol of life and fertility. From this comes the custom in the United States of throwing rice at weddings. Warm weather and frequent rain makes southern China ideal for growing rice. In fact, three crops of rice a year can be raised.

Rice is highly respected in China. It is never wasted. Leftover steamed rice is the basis for fried rice. Fried Rice is a good way to use bits of leftover meat and vegetables. It is a popular snack, as well as a speedy and nutritious main dish. Fried Rice is served all over China.

ONION CAKES*

Food Category: Dough *Low Cost*

3 cups flour
1 cup of water

10 to 15 scallions or green onions
1½ tsp. sesame oil

2 tsp. salt
6 tbsp. peanut oil

1. Mix flour and water together until a stiff dough forms. Set aside for 30 minutes so dough will absorb water and become stiffer.
2. Wash and trim scallions (or green onions). Chop green and white parts very fine.
3. Sprinkle bread board with oil to prevent sticking. *Knead* dough 1 minute. Divide in half for easy handling. Using rolling pin, roll a dough ball into 8-inch × 10-inch rectangle.
4. Sprinkle 1 tsp. salt over rectangle of dough, pressing into dough. Brush with ½ of sesame oil. Sprinkle with half the chopped scallions. Roll up like a jelly roll from the long edge. Pinch ends to keep filling inside.
5. Divide roll into 3 sections, twisting ends of each piece to keep filling from falling out. Repeat with remaining dough, oil, and scallions.
6. Just before cooking, flatten one ball into a circle 8 inches in diameter. Heat frying pan with ¼ inch oil. When oil is hot, fry scallion cake 3 minutes on each side. *Drain* on paper towel. Repeat with rest of dough. Cut each cake into 8 pieces. Salt after frying if desired. *Makes 48 pieces.*
Serves 8.

Recipe Tip

- *Oiling the rolling pin will prevent the dough from sticking to it.*

EGG FOO YUNG*

Food Category: Eggs *Moderate Cost*

½ cup fresh bean sprouts
4 fresh mushrooms, diced
½ lb. shrimp
2 to 4 tbsp. oil
3 eggs

Sauce

¾ cup chicken broth
1 tbsp. soy sauce
½ tsp. salt
1 tbsp. cornstarch dissolved in 2 tbsp. cold water

1. Bring broth to boil.
2. Add soy sauce, salt and cornstarch mixture.
3. Reduce heat. Cook for 2 minutes until sauce is thick and clear. Keep warm.
4. Rinse fresh bean sprouts. Drain and pat dry.
5. Rinse shrimp under cold water. Pat dry. *Dice* into ¼-inch pieces.
6. Place bean sprouts, shrimp, mushrooms, eggs, oil, stock, soy sauce, salt, and cornstarch mixture within easy reach.
7. Set *wok* over high heat for 30 seconds. Pour in 1 tbsp. oil, swirl around wok, and heat for another 30 seconds. Add shrimp and *stir-fry* 1 minute. Transfer to plate.
8. Beat eggs well. Add shrimp, bean sprouts, and mushrooms. Set wok over high heat for

This recipe is typical of the earthy, savory cooking found in Sichuan. It involves cooking in a large quantity of oil, a method unique to the cooking of this western province.

The land in western China is mountainous and isolated and humid, with much rain and fog. Crops grow well in this type of climate. Year-round agriculture produces wheat in the winter and rice in the summer.

These crisp, salty Onion Cakes were originally made in open-air restaurants and sold in the streets. Today they are served with drinks or as the final course of a large meal.

---

30 seconds. Add 1 tbsp. oil, swirl it around pan, reduce heat to low, and pour in ¼ cup of egg mixture. Let cook undisturbed for 1 minute until lightly browned. Turn pancake. Cook another minute. Transfer to warm platter, cover with foil to keep warm. Make 5 more pancakes with remaining mixture, adding 1 tsp. oil to pan as necessary.

9. Serve with sauce poured over each pancake.
Serves 6.

Recipe Tip

- *To warm platter, place in oven preheated to lowest setting.*

Egg Foo Yung is a Chinese omelet. It was named after the big foo yung flower, which we know as the hibiscus. The vegetables inside the omelet are crunchy; the eggs are soft and creamy. This Cantonese dish can be served as a quick and delicious main dish. This recipe is an American adaptation because it is served with a sauce, instead of plain, as in Canton.

Eggs are an important source of protein in China. In a Chinese market you will see many varieties: speckled quail eggs, duck eggs, brown hen eggs, and preserved eggs called thousand-year-old eggs. Hard-cooked eggs are eaten as snacks, and eggs are added to soups.

ALMOND COOKIES*

Food Category: Sweets

Low Cost

1 cup butter, softened	1 tsp. almond extract	2½ cups flour	⅛ tsp. salt
1 cup sugar	1 egg	1 tsp. baking soda	red food coloring or Spanish peanuts

1. Cream butter with sugar until light and fluffy.
2. Add egg and mix well. Add almond extract.
3. Sift dry ingredients together. Add to creamed mixture and mix well.
4. Shape into 1-inch balls. Place on ungreased cookie sheet. Flatten slightly by pressing center of cookie with thumb. Dip end of toothpick into food coloring and touch top of cookie or place Spanish peanut in center of each cookie. Bake in preheated oven at 350 degrees for 10 minutes.

Makes 4½ dozen.

Recipe Tips

- If dough is too dry to shape into balls, add a drop or so of water.
- Cookies do not become brown while baking. They will feel somewhat firm to the touch when done.

Most Chinese homes do not have ovens, so very few Chinese recipes require baking. This recipe is an exception. Historically, land has been too valuable in China to raise dairy cattle for products such as butter. This recipe may have originated in northern China because butter is used in the northern region of Inner Mongolia. However, the majority of the Chinese provinces do not use butter at all. Because commercial bakeries in China use lard instead of butter, most pastries are not sweet as we know them. This recipe, using butter instead of lard, is an American adaptation of the Chinese recipe.

Almond Cookies are eaten with tea for a break during the day, but they are not served with a meal. The Chinese explain that they do not eat sweets after a meal because the memory of the foods is the best dessert.

NOTES

NOTES

NOTES

NOTES

Exploring International Foods

Travel Italy

Section Four

INTRODUCTION TO ITALIAN FOODS

BENVENUTO!

Welcome to Italy! Your culinary tour of Italy begins with the roots of Italian cooking traditions. You will learn how traditional Italian foods were created, and why Italy is now considered to have had the greatest influence on western European cuisine.

Reading the recipes will give you a chef's tour through Italy's 20 diverse regions. These 23 recipes are classic examples of Italian first courses, breads, vegetables, meat dishes, salads, and desserts. As you read the recipes and learn what ingredients are used in Italian foods, you will begin to understand Italian cooking style. After you identify the region on the map where each dish is prepared, you will feel as if you have traveled throughout Italy.

The highlight of your introduction to Italy will involve your observing the preparation of Calzone (kahl-TSOH-neh), a pizza turnover, and Deep-Fried Rice and Cheese Balls. Sampling these demonstration dishes will reveal what you have to look forward to when you cook your own Italian meal. In this section you will find

- an Italian food history
- a map of Italy's regions
- 23 Italian recipes

9
ITALIAN FOOD HISTORY

The more you know about the history of Italian food, the better you will understand the influence that food has had on Italian culture. By reading this history, you will discover why cooking of the north differs from that of the south. You will learn that hundreds of years ago, America helped Italy develop particular foods, most of which are still popular today. You will learn how the Italians, in turn, have influenced American cooking.

Much of what we know about the history of Italian cooking has been learned from two major sources: the records kept by poets and philosophers, and the artifacts discovered in the remains of ancient Italian cities. About 3,000 years ago, the Etruscans, people from the eastern shore of the Mediterranean, settled in northern central Italy and established a flourishing civilization. There is evidence of an Etruscan tomb in northern Italy from the 4th century B.C. on whose columns pictorial carvings depict utensils for making *pasta* (PAH-stah), a flour and water dough, either fresh or dried, made in various shapes and sizes.

The Greeks also knew of pasta and are credited for bringing "lasanon," now called *lasagna* (lah-ZAHN-ya), into southern Italy. The Arabs used dried pasta to preserve flour and make cooking easier on their long trips through the desert. They were responsible for introducing pasta into Sicily, an island off the coast of southern Italy. Marco Polo is credited with introducing a pasta noodle similar to spaghetti (spa-GET-e) as a result of his travels to China. Pasta was considered so valuable that in 1279 it was listed as part of an inheritance in an Italian will.

Salt was also very important. The early Romans were shepherds and learned how to obtain salt for their sheep by evaporating sea water. Salt became very valuable and was used in trade between the Etruscans of northern Italy and the Greeks of the south. In fact, our word "salary," which comes from the Latin word *salarium*, was derived from the Latin word *sal*, meaning salt. Salt had such high value, it was used as a portion of the wages paid to Roman soldiers.

Eventually, trade routes expanded outside Italy with the rise of the Roman Empire. The Romans already had conquered and were ruling a great part of the area we now call western Europe. By 200 B.C., Cato the Censor, a Roman statesman, became one of the earliest promoters of good nutrition. He wrote an encyclopedia that included essays on agriculture and medicine. He preached the benefits of cabbage, although he lacked the knowledge that cabbage was a good source of vitamin C. At that time, dried and cooked cereals lacking vitamin C were staples of the diet, but the advice of authorities such as Cato was followed. Those who could not afford cabbage ate boiled greens, a variety of chard, and the mallow plant, a European herb. Then, as today, it was considered good nutrition to eat a variety of foods in order to obtain the recommended nutrients.

Polenta (poe-LEN-tah) (a mush), served in northern Italy today, originated in early Roman times when *pulmentum*, a thick, cooked cereal, was a dietary staple. The Roman soldiers carried a primitive grain, usually millet, which they toasted on a hot stone over a campfire. They carried this roasted grain with them in their haversacks (knapsack-type bags) as a field ration. When a soldier was ready to eat, he boiled the grain and ate it as a mush, or he let it harden and ate it in the form of a cake. After Columbus discovered the New World, a source for corn, millet was eventually replaced by corn, and polenta became similar to cornmeal mush in the soft variety and cornbread in the hard variety.

The period between A.D. 1600 and A.D. 1300 is known as the Italian Renaissance. The culture was highly sophisticated, and cooking advanced to a fine art. Cooking schools were established, and the upper class enjoyed eating complicated and elaborate foods. Famous sculptors, architects, and artists were hired to prepare banquets for the upper class. Sculptures made of butter, ice, or sugar were popular. Prepared food looked like its natural form; for example, meat was cooked and then put back together to look like the animal from which it originated. Birds, such as the peacock, were stuffed, cooked with the head and feet still intact, and then the feathers were put back.

There were other foods important to Italian cooking that were introduced as a result of explorations of the New World. From America came potatoes, peppers, the white kidney beans used in *minestrone* (mee-nee-STRO-neh), and turkey, which became a substitute for peacock. No European had ever seen a tomato before Cortez conquered Mexico. The first tomato seen in Europe was golden and cherry-sized. At first it was used as a salad vegetable. It took 200 years for the Italians to develop the tomato into bigger red varieties and use it regularly in cooking. The tomato is still one of Italy's most popular staples for sauces.

TABLE MANNERS

During the Renaissance, table manners were important. Then,

as now, manners were based on logic. A 1475 Italian book on manners advised against disputes at the table, saying, "The stomach needs natural warmth, little motion, and little agitation; otherwise, it becomes weak and unable to produce its digestive juices." In 1480, an Italian book, *The Fifty Courtesies of the Table*, stated, "Do not stuff too large mouthfuls in both cheeks. Do not keep your hand too long in the platter, and put it in only when the other has withdrawn his hand from the dish."

Eating with forks became fashionable. A Byzantine princess had introduced a two-pronged fork to Italian upper-class society in the 11th century, but until the Renaissance, people ate with their fingers.

Table etiquette was expected. Weapons had to be left at the door, and hands had to be washed before eating. It was the custom to keep one's hands above the table, except when tossing scraps to the dogs, to make it evident that one did not have a concealed dagger.

Until napkins were introduced in Italy, fingers were wiped on the floor-length tablecloth. In upper-class homes, tables were set with many layers of tablecloths so that, one by one, soiled cloths could be removed during long, multi-course meals. It was the custom for Romans to clean their hands between courses by dipping their fingers in perfumed water. When napkins finally made their appearance, guests often brought their own so that choice leftovers could be taken home.

The Italians were responsible for the first fully developed cuisine in Europe, and it became the inspiration for many other European countries. In 1533, Catherine dé Medici, a 14-year-old Italian princess, married a French prince, who later ruled France as King Henry II. When Catherine recognized that French cooking was not as advanced, and eating not as refined, as it was in Italy, she decided to further improve French cooking. She had expert Italian chefs travel to France and introduce fine pastry, desserts such as ices and ice cream, and vegetables such as artichokes, broccoli, and peas. The elegant customs and table manners of Italian royalty were adopted, including the use of imported Venetian glassware, silver and gold table ornaments, fine chinaware, and linen tablecloths. As a result of this great influence, Italy became known as the "mother" of French, as well as western European, cuisine.

REGIONAL DIFFERENCES

For centuries, Italy was divided into rival city-states. Politically separated, each city-state developed its own identity, which included regional forms of speech and cooking. Foods and dishes of each state were different, and even after Italy was united in 1861, the regional characteristics of Italian cooking continued. Cooking is still well defined within Italy's 20 regions.

Figure 9.1. Twenty Culinary Regions of Italy

Italy's geographical makeup also contributed to its regional cooking (see Figure 9.1). Italy is a peninsula, about as large as the state of Arizona, with an area of 116,000 square miles. It is shaped like a boot, with the toe pointing towards Africa. The Apennine mountain range runs through the center of Italy. Dividing the country and making travel across Italy difficult, the mountains so isolated some areas that people could eat only what was grown and produced locally. Fresh seafood was

86 Section Four • Introduction to Italian Foods

eaten along the 2,500 miles of coastline, while in the mountains, wild game, such as rabbit, was hunted for food.

There is also a difference between the northern and southern terrain in Italy. Northern Italy's regions have fertile soil and flat land and are now more industrialized and prosperous than those in the south. The flat land is suitable for raising dairy cattle, and as a result, butter is used as fat for cooking. Northern cooking is much lighter, more subtle, and more varied than that of the southern regions that lie in the "heel" of Italy. The herbs sage and rosemary are used with a light hand in the north. The pasta is usually noodles, the flat variety of pasta, freshly made with eggs.

In the poorer south, flavors are stronger through the use of garlic, basil, oregano, olives, and tomatoes. The mountainous countryside is not appropriate for raising cattle, so olives grown on the slopes provide oil for use as cooking fat. Pasta is manufactured in tubular form and made without eggs. *Macaroni* is a common variety.

Today when you eat spaghetti or lasagna, you probably don't think that you are eating Italian food. These dishes don't seem foreign anymore. Americans have adopted many of the dishes that were brought here by Italians emigrating from southern Italy. After World War II, pasta dishes, with their heavy spices and thick mushroom, tomato, and cheese sauces, quickly appealed to Americans because of their low cost, good nutrition, pleasing taste, and easy preparation.

Both northern and southern Italians insist upon the use of fresh ingredients. Many prefer to shop daily in specialty shops, such as the dairy, bakery, and meat, fruit, and vegetable markets. The fruit and vegetables sold in the marketplace come from farms only a few miles away, and produce is eaten seasonally, when it is at its peak of flavor and texture. The cooking methods of Italy stress retaining the quality of the ingredients—their taste, color, shape, and freshness. Cooking is simple, direct, and careful; and, the Italian home is where Italian cooking is at its best.

The most common ingredients in Italian foods are listed in Table 9.1.

MEAL PATTERNS

To eat in Italy is to eat in the "continental" style. Breakfast is usually light—tea, chocolate, or coffee with milk is served with bread and jam. The main meal is usually eaten about 1 o'clock, often on the patio of the house, as the weather is warm much of the year. An italian special-occasion dinner consists of four or five courses: *antipasto*, (ahn-tee-PAHS-toh), which is the appetizer; pasta, soup, or rice; fish or meat served with a vegetable; salad; and cheese and fruit. Fresh green salads are served after the main course and are tossed with olive oil, wine vinegar, and a bit of garlic.

Table 9.1 Ingredients Common to Italian Recipes

*artichokes	geese	**Seasonings**
*asparagus	*mushrooms	*basil
broccoli	*olives	*bay leaf
*carrots	*onions	cloves
*celery	*pastas	coriander
*cheese—parmesan,	*peppers	*garlic
mozzarella,	*pork	marjoram
romaine, ricotta	rabbit	mint
*chicken	*rice	*oregano
duck	*sausage—salami,	parsley
eggplant	mortadella	*rosemary
fish—shellfish	*spinach	saffron
game in season	*tomatoes	sage
		tarragon
		thyme

*Foods used in one or more of the Italian recipes.

Elaborate desserts do not have a place in the everyday Italian meal. Homemade desserts are simple cookies, cakes, or puddings. For special occasions, such as Christmas, desserts similar to *panettone*, (pah-neh-TO-neh) a rich, sweet, cakelike bread filled with nuts, raisins, and candied fruit, are purchased and eaten at home. Italy is famous for fruit ices, called *granite* (grah-NEE-teh), and *gelata*, which is similar to ice cream that is very rich and dense with little air. *Espresso* (ess-PRESS-o), extremely black and strong coffee, ends the meal. It is usually served in small cups.

The evening meal in Italy is light. A one-dish meal might be served, such as pasta, fish, stew, rice, a *frittata* (free-TAH-tah) (nonfolded omelet), or stuffed vegetables.

Now turn to the Activities for the Italy unit and remove Activity 1, Italian Food History Review. Complete the Italian Food History Review and give it to your instructor for evaluation.

10
EXPLORING ITALIAN RECIPES

In this chapter, you will use the Italian recipes provided at the end of the Italy unit. You will become familiar with Italian cooking by reading each recipe and completing two related activities. The recipes are yours to keep when your culinary tour is concluded. Complete this chapter by following Steps 1 through 4:

Step 1: Remove the Italian recipe sheets and cut them apart.

Step 2: Read the Italian recipes and descriptions. The recipes are labeled in the following categories: First Course, Bread, Vegetable, Meat, Salad, and Dessert. The last five recipes are marked with an asterisk (*). Read and use these recipes to complete some of the activities but *do not* use them in your menu plans. These recipes are added for you to prepare at home.

    To indicate approximately how much the recipe will cost to prepare, each recipe is rated either low cost, moderate cost, or high cost. The cost is based on the prices of the ingredients, which may vary because of different seasons and your location. On the back of each recipe is a brief history of each dish and information about the region where the dish is popular.

Step 3: Remove Activity 2, Italian Recipe Match. Completing this activity will make you aware of recipe histories, names, food categories, and ingredients. Review both sides of each recipe in order to finish this activity. When finished, give your Italian Recipe Match to your instructor for evaluation.

Step 4: Remove Activity 3, Italian Map Review. Completing this activity will help you become familiar with the various culinary regions of Italy and the regions where the recipes are popular. Review the descriptions of the recipes as you do this activity. When finished, give your Italian Map Review to your instructor for evaluation.

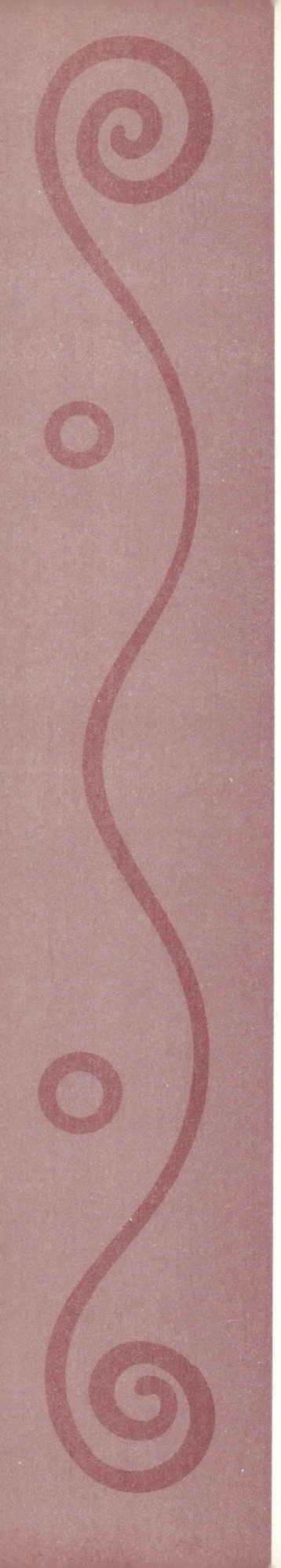

11

ITALIAN RECIPE DEMONSTRATIONS

In this chapter you will get to the heart of Italian food by tasting classic Italian cooking. Two Italian recipes will be demonstrated, and you will learn how to prepare them. While the recipes are being demonstrated, be sure to take good notes. The information in your notes will help you prepare the dishes later. The answers to the questions below will add to your knowledge of the recipes. Having the answers explained during the demonstrations and in the recipes will ensure your success.

DEEP-FRIED RICE AND CHEESE BALL DEMONSTRATION

Notes: _____

_____

_____

_____

_____

_____

_____

_____

_____

_____

_____

QUESTIONS ON THE DEEP-FRIED RICE AND CHEESE BALL DEMONSTRATION

1. What are the correct proportions of water to rice when cooking rice?

_____
_____
_____

2. Why is it important not to "peek" while rice is cooking?

_____
_____
_____

3. When rice is done, how must it look on top?

_____
_____
_____

4. Why is it better to prepare the rice ahead of time for this recipe?

_____
_____
_____

5. Why are eggs an essential ingredient in this recipe?

_____
_____
_____

6. What does the cooking term *cube* mean?

_____
_____
_____

7. Why is the correct temperature of the oil for deep-fat-frying so important?

_____
_____
_____

PIZZA DOUGH FOR CALZONE AND CALZONE DEMONSTRATION

Notes: _____
_____
_____
_____
_____
_____
_____
_____
_____

QUESTIONS ON THE PIZZA DOUGH FOR CALZONE AND CALZONE DEMONSTRATION

1. Yeast is available in what two forms?

_____
_____
_____

2. What is the correct water temperature for dissolving dry yeast?

_____
_____
_____

92   Section Four ● Introduction to Italian Foods

3. How can you determine the correct temperature of the water?

4. What does sugar do to yeast?

5. What does salt do to yeast?

6. What does yeast do to dough?

7. What is kneading and what does it do to the dough?

8. What is gluten and why is it necessary in dough?

Section Five

PLANNING YOUR ITALIAN MEAL

You have already explored Italy by way of map, history, recipes, and sample tasting. Now your class will prepare an Italian meal. This meal will be similar in flavor to the native Italian cuisine that you would find if you were actually in Italy.

The success of your Italian meal depends upon the combined effort of all students in each kitchen group. The food should be well prepared and attractively displayed on the buffet. The dining table should be properly set, and the kitchen should be clean. Remember that good table manners enable you to have an enjoyable dining experience.

While working in your assigned kitchen group, you must have your duties clearly in mind to ensure that the Italian meal is a success. Planning ahead of time for the cooking and evaluation days will give you the confidence necessary to carry out your duties smoothly. Each part of this section is designed to prepare you for both the cooking and evaluation days. In this section you will find

- a guide to help you select your Italian menu
- guides for Italian recipe nutrition, convenience, and cost
- directions for setting a buffet and dining table
- seven ways to improve table manners
- a planning form for the cooking and evaluation days

12

SELECTING YOUR ITALIAN MENU

Your meal will be similar to an Italian midday meal—the main one of the day. People come home from work, and children come home from school, making this meal an important family event.

You will select your menu from recipes in the following food categories: first course, bread, vegetable, meat, salad, and dessert. Each food category has three recipes. You will choose one recipe from each category. Remember that the recipes marked with an asterisk are for home use only.

After selecting one recipe from each of the food categories, you will have a total of six recipes, one of which you and your kitchen group will prepare.

A brief description of the food categories from which you will choose is as follows:

first course The first-course recipes represent the many pasta, rice, gnocchi, and soup dishes that are served throughout Italy. Pasta is always served as a separate course before the meat dish.

breads Bread accompanies the main meal, although butter is never put on the table.

vegetables Simple vegetable dishes are usually considered as side dishes and are served with the meat course. However, when vegetable dishes are substantial, as in the recipes presented here, they are treated as a separate course.

meat course Steaks, chops, and roasts are simply prepared to complement the many course main meals in Italy, yet there is a variety of chicken dishes and veal specialties throughout Italy represented by the recipes included here. Also, fish, from Italy's extensive coastline and inland waterways, is a popular staple and an alternative to meat.

salads   Salad follows the meat course in order to clear the palate, or freshen the taste buds.

desserts   Dessert in an Italian meal is usually cheese and fruit; the dessert recipes presented here would only be served for a special event.

Italians are careful to choose dishes that together balance the meal. Each dish adds to the appearance, texture, and flavor of the meal, while providing the necessary nutritional balance. As you read the Italian recipes, decide what you think would make the most appealing combination of dishes for the buffet. Incorporate foods with different colors and shapes to add interest to the meal. Be sure not to repeat major ingredients when you select the recipes. For example, if you choose *Tortellini* (tor-teh-LEE-nee) to start the meal, you should not repeat pasta in another dish. This way, your meal will not become monotonous, with several of the dishes having the same texture and the same taste. Moreover, by not repeating major foods in your menu, your meal will be nutritionally balanced.

When selecting a menu, be adventurous! Choose recipes you have neither tasted nor prepared. Look for ingredients that you have not tried. New taste experiences contribute to the excitement of cooking recipes from other countries. You may be pleasantly surprised, and as a result, you will develop a broader taste palate. Don't be concerned with unfamiliar or complicated directions. Remember, your kitchen group will prepare only one recipe, so you will have ample time to study it and clear up anything that you do not understand.

Select your menu in these two easy steps:

Step 1: Read the Italian recipes. After you are familiar with them, proceed to Step 2.

Step 2: Remove Activity 4, Selecting Your Italian Menu. Complete the activity and give it to your instructor for evaluation. He or she will tell you how the class menu will be selected and how each kitchen group will determine which recipe it will prepare.

13

ITALIAN RECIPES: NUTRITION, CONVENIENCE, AND COST

In this chapter, you will learn the nutritional value of your menu. You will learn how to determine if your recipes are convenient to prepare and how much your meal will cost. The knowledge that you gain from completing this part will give you a good background for selecting recipes and planning meals when you are cooking on your own.

NUTRITION

A variety of healthy food is essential to good nutrition. Because people eat not only to enjoy the taste of food, but also to remain healthy, it is necessary to consider the nutritional value of your recipes. For example, spaghetti is a grain product and a good source of carbohydrates for energy, but it would be poor nutrition to eat just plain spaghetti all day.

Your body requires more than just energy foods: it needs the nutrients that are found in the four major food groups:

- meat, poultry, fish, eggs, and legumes (dried beans and peas)
- milk products
- fruit and vegetable
- bread and cereal

Eating the recommended amount of food from each group provides the required nutrients needed in your daily diet.

Table 13.1 shows the necessary servings per day from each food group for your age.

Table 13.1 Necessary Servings Per Day

Food Group	Servings
Meat/Poultry/Fish/Eggs/Legumes	2
Milk Products	4
Fruit/Vegetable	4
Bread/Cereal	4

Table 13.2 will help you determine the number of servings from these food groups provided by your Italian meal. The completed chart will indicate to you which food group your meal has too much or too little of. If it is low in one group, you simply include food from that group in another meal that day. If it is high in another group, you decrease the amount of food in that group at another meal.

Italians, by virtue of their meal planning, maintain a well-balanced diet. Italian meals consist of a variety of foods, although it is common for the meals to be high in carbohydrates. Pasta and bread are both eaten during a meal; however, the portions of pasta in the first course are always small. Because vegeta-

Table 13.2 Food Group Menu Chart

Food Groups	Meat/Poultry Fish/Eggs/ Legumes	Milk Products	Fruit/ Vegetable	Bread/ Cereal
Daily Necessary Servings*	2	4	4	4
First Course:				
Bread:				
Vegetable:				
Meat Course:				
Salad:				
Dessert:				
Totals				
Servings Still Needed				

*for your age group

98   Section Five ● Planning Your Italian Meal

bles and fruits play an important role in Italian meals, the daily requirement of four servings of vegetables is met easily.

Follow these directions for completing the Food Group Menu Chart.

1. List the recipes your class has selected in the Recipes column on the chart.
2. Read the ingredients of each recipe and check (√) the major food group into which each falls. A recipe may fall into more than one food group. When this occurs, only major ingredients are classified.
3. Total the number of servings in each food group column.
4. Using Table 13.2, write the number of servings still needed to attain the necessary daily food group recommendations.

CONVENIENCE

You will know a recipe is convenient if

- you easily can obtain the ingredients
- you have the necessary equipment to make the dish
- you have adequate time to prepare it

Because some ingredients are too expensive or not available, other ingredients, which still assure the desired results, can be substituted. For example, the veal in Veal Scallopini (skah-lo-PEE-neh) can be very expensive. However, less costly filleted chicken breasts can be substituted without altering the flavor of the dish.

First, make a list of the equipment needed. Then check the kitchen to see if all the equipment is there. The correct equipment is essential for the smooth and efficient preparation of your recipe. Carefully read the recipe to determine how much time will be required, and make sure the recipe fits into your time schedule. Preparing part of the recipe one day and completing it the next also will be more convenient to prepare.

The decision to prepare Italian food may result in some minor inconveniences. You might have to search the grocery store for certain ingredients, such as artichoke hearts, that you are not accustomed to buying. You might have to purchase new equipment or figure out how to improvise with what you have, in order to prepare a recipe at home. For example, the recipe for Biscuit *Tortoni* (tor-TOE-nee) calls for a *springform pan*, which you might not have. You will find, however, that the opportunity to expand your Italian cooking knowledge is worth the purchase of a piece of special equipment.

Answer the following questions, which will help your recipe preparation. Planning ahead will ensure efficiency on preparation day.

1. What recipe ingredients are not available? _____

   _____

2. What major pieces of equipment (pans, bowls) will be necessary? _____

   _____

3. What utensils will be necessary? _____

   _____

4. What necessary equipment is missing? _____

   _____

5. How might you improvise this missing equipment?

   _____

   _____

6. How much time will your recipe take to prepare?

   (Estimate) _____

7. How do you rate the convenience of your recipe? Check (✓) one:

   ____ quick and easy

   ____ somewhat involved

   ____ difficult but worth the effort

COST

In this activity, each kitchen group will compute the cost of its recipe. Afterwards, you will total the cost of all recipes and find out the cost of the entire meal.

Soon you will be responsible for your own food budget. You will want to keep your food costs within the amount of money you have budgeted. You must know if you can feed the desired number of people within your budget. Knowing the cost of individual servings will help you determine if you can.

If a recipe costs $10.00 to prepare and makes ten servings, it costs only $1.00 per serving; however, if that dish made only four servings, the cost would more than double to $2.50 per serving. The cost of the recipe per serving is the meaningful figure.

SECTION A   Name of Recipe: *Calzone*

(1) Recipe Ingredients	(2) Amount Required	(3) Price Per Item	(4) Amount of Store Container	(5) Cost Computation	(6) Total Ingredient Cost
yeast	2 pkgs.	.59	strip of 3	.59 ÷ 3 = .19⅔ or .20 .20 × 2 = .40	.40
flour	3½ cups	.85	5 pounds	.85 ÷ 5 = .17 ÷ 4 = .04 .04 × 3.5 = .14	.14
oil	7 tbsp.	1.81	quart	1.81 ÷ 64 = .02 53/64 .03 .03 × 7 = .21	.21
salami	½ pound	3.81	10 ounces	3.18 ÷ 10 = .31 8/10 .32 .32 × 8 = 2.56	2.56
onion	¼ cup	.48	pound	.48 ÷ 3 = .16 ¼ × 16/1 = .04	.04
mushrooms	½ pound	1.77	pound	1.77 ÷ 16 = .11 .11 × 8 = .88	.88
green pepper	⅓ cup	.83	pound	.83 ÷ 4 = .20 ⅓ × 20/1 = .07	.07
tomato sauce	8 ounce can	.29	8 ounce can	exact amount needed (.29)	.29
olives	2¼ ounce can	.69	2¼ ounce can	exact amount needed (.69)	.69
mozzarella	2⅓ cups	2.56	16 ounce ball	2.56 ÷ 4 = .64 2⅓ C = 7/3 × .64/1 = 1.49	1.49

SECTION B ──────────────────────► Total Recipe Cost: **$6.77**

SECTION C ──► Total Recipe Cost ÷ Number of Servings = Cost Per Serving
($6.77) ÷ (6) = ($1.13)

Figure 13.1. Sample Filled-in Activity 5

Study the example of the Italian Meal Cost Sheet (Figure 13.1). The cost per serving of Calzone has been determined. By studying these steps, you will be able to follow the directions for completing your own Italian Meal Cost Sheet. See how Jennifer Chin determined the cost of Calzone.

Step 1:   Jennifer read the recipe to determine what ingredients should be included in figuring the cost of the recipe (see Figure 13.2). Ingredients such as salt, pepper, vanilla, baking soda, baking powder, lemon juice, vinegar, and most spices are on hand in the kitchen, so it is not necessary to include small amounts of these items when figuring per serving cost. Jennifer determined that the cost of the sugar, salt, garlic, basil, and red pepper did not have to be included. She recorded the remaining ingredients for the Calzone in Column 1 of the Italian Meal Cost Sheet.

Chapter 13 • Italian Recipes: Nutrition, Convenience, and Cost

Calzone

½ lb. dry salami, finely chopped
¼ cup finely chopped onion
1 clove garlic, crushed
½ lb. mushrooms, chopped
⅓ cup finely chopped green pepper
3 tbsp. oil
8 oz. can tomato sauce
2¼ oz. can sliced olives, drained
1 tsp. dry oregano, crushed
1 tsp. dry basil, crushed
½ tsp. sugar
¼ tsp. crushed red pepper
2⅓ cups shredded mozzarella cheese

Pizza Dough for Calzone

2 pkgs. dry yeast
1 pinch sugar
1¼ cups lukewarm water
3½ cups all-purpose flour
1 tsp. salt
¼ cup oil
Makes 36 small for appetizers
 or 6 for a main course

Figure 13.2. Recipe for Calzone

Step 2: Jennifer wrote the amount of each ingredient she needed in Column 2. Because oil was called for twice, the amount of oil recorded in column two was the total.

Step 3: Jennifer took the Italian Meal Cost Sheet to the grocery store. She listed the price the store charged for each item in Column 3, and then she bought the quantity of each ingredient closest to the amount she needed. For example, she needed one-half pound of salami. The store had 6-ounce and 10-ounce packages of salami. Jennifer purchased the 10-ounce package of

Table 13.3 Table of Weights and Measures

3 teaspoons	1 tablespoon
4 tablespoons	¼ cup
5⅓ tablespoons	⅓ cup
8 tablespoons	½ cup
16 tablespoons	1 cup or 8 ounces (oz.)
2 cups	1 pint
2 pints	1 quart
4 cups	1 quart
4 quarts	1 gallon
16 ounces	1 pound (lb.)

salami because it was less expensive than buying two 6-ounce packages.

Step 4: Jennifer listed the amount of the item's store container in Column 4. Stores sell items in different measurements, weights, or quantities, depending on the item itself. Pints, quarts, gallons, ounces, pounds, bunches, or "per each" are common quantity terms.

Step 5: Jennifer computed the cost of each ingredient in Column 5. When necessary, she referred to the Table of Weights and Measures or to the Table of Equivalent Amounts (see Tables 13.3 and 13.4).

Table 13.4 Equivalent Amounts (Approximate)

Item	Common Weights or Units	Equivalence in Cups or Spoons
Asparagus	1 pound	2 cups
Bacon, uncooked	1 pound	2⅔ cups diced
	1½ ounces	¼ cup
Butter	1 pound (4 sticks)	2 cups
	1 stick	½ cup
Beans, dry	1 pound (2½ cups) raw	5 to 7 cups cooked
	¼ pound (½ cup) raw	1¼ to 1¾ cups cooked
green	1 pound raw or cooked	3 cups
Bread Crumbs	3 to 4 slices dried bread	1 cup fine dry crumbs
	1 slice fresh bread	½ cup fresh crumbs
Carrots	1 pound (6 medium)	2 cups sliced
Cauliflower	2 pounds (average with leaves and core removed)	4 cups flowerets
	½ pound	1 cup flowerets
Celery	10 stalks per bunch (average)	5 cups
	1 stalk	½ cup sliced
Cheese, hard	1 pound	5 cups
Parmesan freshly grated	1 pound	4 cups
Chicken, uncooked	3½ pound	2 cups cooked diced

Table 13.4 (Continued)

Item	Common Weights or Units	Equivalence in Cups or Spoons
Corn Meal, uncooked	1 cup	4 cups cooked
Flour, wheat	1 pound	4 cups unsifted
Grapefruit	1 pound (1 large)	1 to 1½ cups sectioned
Greens, salad	1 serving 1 head or 1 bunch (4 servings)	2 cups loosely packed 8 cups loosely packed
Ham (see Bacon)		
Lemons	1 medium	1 to 2 tablespoons juice, 1 tablespoon grated peel
Macaroni	⅛ pound (½ cup) dry ½ pound (2 cups) dry 1 cup dry	1 cup cooked 4 cups cooked 2 cups cooked
Mushrooms, uncooked	1 pound	4 to 5 cups sliced
Noodles (see Macaroni)		
Onions, dry	1 pound (3 large, 4 medium, 5 small) 1 large (⅓ pound)	3 cups 1 cup
green	1 bunch with tops (5 onions)	½ cup
Oranges	½ pound 1 pound (3 medium) 1 medium	1 cup sectioned 2 cups sectioned 2 to 3 tablespoons peel or rind
Peas, green frozen	1 pound 10 ounces ¼ 10-ounce box	1 cup shelled 2 cups cooked ½ cup
Peppers, bell	1 pound (3 to 6 small) ¼ pound	4 cups chopped 1 cup chopped
Potatoes	1 pound (3 medium)	2 cups mashed, 3 cups sliced
Rice	½ pound (1 cup) raw	3 cups cooked
Spaghetti (see Macaroni)		

104 Section Five ● Planning Your Italian Meal

Table 13.4 (Continued)

Item	Common Weights or Units	Equivalence in Cups or Spoons
Spinach	1 pound (3 cups) raw	1 cup cooked
Strawberries	1½ pound basket	4 cups
Sugar, granulated	1 pound	2 cups
Tomatoes, fresh	1 pound (3 medium, 4 small)	1½ cups peeled and chopped
Vanilla Wafers	¼ pound (22 wafers)	1 cup fine crumbs
Zucchini	1 pound (6 small, 4 medium)	3½ cups sliced
	1 medium	1 cup

The Tables 13.3 and 13.4 will help you figure the cost of the ingredients in a recipe. To use the tables, you need to know the amount of each ingredient required for your recipe. Here are two examples:

1. Suppose your recipe calls for 7 tablespoons of oil and you want to figure the cost. Table 13.3 shows that 16 tablespoons equal 1 cup, and 4 cups equal 1 quart. Multiply 4 × 16, which is 64—the number of tablespoons in 1 quart. Next, divide the current market price for 1 quart of oil by the number of tablespoons in 1 quart (64). This gives you the price per tablespoon: $1.84 ÷ 64 = $.028, which is approximately 3 cents per tablespoon. Finally, 7 × $.03 = $.21 which is 21 cents, the cost of 7 tablespoons of oil.

2. Your recipe calls for ½ cup of butter, and you want to figure the cost. Table 13.4 shows that 4 sticks equal 1 pound of butter, and 1 cube equals ½ cup of butter. Divide the current market price for one pound of butter by 4: $1.89 ÷ 4 = $.471, or 47 cents, the cost of ½ cup of butter.

Figure 13.3 shows an explanation of the computation Jennifer did in Column 5, using both tables.

Step 6: In Column 6, Jennifer recorded the answers she had computed in Column 5.

Now you are ready to figure the cost of your recipe. Remove Activity 5, Italian Meal Cost Sheet. Follow the directions given here to complete this activity. Refer to the example of Jennifer Chin if you need help. Remember, the recipe cost you compute should be *approximate*. Current market prices should be used to determine the cost of your recipes. You can read grocery store advertisements or go to the market to find out current prices.

Cost Analysis

1. Yeast
   Store quantity . . . . 3 packages
   Store cost (in dollars) 59
   Cost per package . . . . .59 divided by 3 = .196 or .20
   Amount required (2 pkg.) × cost for one (.20) = Cost for ingredient (.40)
2. Flour
   Store quantity . . . . 5 pounds
   Store cost (in dollars) 85
   Cost per cup . . . . .85 divided by .17 for 1 lb. or .04 a cup
   Amount required (3½ cups) × cost for one (.04) = Cost for ingredient (.14)
   In Table 13.4, Jennifer found that 4 cups of flour = 1 lb. So 1 cup = ¼ pound.
   17 divided by 4 = .04 (rounded off).
3. Oil
   Store quantity . . . . quart
   Store cost (in dollars) . . . . 1.81 quart
   Cost per tablespoon . . . . 1.81 divided by 64 = .03
   Amount required (7 tablespoons) × cost for one (.09) = Cost for ingredient (.21)
   In Table 13.3, Jennifer found that 64 tablespoons of oil = 1 qt.
4. Salami
   Store quantity . . . . 10 ounces
   Store cost (in dollars) 3.18
   Cost per ounce . . . . 3.18 divided by 10 = .32
   Amount required (8 ounces) × cost for one (.32) = Cost for ingredient (2.56)
5. Onion
   Store quantity . . . . 1 pound
   Store cost (in dollars) 48/pound
   Cost per cup . . . . .48 divided by ⅓ = .16
   Amount required (¼ cup) × cost for one (.16) = Cost for ingredient (.04)
   In Table 13.4, Jennifer found that 3 cups of onions = 1 pound. So 1 cup = ⅓ pound.
6. Mushrooms
   Store quantity . . . . 1 pound
   Store cost (in dollars) 1.77/pound
   Cost per ounce . . . . 1.77 divided by 16 = .11
   Amount required (8 ounces) × cost for one (.11) = Cost for ingredient (.88)
   In Table 13.3, Jennifer found that 16 ounces of mushrooms = 1 pound. She needed 8 ounces, which is ½ pound.
7. Green Pepper
   Store quantity . . . . 1 pound
   Store cost (in dollars) 84/pound
   Cost per cup . . . . .84 divided by 4 = .21
   Amount required (⅓ cup) × cost for one (.21) = Cost for ingredient (.07)
   In Table 13.4, Jennifer found that 1 pound of green peppers = 4 cups.
8. Tomato Sauce
   Store quantity . . . . 8 ounce can
   Store cost (in dollars) 29
   Cost per can 29
   Amount required (8 ounce can at .29) = Cost for ingredient (.29)
9. Olives
   Store quantity . . . . 2¼ ounce can
   Store cost (in dollars) 69
   Cost per can 69
   Amount required (2¼ ounce can at .69) = Cost for ingredient (.69)

Figure 13.3. Recipe Cost Analysis

> **10.** Mozzarella
> Store quantity .... 16-ounce ball
> Store cost(in dollars) 2.56
> Cost per cup .... 2.56 divided by 4 = .64
> Amount required (2⅓ cups) × cost for one (.64) = Cost for ingredient (1.491 or 1.49)
> In Table 13.4, Jennifer found that 1 pound of cheese = 4 cups.

Note: All costs should be approximate. When a price per unit comes out unevenly, round up (as stores do) to the nearest cent.

First, fill in the name of the recipe your kitchen group will prepare in the space provided. Then do as follows:

Section A
Column 1: Determine what ingredients should be figured in the cost of the recipe. List each of these ingredients.
Column 2: List the amount of the ingredient your recipe requires.
Column 3: List the price of the item.
Column 4: List the amount of the ingredient in store container.
Column 5: Show your computation of the cost per ingredient.
Column 6: List the cost of each ingredient.

Section B
Add the cost of each ingredient in Column 6 to get the total cost of the recipe. Write that figure in Section B.

Section C
Divide the total cost of the recipe by the number of persons it serves to determine the cost per serving. Write these figures in Section C.

Section D
Column 1: List the recipes prepared by other kitchen groups.
Column 2: List the total cost of each recipe.
Column 3: List the cost per serving of each recipe.

Section E
Add the cost of each recipe in Column 2 to get the cost of the total meal. Write that figure in Column 2. Add all of the recipe costs for each serving in Column 3 to determine the total cost of the meal per serving. Write that figure in Column 3.

Give your completed Italian Meal Cost Sheet to your instructor for evaluation.

14
TABLE SETTINGS AND TABLE MANNERS

BUFFET SETTINGS

It is important to know how to set the buffet and dining tables properly when you serve your Italian meal on evaluation day. If you are the host or hostess, setting the tables is one of your duties. You will place the dish your kitchen group prepares on the buffet table and set your kitchen group's dining table. Even if you are not the host or hostess, it is every kitchen group member's responsibility to make sure that the buffet and dining tables are set properly. A properly set table adds to the enjoyment of the meal.

Serving a meal buffet-style is extremely efficient for entertaining. A buffet enables a large group of people to serve themselves easily in a short period of time. This is particularly important at school.

An attractive centerpiece of Italian ceramics, straw baskets filled with fresh vegetables or flowers, or hand-embroidered linens would add to the beauty of the table and the room. To create the atmosphere of an Italian *trattoria* (restaurant), use a checkered tablecloth, and a wicker-covered wine bottle holding a candle as the centerpiece.

The correct placement of the food is important. Everything should be organized to assure ease in serving. The foods for each course are placed next to each other on the table, in the order in which you wish them to be selected. The foods for the Italian meal designed for your class are placed on the buffet table and served in the following order:

- Antipasto
- First Course
- Bread
- Vegetable
- Meat Course
- Salad
- Dessert

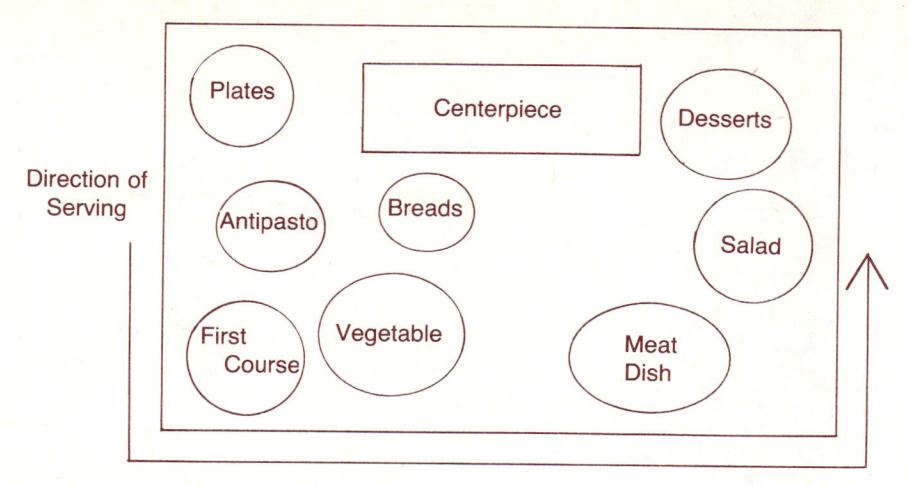

Figure 14.1. Buffet Table

Figure 14.1 illustrates a correctly set buffet table for your Italian meal.

Marinated vegetables can be served as the antipasto, in which case the salad would be eliminated. In many Italian meals, the vegetable dish accompanies the meat dish and is placed on the buffet table after the meat. However, the vegetable dishes for which recipes are given in this book are substantial and are eaten before the meat; therefore, they are placed on the buffet in that order.

DINING TABLE SETTINGS

How you set the dining table in your classroom depends on the equipment available. The following directions tell how a basic table should be set. Refer to Figure 14.2 as you read the instructions.

1. The napkin, plate, and flatware should be placed one inch from the edge of the placemat. If you have trouble judging an inch, use your thumb as a ruler. From the tip of your thumb to the first joint is approximately one inch.
2. If you are serving buffet style, the plates will be on the buffet table. The utensils must be correctly positioned on the dining table so that there will be room for the plate after it has been filled from the buffet. To set the table properly, use one plate as a guide to position the utensils correctly.
3. The knife is placed to the right of the plate with the sharp edge facing the plate.
4. The spoon is placed next to the knife.
5. The waterglass is placed at the tip of the knife.
6. The fork is placed to the left of the plate, with the tines facing up.
7. The napkin is placed beside the fork and folded so that it opens like a book.

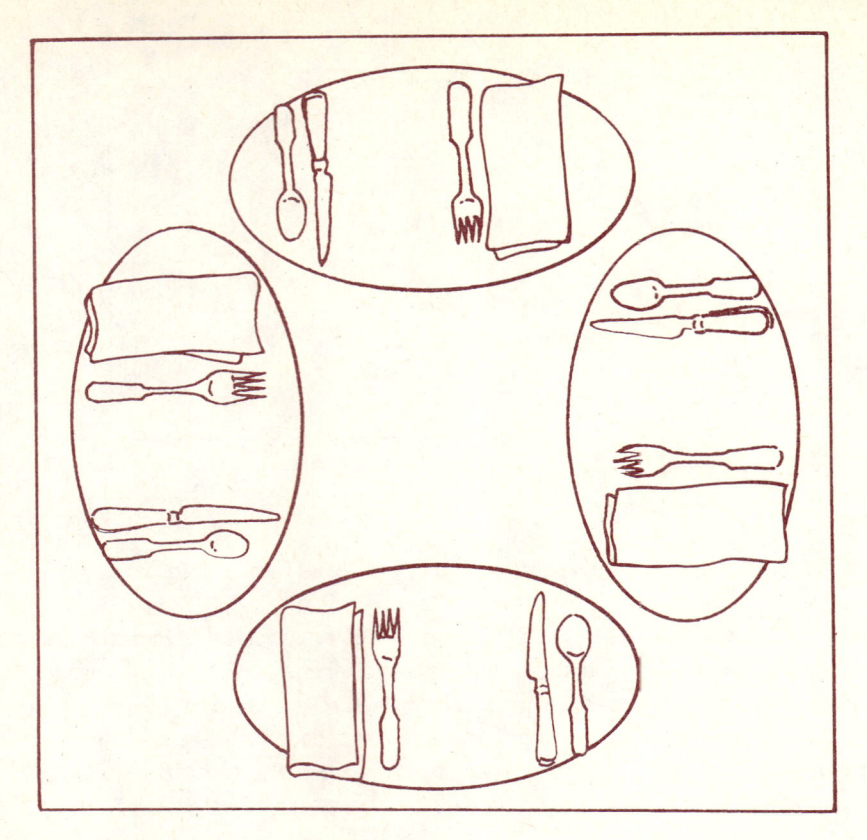

Figure 14.2. Dining Table

Now that you are familiar with the way to set a dining table, draw a place setting on the placemat in Figure 14.3. Include the table equipment that you have available for your kitchen group. The completed drawing will remind you how the table should be set for your Italian meal.

TABLE MANNERS

Good table manners allow you and your companions to have a pleasant mealtime experience. Your concern for the pleasure of others at the table is obvious from your good manners. Be aware of good table manners and practice them while eating at all times—not just in the classroom. Eventually good manners will become second nature.

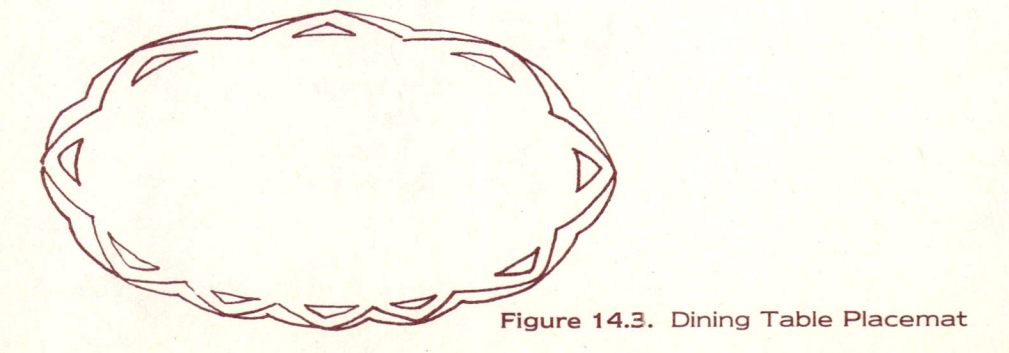

Figure 14.3. Dining Table Placemat

110 Section Five ● Planning Your Italian Meal

After your meal is finished, you will evaluate the manners you observed during the meal with your kitchen group. Here are some suggestions for good table manners.

1. Make sure you are well-groomed before you serve yourself at the buffet table. Check that your hands and fingernails are clean and your hair and clothes are neat.
2. After you have served yourself, put your plate at your table setting, then sit down from the left side of your chair.
3. Unfold your napkin when the host or hostess does. Do not shake it open. A small napkin may be opened completely, while a large one may be left folded in half.
4. Begin eating when your host or hostess does. Eat slowly, one piece of food at a time. Do not talk with your mouth full. If you take small bites that can be easily swallowed, you will be able to talk when you want. Chew your food quietly with your mouth closed.
5. Sit upright when you eat. Keep your arms off the table and your hands away from your face and hair. Do not play with anything on the table.
6. It is the responsibility of the host or hostess to keep the conversation moving while making sure that everyone is included. Each person, however, should contribute to the conversation. Listen to others and acknowledge what they say.
7. When you have finished eating, place your knife (carving end well in the center of the plate) and fork (tines up) across the center of your plate, parallel to each other. When everyone has finished eating, the host or hostess will put his or her napkin on the table. This signals that the meal is completed. Place your napkin on the table without refolding or crumpling it. Return it, loosely gathered, to its original place to the left of the plate. If you have to get up during the meal, put your napkin on your chair. If you put it on the table, it may get in the way of the person sitting next to you. Also, if your napkin is messy, it isn't an attractive sight for anyone to see while eating.

15

YOUR ITALIAN MEAL PLANNING FORM

You will use your Italian Meal Planning Form during the cooking and evaluation days. On the cooking day you will prepare as much of the recipe as possible. On evaluation day, you will finish preparing the recipe, set the dining table, arrange the food on the buffet, serve yourself, eat, and write an evaluation of your recipe. The planning form has a time schedule to follow, so you will easily be able to complete all your responsibilities on both days. If you do run behind, the time schedule on your planning form lets you know what still must be completed.

The success of both the cooking and evaluation days depends on the ability of the kitchen group members to work together to ensure that all the duties are completed correctly. You are expected to help other students in your kitchen if you finish your job duties early. Your completed planning form will have the names and duties of the members of your kitchen group, so you will know how you can help each of them. For example, if you, as the host or hostess, finish your assigned duties early and see that the cook has not completed the recipe, you can offer to help. You will know how to help because you have read the recipe and are familiar with the ingredients. Carefully check to see that the place settings are correct on the dining table (refer to Chapter 14). Be aware of all your kitchen group's duties, and if you see something has not been done right, alert the person who has that job responsibility and offer to help if you can.

HOW TO COMPLETE YOUR PLANNING FORM

Remove Activity 6, Italian Meal Planning Form. Figure 15.1 shows a sample filled-in Italian Meal Planning Form. Use this illustration as a guide for completing Activity 6. Use the front of

Class Menu (1) **Calzone** (2) **minestrone** (3) **bread sticks**
(Your Kitchen's Recipe)
(4) **Italian celery** (5) **citrus-artichoke salad** (6) **granite**

Name	Kitchen Job	Preparation Duties	Cleanup Duties
Jennifer Chin	Cook	Prepare the recipe; prepare food for serving	Check kitchen (canisters, cupboards, drawers, counters) for cleanliness and order
Carlos Ramirez	Assistant Cook	Assist cook	Wash equipment; scour sink
Mary Hughes	Host or Hostess	Obtain supplies needed; set table/set buffet	Clear table; clean table and chairs
Diane Stoltz	General Assistant 1	Assume duties of anyone absent; assist where needed	Dry dishes
Bob Iversen	General Assistant 2	Do weekly duty (see instructor); turn in evaluations; assist where needed	Put dishes away; clean range

Recipe Ingredients not in the Kitchen: 1 package yeast, ½ lb. salami, ¼ c. onion, 1 clove garlic, ½ lb. mushrooms, ⅓ c. green pepper, 3 T oil, 8 oz. can tomato sauce, 2 ¼ oz. can sliced olives, 1 tsp. oregano, 1 tsp. basil, ¼ tsp. crushed red pepper, 2 ½ c. shredded mozzarella cheese

Equipment not in the Kitchen: mushroom brush

Cooking-Day Time Schedule		Evaluation-Day Time Schedule	
Time	Duty	Time	Duty
8:00-8:05	Read Recipe	8:00-8:05	Read Recipe
	Make dough, let rise; saute vegetables, add all ingredients but cheese	8:05-8:20	Preheat oven to 475° Bake and place on buffet.
8:05-8:40	Simmer, cool, add cheese Roll out dough + fill wrap; refrigerate overnight	8:20-8:35	Serve Yourself and Eat
		8:35-8:40	Cleanup: check kitchen
8:40-8:50	Cleanup: check kitchen	8:40-8:50	Written Evaluation: Refer to Italian Sample Activity 7.

Figure 15.1. Sample Filled-in Activity 6

Chapter 15 • Your Italian Meal Planning Form

Activity 6 for a five-member kitchen group and the back for a four-member kitchen group.

Follow these directions when completing Activity 6.

Write your name, class period, kitchen number, and date due. Write the names of each recipe your class will prepare. List your kitchen group's recipe first.

Write the names of each kitchen group member next to the appropriate kitchen job.

List recipe ingredients not in the kitchen. Carefully read the recipe your kitchen group will prepare, and determine what ingredients will have to be obtained from outside your assigned kitchen.

Once you have determined which ingredients are not in your kitchen, list those ingredients and the amounts you will need. This will enable your teacher to know what has to be purchased from the grocery store or obtained from another storage area.

Each kitchen will have some staples such as salt, pepper, flour, sugar, baking powder, and baking soda. Check to see what staples are available in your kitchen. List these staples below:

Staples in the Kitchen

1. _____   4. _____   7. _____
2. _____   5. _____   8. _____
3. _____   6. _____   9. _____

List equipment not in the kitchen in this space. Refer to Figure 15.1. The missing equipment will be placed in the supply area ready for your kitchen group's use at the beginning of your cooking day.

Devise a time schedule for all duties assigned to you on *cooking day.*

- Write the time you allot to read the recipe on cooking day.
- Write the time you allot for preparation duties assigned to you for cooking day. Write a few notes that will help you perform these duties.
- Write the time you allot for cleanup duties. Write your cleanup duty assignments.

Devise a time schedule for all duties assigned to you on *evaluation day.*

- Write the time you allot to read the recipe on evaluation day.
- Write the time you allot for preparation duties assigned to you for evaluation day. Include the time for final food prep-

aration and setting the buffet and dining table. Write a few notes that will help you perform these duties.
- Write the time you allot to serve yourself and eat.
- Write the time you allot for cleanup duties. Write your cleanup duty assignments.
- Write the time you allot for the written evaluation.

Give your completed Italian Menu Planning Form to your instructor for evaluation.

ARE YOU READY?

The success of your dish depends on your following recipe directions exactly and on your ability to complete your duties on time. On cooking day, use your completed Italian Meal Planning Form to guide you through your duties and time schedule. All the duties must be finished and as much of the recipe prepared as possible, so that everything can be completed on evaluation day.

Before you start your duties, a quick review is necessary. Read the following questions. If you answer no to any of these questions, check your notes or any other source of information you have for help.

1. Are you familiar with your kitchen group's recipe?
2. Do you know what the cooking terms mean in your recipe?
3. Do you know your kitchen job assignment?
4. Do you know your preparation duties?
5. Do you know your cleanup duties?
6. Are you aware of your time schedule?
7. Do you know your co-workers' duties?
8. Are you prepared to help your co-workers if you finish your duties early?
9. Do you know where the equipment is located in the kitchen so that preparation and cleanup will be efficient?

When you have answered yes to all the questions, you are ready to begin your cooking-day duties. Enjoy your experience with Italy's cuisine.

GODERE!

Section Six

EVALUATING YOUR ITALIAN MEAL

Whether you are evaluating a trip you have taken, a movie you have seen, or a meal you have helped prepare, you should always be aware of what did not meet your expectations. Your judgments and observations are important.

Consider the following questions concerning your Italian meal:

- Did your kitchen group prepare a dish of the quality and taste you expected? How did the dish vary from your expectations?
- After tasting the dish, what changes would you suggest in the ingredients for the next time?
- How would you rate the appearance, texture, and flavor of all the dishes?
- What one dish did you especially enjoy? Give your reasons for this choice.

Answers to these questions will help in your evaluation of the foods that were prepared by you and your class. Remember, constructive criticism is the key to becoming a better cook, and an honest evaluation will improve your cooking in the future. In this section you will find

- a sample Italian Product Evaluation Form
- an Italian Product Evaluation Form for you to complete

16
ITALIAN PRODUCT EVALUATION

Three criteria will be used to evaluate the food your class has prepared. These are appearance, texture, and flavor.

Appearance

Appearance is the color, size, and shape of the product. Italian bread sticks have a good appearance if they are nicely browned, uniform in length and thickness, and straight. If a product looks so attractive to you that you can hardly wait to taste it, it should rate high in appearance.

Texture

The texture of a product is described as crisp, crunchy, flaky, moist, dry, tender, light, soft, or hard. A variety of textures in one dish is appealing. For example, Veal Scallopini has a smooth tomato sauce over tender mushrooms and moist, juicy veal. This delicious dish is a wonderful combination of textures. A dish with pleasing texture should earn a high rating.

Flavor

Flavor is a blend of taste and aroma and can be described as salty, sweet, sour, bitter, bland, delicate, or rich. The aroma of food influences its flavor. For example, much of the flavor of minestrone comes from the aroma of the blended ingredients. The long, slow cooking of the vegetables results in a soup of mellow, dense flavor. If you enjoy the flavor of a food, you should rate it high.

If the appearance, texture, or flavor of a particular dish is not what you think it should be, try to determine what caused the disappointment. Improper cooking techniques negatively affect a recipe. For example, when making pizza, if you sift the flour before measuring it instead of afterward you will not have enough flour, since sifting adds air. When making a marinade,

Calzone

pizza dough
½ lb. dry salami
¼ cup onion
1 clove garlic
½ lb. mushrooms
⅓ cup green pepper
3 tbsp. oil
8 oz. can tomato sauce
2¼ oz. can sliced olives
1 tsp. dry oregano
1 tsp. dry basil
½ tsp. sugar
¼ tsp. crushed red pepper
2⅓ cups mozzarella cheese

Figure 16.1. Calzone Recipe

you should crush the dried basil or oregano to release the oils; otherwise their flavor will not be incorporated into the marinade.

Evaluating the Italian dish you have made will help you improve it the next time you make it. By altering the ingredients, you can create a different, but just as pleasing, dish. Your sight, taste, and imagination will provide you with clues on what to add or eliminate. Figure 16.1 is an example of a basic recipe for Calzone that can be altered with the following variations.

By applying one or a combination of the following ideas, you change the flavor of Calzone:

1. Sauté and add 1 small, thinly sliced carrot.
2. Reduce mozzarella cheese to 2 cups and add ½ cup grated parmesan cheese.
3. Substitute for salami 10 ounces of mild Italian sausage (casing removed) crumbled and browned.
4. Omit salami and increase mushrooms, oregano, and mozzarella.
5. Substitute ricotta cheese for mozzarella cheese and add 1 cup diced provolone cheese.
6. Substitute ham for salami.

EVALUATION FORM

Evaluation forms are used to help improve your cooking. Study the example of a completed evaluation form for Jennifer Chin (see Figure 16.2).

Note that Jennifer wrote the names of the Italian recipes her class prepared. She evaluated the foods by indicating in the appropriate column her opinion of their appearance, texture, and flavor. She then suggested a change in the ingredients for the dish she helped prepare. Next, she discussed her questions concerning the preparation of the recipe with her kitchen group

Write the names of the products that will be evaluated, and check (✓) the space that best describes the product: E = Excellent, G = Good, P = Poor.

	Appearance			Texture			Flavor		
	E	G	P	E	G	P	E	G	P
1. Calzone	✓				✓			✓	
2. Minestrone	✓			✓			✓		
3. Bread Sticks		✓		✓				✓	
4. Italian Celery		✓		✓			✓		
5. Citrus Artichoke Salad	✓			✓			✓		
6. Granite	✓			✓			✓		
7.									
8.									

Write the name of the recipe your kitchen group prepared: __Calzone__

Describe how you would change the ingredients of your recipe to make a different product:

I would substitute sausage for salami, frying it and draining the grease before adding to the tomato sauce mixture.

Answer these questions about your recipe preparation. Check (✓) the appropriate space.

	Yes	No
1. Were the ingredient amounts measured correctly?	✓	
2. Were the proper utensils used for the measuring?	✓	
3. Were the correct techniques used to prepare the ingredients?		✓
4. Were the ingredients added in the right order?	✓	
5. Was the correct size cookware used?	✓	
6. Was the cookware prepared correctly?	✓	
7. If the oven was used, was it preheated?	✓	

Write a paragraph that explains what contributed to the product's success and what could have been done to improve the product.

The combination of ingredients, salami, garlic, onion, green peppers,

Figure 16.2. Sample Filled-in Activity 7 (Continued)

> mushrooms, and seasonings created a hearty blend of flavors and textures. We should have let the tomato mixture cool a bit longer. Then the cheese would not have melted as much. Nevertheless, the quality still was excellent.
>
> Describe the good table manners that made the Italian meal more enjoyable for your kitchen group:
>
> We had fun talking and everyone had something to add to the conversation. Our hostess did a good job of keeping the conversation on subjects that interested everyone. We all remembered to place the flatware correctly on the plate when we finished to tell our hostess we were finished eating.

Figure 16.2. (Continued)

and checked the appropriate space for the answers. After doing this, Jennifer found out why her dish did not turn out as well as she had expected. She then wrote a paragraph telling what was successful about the dish and how it should be prepared the next time to ensure the best results. Finally, after a discussion with her kitchen group, Jennifer described the good table manners that made the Italian meal with her group members pleasant and enjoyable.

Remove Activity 7, the Italian Product Evaluation Form. Use the sample Figure 16.2 to complete Activity 7 and give it to your instructor for evaluation.

Name _____ Class Period _____ Kitchen Number _____ Date Due _____

Activity 1 ITALIAN FOOD HISTORY REVIEW

Test your knowledge of Italian Food History by completing the following sentences with the proper word or words. Place your answer in the answer column at the right.

Answers

1. Evidence found on columns in an Etruscan tomb show that __?__ was made in Italy in the 4th century B.C.

2. Bread was not known in the time of the Roman Empire. Soldiers ate a form of __?__, which they made by cooking a coarse wheat grain.

3. The upper class enjoyed complicated and elaborate food during Italy's __?__.

4. Explorations of the New World brought new foods to Italy. The __?__ became a substitute for the peacock, and the __?__ was first eaten as a salad vegetable.

5. The table manners of Italy were advanced greatly by the introduction of the __?__.

6. Many French dishes owe their origins to Italian chefs, who were brought to the French court by Catherine dé Medici; thus Italy became known as the __?__ of French cooking as well as western European cuisine.

7. Before becoming united in 1861, Italy was divided into rival __?__ __?__, and as a result, each developed unique cooking styles and dishes.

8. People ate only what was grown and produced in their region because the __?__ __?__ __?__ made travel difficult.

9. Italy is a peninsula, and much of the food is obtained from the __?__.

10. The geography of the north provides the best __?__ land for cattle. As a result, the fat for cooking in the north is __?__.

11. In mountainous southern Italy, __?__ trees provide __?__ used for fat in southern Italian recipes.

12. Americans are most familiar with dishes that are common to __?__ Italy.

13. In Italy the main meal is eaten about __?__ o'clock.

14. In Italy fresh green salads are served __?__ the main course.

15. A favorite dessert is __?__, a fruit flavored ice.

Activity 1 • Italian Food History   121

Name _____ Class Period _____ Kitchen Number _____ Date Due _____

Activity 2 ITALIAN RECIPE MATCH

This activity will test your knowledge of popular and classic Italian cooking. In the space provided in the answer column at the right of each definition in Column 2, print the letter of the phrase in Column 1 that matches the definition.

	Column 1		Column 2	Answers
a.	Gnocchi	1.	Served as an antipasto	1. _____
b.	Noodles	2.	Follows the main course in an Italian meal	2. _____
c.	Flat Bread	3.	A fried dessert	3. _____
d.	Frittata	4.	Made with a pizza dough crust	4. _____
e.	Veal	5.	A frozen dessert that is flavored with almond extract	5. _____
f.	Bread Sticks	6.	A fine, ice-crystal sherbet	6. _____
g.	Tortellini	7.	Found in the supermarket by the name, "grissini"	7. _____
h.	Chicken			
i.	Minestrone	8.	An Italian dumpling made with potatoes and flour	8. _____
j.	Celery	9.	The flat form of pasta	9. _____
k.	Cacciatore	10.	The Italian word for "bread"	10. _____
l.	Pane	11.	In Italian the word means "pie"	11. _____
m.	Polenta	12.	An open-faced omelet	12. _____
n.	Lasagna	13.	A kind of beef for which Italy is well known	13. _____
o.	Calzone	14.	One of the varieties of vegetables, elevated to first or second courses in the Italian meal	14. _____
p.	Salad			
q.	Tortoni			
r.	Granite	15.	Italians serve this on Christmas and New Year's	15. _____
s.	Pizza			
t.	Cenci	16.	A staple grown and eaten primarily in northern Italy	16. _____
u.	Marinated Vegetables			
v.	Rice	17.	The "bread" of northern Italy	17. _____
w.	Artichoke	18.	A broad noodle casserole dish	18. _____
		19.	Known for its distinctive, stout, globelike shape, which Italians boil, bake, or fry, and put on pizza, in pasta sauce, or on salad	19. _____
		20.	The way chicken is cooked in sauce	20. _____
		21.	A form of poultry which, along with capon, duck, goose, and turkey, is popular throughout Italy	21. _____
		22.	Originally cooked on the hearth under ashes	22. _____
		23.	The Italian word for "big soup"	23. _____

Name _____ Class Period _____ Kitchen Number _____ Date Due _____

Activity 3 ITALIAN MAP REVIEW

To complete this activity, match the recipe with the culinary region for which it is known. Write the letter of the recipe on the line(s) provided within the regions. For example, the first recipe is Gnocchi. After reading the recipe for Gnocchi, you know it is identified with the Latium region. The letter "a" is written on the line in the Latium region as an example.

Recipe

a. Gnocchi
b. Minestrone
c. Tortellini
d. Bread Sticks
e. Italian Bread
f. Italian Flat Bread
g. Celery Italian Style
h. Frittata
i. Springtime Vegetables with Noodles
j. Chicken Cacciatore
k. Stuffed Chicken Breasts
l. Veal Scallopini
m. Citrus-Artichoke Salad
n. Green Salad
o. Marinated Vegetables
p. Biscuit Tortoni
q. Deep-Fried Sweet Pastry
r. Strawberry Flavored Granite
s. Calzone
t. Deep-Fried Rice and Cheese Balls
u. Lasagna
v. Pizza
w. Polenta with Sausage

Culinary Regions of Italy

Activity 3 ● Italian Map Review   125

Name _____ Class Period _____ Kitchen Number _____ Date Due _____

Activity 4 SELECTING YOUR ITALIAN MENU

By completing this activity, you will have a better understanding of the Italian recipes. This will make choosing your menu easier.

	FIRST COURSE			BREAD			VEGE- TABLE			MEAT COURSE			SALAD			DESSERT	
	Gnocchi	Minestrone	Tortellini	Bread Sticks	Italian Bread	Italian Flat Bread	Celery Italian Style	Frittata	Springtime Vegetables with Noodles	Chicken Cacciatore	Stuffed Chicken Breasts	Veal Scallopini	Citrus-Artichoke Salad	Green Salad	Marinated Vegetables	Biscuit Tortoni	Deep-Fried Sweet Pastry	Strawberry Flavored Granite
Place a check mark (√) in the appropriate column(s) to complete the following activity.																		
1. The recipes that use cooking techniques you have not tried.																		
2. The recipes that have unfamiliar ingredients.																		
3. The recipes that you have tasted before.																		
4. The recipes that you have tasted and would like to taste again.																		
5. The recipes that you have not tasted but would like to taste.																		
6. The first course recipe that would be your first choice to taste.																		
7. The bread recipe that would be your first choice to taste.																		
8. The vegetable recipe that would be your first choice to taste.																		
9. The meat course recipe that would be your first choice to taste.																		
10. The salad recipe that would be your first choice to taste.																		
11. The dessert recipe that would be your first choice to taste.																		

(Continued)

Activity 4 (Continued)

You have now selected the dishes you would like to taste. Will your choices provide a variety in color, shape, texture, and flavor? After carefully considering this question and making any changes, write your recipe selections for the menu you would like your class to prepare.

First Course _____   Meat Course _____

Bread _____   Salad _____

Vegetable _____   Dessert _____

Name _____ Class Period _____ Kitchen Number _____ Date Due _____

Activity 5 ITALIAN MEAL COST SHEET

SECTION A   Name of Recipe:

(1) Recipe Ingredients	(2) Amount Required	(3) Price Per Item	(4) Amount of Store Container	(5) Cost Computation	(6) Total Ingredient Cost

SECTION B ———————————————→ Total Recipe Cost: _____

SECTION C   Total Recipe Cost ÷ Number of Servings = Cost Per Serving
———→ (_____) ÷ (_____) = (_____)

SECTION D

Final Class Meal Cost		
(1) Recipe	(2) Recipe Cost	(3) Cost Per Serving
First Course:		
Bread:		
Vegetable:		
Meat Course:		
Salad:		
Dessert:		

SECTION E   TOTALS: Meal Costs: _____   Meal Cost Per Serving: _____

Activity 5 • Italian Meal Cost Sheet   129

Name _____ Class Period _____ Kitchen Number _____ Date Due _____

Activity 6 ITALIAN MEAL PLANNING FORM (FOUR-MEMBER KITCHEN)

Class Menu (1) _____ (2) _____ (3) _____
(Your Kitchen's Recipe)
(4) _____ (5) _____ (6) _____

Name	Kitchen Job	Preparation Duties	Cleanup Duties
	Cook	Prepare the recipe; prepare food for serving	Check kitchen (canisters, cupboards, drawers, counters, etc.) for cleanliness and order
	Assistant Cook	Assist cook	Wash dishes; scour sink
	Host or Hostess	Obtain supplies needed; set table/set buffet; do weekly duty (see instructor)	Clear table; clean table and chairs
	General Assistant	Assume duties of anyone absent; turn in evaluation; assist where needed	Dry dishes; put dishes away

Recipe Ingredients not in the Kitchen: _____
_____
_____

Equipment not in the Kitchen: _____

Cooking-Day Time Schedule		Evaluation-Day Time Schedule	
Time	**Duty**	**Time**	**Duty**
_____	Read Recipe	_____	Read Recipe
_____	_____	_____	_____
_____	_____	_____	_____
_____	_____		Serve Yourself and Eat
_____	_____		Cleanup: _____
	Cleanup: _____		Written Evaluation: Refer to Activity 7.

Name _____ Class Period _____ Kitchen Number _____ Date Due _____

Activity 6 ITALIAN MEAL PLANNING FORM (FIVE-MEMBER KITCHEN)

Class Menu (1) _____ (2) _____ (3) _____
            (Your Kitchen's Recipe)
            (4) _____ (5) _____ (6) _____

Name	Kitchen Job	Preparation Duties	Cleanup Duties
	Cook	Prepare the recipe; prepare food for serving	Check kitchen (canisters, cupboards, drawers, counters, etc.) for cleanliness and order
	Assistant Cook	Assist cook	Wash equipment; scour sink
	Host or Hostess	Obtain supplies needed; set table/set buffet	Clear table; clean table and chairs
	General Assistant 1	Assume duties of anyone absent; assist where needed	Dry dishes
	General Assistant 2	Do weekly duty (see instructor); turn in evaluations; assist where needed	Put dishes away; clean range

Recipe Ingredients not in the Kitchen: _____

_____

Equipment not in the Kitchen: _____

Cooking-Day Time Schedule		Evaluation-Day Time Schedule	
Time	**Duty**	**Time**	**Duty**
_____	Read Recipe	_____	Read Recipe
_____	_____	_____	_____
_____	_____	_____	_____
_____	_____	_____	_____
_____	_____	_____	Serve Yourself and Eat
_____	_____	_____	Cleanup: _____
_____	Cleanup: _____		Written Evaluation: Refer to Activity 7.

132   Activity 6 • Italian Meal Planning Form (Five-Member Kitchen)

Name _____ Class Period _____ Kitchen Number _____ Date Due _____

Activity 7 ITALIAN PRODUCT EVALUATION FORM

Write the names of the products that will be evaluated, and check (✓) the space that best describes the product: E = Excellent, G = Good, P = Poor.

	Appearance			Texture			Flavor		
	E	G	P	E	G	P	E	G	P
1.									
2.									
3.									
4.									
5.									
6.									
7.									
8.									

Write the name of the recipe your kitchen prepared: _____

Describe how you would change the ingredients of your recipe to make a different product:
_____
_____
_____
_____

Answer these questions about your recipe preparation. Check (✓) the appropriate space.

	Yes	No
1. Were the ingredient amounts measured correctly?		
2. Were the proper utensils used for measuring?		
3. Were the correct techniques used to prepare the ingredients?		
4. Were the ingredients added in the right order?		
5. Was the correct size cookware used?		
6. Was the cookware prepared correctly?		
7. If the oven was used, was it preheated?		

Activity 7 (Continued)

Write a paragraph that explains:
1. What contributed to the product's success?
2. What could have been done to improve the product?

_____
_____
_____
_____
_____
_____

Describe the good table manners that made the meal more enjoyable for your kitchen group:

_____
_____
_____
_____
_____

GNOCCHI

Food Category: First Course   *Low Cost*

4 lb. potatoes
5 cups unsifted flour

salt to taste
butter

grated parmesan cheese

1. Boil and *rice* potatoes.
2. Gradually add flour. Do not add too much, or the gnocchi will become too dry. *Knead* until the dough is smooth, adding flour as necessary.
3. Roll dough on lightly floured board. Cut into 12-inch-long rope-like strips about ¾ inch thick. Cut strips into 1-inch pieces. Dip in flour.
4. To make dented design (see illustration), just press pieces of dough against prongs of fork.
5. Bring water and salt to boil in large pan. Drop gnocchi (a few at a time so that they don't touch each other) into rapidly boiling water. Cook for about 10 minutes until they float to the surface. Then cook for 8 to 10 seconds more. Lift from water with slotted spoon, or pour into strainer or *colander* if all are cooked at once. If not, keep first batch warm in 350-degree oven until next batch is done.
6. Serve on large, warmed platter with melted butter and grated parmesan cheese.

Serves 6

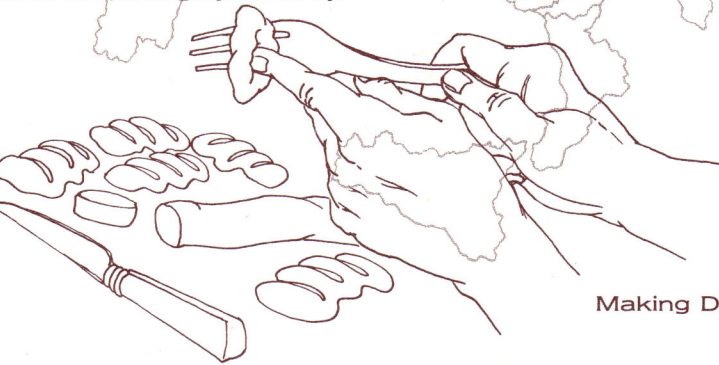

Making Dented Design in Gnocchi

MINESTRONE

Food Category: First Course   *Low Cost*

1 cup water
½ cup dried great northern or kidney beans
4 cups chicken broth

2 small tomatoes, chopped
2 medium carrots, sliced
1 stalk celery, sliced
1 medium onion, chopped

1 clove garlic, chopped
½ cup uncooked macaroni
1 tsp. salt
½ tsp basil

⅛ tsp. pepper
1 bay leaf
¾ cup green beans, cut in 1-inch pieces
2 small zucchini, cut in 1-inch slices

1. Heat water and dried beans to boiling in *Dutch oven*. Boil for 2 minutes. Remove from heat. Cover. Let stand 1 hour.
2. If necessary, add more water to cover beans. Heat to boiling. Reduce heat. Cover. Simmer until tender, about 1 to 1½ hours. Do not boil or the beans will burst. (Steps 1 and 2 may be eliminated if canned beans are used.)
3. Add chicken broth, tomatoes, carrots, celery, onion, garlic, macaroni, salt, basil, pepper, and bay leaf to beans. Heat to boiling. Reduce heat. Cover. Simmer 15 minutes.
4. Add green beans. Heat to boiling. Reduce heat. Cover. Simmer until macaroni and vegetables are tender, about 15 minutes.
5. Add zucchini and heat until zucchini is hot. Remove bay leaf and serve.

Serves 6

Recipe Tips

- *Crush basil to release oils.*
- *To divide preparation time into two days, soak beans at room temperature overnight. This will take the place of Step 1. The next day begin with Step 2 and reduce cooking time to about 1 hour.*

Recipe Tips

- *White corn meal may be substituted for potatoes; however, the potato version is easier to handle.*
- *The indentations in gnocchi thin the middle section of dumpling so that it will cook evenly. Also, little grooves will trap melted butter.*
- *Warm platter by letting stand in hot water. If platter is oven proof, place in oven a few minutes at lowest setting.*
- *To divide preparation into two days, complete Steps 1 through 4. Store gnocchi in tightly sealed plastic bag and refrigerate overnight. Begin with Step 5 the next day.*

Gnocchi (NYOHK-kee) are dumplings, which are considered a staple like *polenta* (bread) and *pasta*. The word itself means "lumps," which well describes gnocchi shapes, from perfect spheres to elongated cylinders. Gnocchi dough is sometimes stamped with small cutters and then baked in layers in an oven. The shaped gnocchi are either poached or baked and can be seasoned with almost any sauce—tomato or a mixture of butter and parmesan cheese, as in this recipe. In northeastern Italy, very small gnocchi are sometimes added to broth and are even used in stews.

In early Roman times, Gnocchi was made with flour and milk, then fried and served with honey. After potatoes were introduced from the New World, Gnocchi was made with a flour and potato mixture, as in this version which is popular in Rome. Other varieties are now made by adding meat, cheese, or spinach to the filling.

Minestrone (mee-nee-STRO-neh) means "big soup" in Italian. It is hearty and rich, made with the freshest available vegetables. Although Milan, in Lombardy, claims to have invented Minestrone, it is a popular soup throughout Italy.

The flavor of Minestrone changes from region to region, from season to season. In the south, a meatless soup with garlic, tomatoes, and olive oil predominates. In central Italy, beans are a major ingredient. In the north, rice is considered essential. Along the Italian Riviera, in the Liguria region, fresh herbs are used in generous quantities.

The recipe here, with its beans and pasta, might be found in the Abruzzi E Molise region on the eastern seacoast of Italy. The Appenine mountains give this region a harsh climate, but they also provide a haven for skiers and scenery lovers. Minestrone makes a great end to a day of skiing.

TORTELLINI

Food Category: First Course   *Low Cost*

Filling
- 2 cups cooked spinach
- 2 tbsp. grated parmesan cheese
- 1 cup ricotta cheese
- 2 eggs, beaten
- 2 tbsp. dry bread crumbs
- ½ tsp. salt

Pasta
- 3 cups flour
- 2 eggs
- 2 egg whites
- 2 tbsp. oil
- 2 tsp. salt
- 4 tbsp. butter
- grated parmesan cheese

1. For filling, *mince* spinach. Drain thoroughly. Combine remaining ingredients. Mix well.
2. For dough, pour flour into large bowl. Make *well* in center. Add eggs, egg whites, oil, and 1 tsp. salt. Mix together with fork or fingers until dough can be gathered into rough ball.
3. *Knead* for 10 minutes, adding flour if dough seems sticky. Dough should be smooth, shiny, and elastic.
4. Divide dough into 4 parts. Wrap in waxed paper. Let rest for 10 minutes.
5. Place one ball on board (covering other balls with damp cloth). Flatten into an oblong, about 1-inch thick. Roll out paper thin.
6. To cut, follow the steps and refer to illustrations (on back):
   (1) Cut in 2-inch rounds with biscuit cutter or small glass. Fill with ¼ tsp. filling. Moisten edges of each circle. Fold in half, pressing edges firmly together.
   (2) Shape into little rings by stretching tips of each circle slightly and wrapping the ring around your index finger. Gently press tip together. Repeat rolling and filling process with all dough.
7. Bring water and 1 tsp. salt to boil in large pan. Drop in tortellini. Boil, stirring occasionally, for 5 to 8 minutes or until *al dente*.
8. Melt butter. Pour into warm serving bowl. Add well-drained tortellini. Sprinkle with grated parmesan cheese. Toss, coating all tortellini. Serve immediately.

Serves 6

BREAD STICKS

Food Category: Bread   *Low Cost*

- 4 to 4½ cups unsifted flour
- 1 tbsp. sugar
- 2 pkg. dry yeast
- ¼ cup oil
- 1¼ cups hot water (120 to 130 degrees)
- 1 egg white beaten with 1 tbsp. water
- coarse salt or sesame seeds

1. In large bowl of electric mixer, mix together 1 cup flour, sugar, salt, and yeast. Add oil. Gradually stir in hot water.
2. Beat at medium speed for 2 minutes. Add ½ cup more flour. Beat at high speed for 2 minutes.
3. Stir in with wooden spoon 1½ to 2 cups remaining flour to make soft dough.
4. Turn dough onto floured board. *Knead* for 10 minutes.
5. Cut into 30 equal pieces. Roll each into a 12-inch rope. Oil all sides lightly. Place 1 inch apart on ungreased baking sheets.
6. Let rise about 15 minutes until puffy. Brush with egg white mixture. Sprinkle with salt or seeds or leave plain. Bake at 375 degrees for 15 to 20 minutes. *Makes 30, foot-long sticks.*

Serves 10

Recipe Tips

- Use candy thermometer to determine water temperature.
- To *divide* preparation into two days, complete Steps 1 through 5. Cover bread sticks with oiled waxed paper and damp towel. Refrigerate overnight. The next day, begin with Step 6, allowing 10 minutes additional rising time.

Step 1　　　　　　　　　　　Step 2

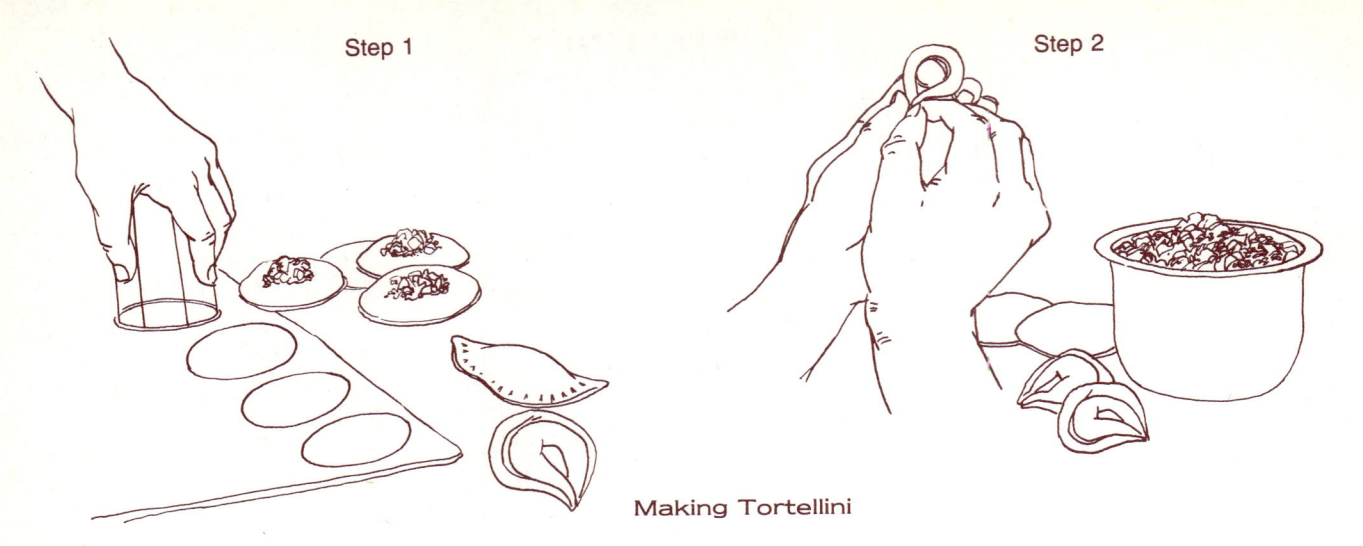

Making Tortellini

Recipe Tips

- *Before cutting tortellini, dip biscuit cutter (or water glass) in flour to keep dough from sticking.*
- *To divide preparation into two days, complete Steps 1 through 6. Store tortellini in tightly sealed plastic bag and refrigerate overnight. Begin with Step 7 the next day.*

At Christmas and New Year's, *Tortellini* (tor-teh-LEE-nee) are served as a first course, floating in broth like dumplings. The whole family gets involved in preparing and wrapping the tortellini. These circles of stuffed, hat-shaped pasta are a specialty of Bologna, in the Emilia-Romagna region, which is almost the width of Italy.

The cheese used in this recipe is Emilia-Romagna's most famous product. Parmesan cheese is named after the city of Parma. Mature Parmesan cheese is used extensively in cooking, but it is also eaten "young," when it is mild.

In the 16th century, a bakery created thin, crisp bread sticks to appeal to the appetite of a young and very ill prince in Turin, the industrial capital of the Piedmont region. Piedmont means "at the foot of the mountains," and the name aptly describes its location near the western and central Alps.

The Piedmont terrain includes mountains, hills, plains, and cities. As a result, many varieties of foods, from country-rustic to city-sophisticated, can be found. Bread sticks are Piedmont's most famous wheat product and are sometimes known by their Italian name, *grissini* (grees-SEE-nee).

ITALIAN BREAD

Food Category: Bread *Low Cost*

1 pkg. dry yeast
2 cups warm water
   (105 to 115 degrees)
1 tbsp. salt
4 to 4½ cups unsifted flour
1 egg white

1. Soften yeast in ¼ cup warm water. Set aside for 5 minutes.
2. Combine remaining 1¾ cups warm water and salt in large bowl. Blend in 3 cups flour. Stir softened yeast. Add to flour mixture. Mix well.
3. Add about ½ the remaining flour to yeast mixture. With a heavy-duty mixer or wooden spoon, beat for about 5 minutes until very smooth. Mix in enough remaining flour to make soft dough. Turn onto lightly floured board. Allow to rest 10 minutes. *Knead* dough about 5 minutes until it is smooth and elastic.
4. Shape dough into smooth ball. Place in large greased bowl. Turn dough over so that top gets greased. Cover with greased waxed paper and damp towel. Let stand in warm place about 45 minutes until dough has doubled.
5. Punch dough down. On lightly floured board, knead again 2 minutes. Divide into 2 equal balls. Cover with towel. Let stand 10 minutes.
6. Roll balls into 14-inch × 8-inch rectangles. Roll up lightly from wide side into long, slender loaf. Pinch ends to seal. Place loaves on lightly greased 15-inch × 10-inch baking sheet. Beat 1 tbsp. water with egg white until frothy. Brush loaves. Cover loosely with towel. Let stand in warm place until doubled.
7. Bake at 425 degrees for 10 minutes. Reduce temperature to 350 degrees. Bake 1 hour or until golden brown. *Makes 2 loaves.*

ITALIAN FLAT BREAD

Food Category: Bread *Low Cost*

1 pkg. dry yeast
1 cup warm water (about 110 degrees)
2 tsp. sugar
¾ tsp. salt
¼ cup salad oil
2⅔ cups unsifted flour

1. In large bowl, sprinkle yeast over warm water. Let stand for 5 minutes to soften. Stir in sugar, salt, and oil. Add 2 cups flour. Mix well.
2. With heavy-duty mixer or wooden spoon, beat for about 5 minutes until dough is smooth and elastic. Stir in ⅔ cup more flour to make soft dough.
3. Turn dough onto lightly floured board. *Knead* about 10 minutes until smooth and springy. Place in greased bowl. Turn dough over so that top gets greased. Cover. Let rise about 1 hour in warm place until doubled.
4. *Punch down* dough. Roll and stretch dough to fit bottom of a well-greased 10- × 15-inch shallow baking pan. With your fingers or the end of a spoon, press holes in dough at 1-inch intervals.
5. Add topping or flavorings as directed in the variations following. Let dough rise, uncovered about 15 minutes until almost doubled.
6. Bake at 450 degrees for 12 to 15 minutes or until well browned. Cut bread into 12 equal pieces. Serve warm or at room temperature.

Serves 12

Variations

- *Raisin Bread* — After dough has risen and been punched down, knead in ⅓ cup raisins. Place in pan. Brush with 3 tbsp. oil. Sprinkle with 1 tsp. sugar.
- *White Pizza* — Place dough in pan. Brush with 3 tbsp. oil.
- *Pizza Bread* — Place dough in pan. Spread with ½ cup canned pizza sauce. Sprinkle with ⅓ cup grated parmesan cheese and ⅓ cup thinly sliced green onion. Drizzle with 3 tbsp. oil.

Recipe Tips

- To increase crustiness during baking, place shallow pan filled with boiling water in bottom of oven.
- To divide preparation into two days, complete Steps 1 through 4. Push dough down. Cover with oiled waxed paper and damp towel. Refrigerate overnight. Begin with Step 5 the next day.

Much of the Apulia region's fertile land is used for growing wheat. Apulia, located in the "heel" of the Italian boot, looks like a peninsula on a peninsula. Apulia has been called the "bread basket" of Italy, and the people there treat bread-making with reverence. Dough from a day's baking is saved and used as the "starter" for the next day's bread. Because of this tradition, it is said that the yeast has been alive in Apulia for generations. *Pane* (PAH-neh) is the Italian word for bread.

- **Onion Bread**—Place dough in pan. Brush with 3 tbsp. oil. Sprinkle with 1 tsp. coarse salt and ½ cup thinly sliced green onions.

Recipe Tips

- Water temperature for dissolving yeast must be between 105 and 115 degrees. If water is too cool, yeast will not activate; if water is too hot, yeast will be killed. Either way, dough will not rise.
- To divide preparation into two days, complete Steps 1 through 3. Cover dough with greased waxed paper and damp towel. Place in refrigerator overnight. Begin with Step 4 the next day after allowing extra time for rising.

Before Pizza became popular around the world, Italians in the Ligurian region baked a thin, flat, crusty bread called *focaccia* (fo-KAH-chah). Its name came from the Latin *focus*, meaning "hearth." Long before the invention of the oven, bread was made by flattening dough on a slab and cooking it on a hearth under a cover of hot coals. When the bread was done, the ashes were brushed off, and the hearth bread was turned over. Similar in texture to thick pizza crust and lightly seasoned, Italian Flat Bread makes a good hot bread with meals.

CELERY ITALIAN STYLE

Food Category: Vegetable
Low Cost

1 large bunch fresh celery
3 tbsp. finely chopped yellow onion
1 tbsp. butter
salt
¼ cup pancetta, prosciutto or smoked ham
freshly ground pepper, about 6 twists of the mill
2 cups homemade meat broth or 1 cup canned beef broth mixed with 1 cup water
1 cup grated mozzarella cheese

1. Trim tops of celery. Detach all stalks from bunch. Lightly peel stalks to remove most of the strings. Cut stalks into 3-inch lengths. Drop into 2 quarts rapidly boiling water. Boil for 2 minutes. *Drain* and set aside.
2. Preheat oven to 400 degrees.
3. In saucepan, *sauté* onion in butter over medium heat until *translucent* but not brown.
4. Add pancetta. Stir and sauté for 1 minute.
5. Add the well-drained celery, pepper, and a light sprinkling of salt. Sauté for 5 minutes, turning celery from time to time.
6. Add broth. Cover pan. Gently simmer until celery is *fork-tender*. If celery is nearly done and there is too much liquid, uncover. Increase heat. Finish cooking while liquid evaporates.
7. Arrange cooked celery in ovenproof serving dish. Spoon sautéed onion and *pancetta* over celery. Add grated cheese. Place dish in preheated oven and bake for 6 to 8 minutes, or until the cheese has melted and formed a slight crust. Allow to settle a few minutes. Then serve.

Serves 6

Recipe Tips
- *Wash celery thoroughly to remove all particles of dirt.*
- *If you are pressed for time, cut celery into smaller pieces and sauté in butter.*

FRITTATA

Food Category: Vegetable
Low Cost

3 cups water
½ tsp. salt
2 tbsp. fresh white bread crumbs
1 cup diced zucchini
3 tbsp. milk
⅛ tsp. grated lemon peel (optional)
¼ tsp. salt
pinch of sugar
4 eggs
2 tbsp. butter

1. Soak bread crumbs in milk for 5 minutes. Stir in zucchini, *grated* lemon peel, ¼ tsp. salt, and sugar.
2. Beat eggs until well mixed. Stir gently into bread crumb–zucchini mixture.
3. Melt butter in 10-inch skillet. Add egg mixture. Cook over moderate heat for 2 to 3 minutes or until the eggs are firm but slightly moist.
4. Place under preheated broiler for 30 seconds to brown top lightly. Slice and serve.

Serves 6

Variations
- *Green Onions*—Add ¼ cup finely chopped green onions for more flavor.
- *Mushrooms*—Add ½ cup sauteed mushrooms into bread crumb–zucchini mixture.
- *Parmesan*—Sprinkle frittata with grated parmesan cheese before broiling.

Recipe Tips
- *Wash lemon before using. Then grate on a grater with small holes, getting only the yellow peel, which is called the zest. (Do not grate any of the white peel, which tastes bitter.)*
- *Clean grater by brushing with pastry brush.*

This dish is associated with the Umbria region, the only region in Italy that does not have a seacoast. Most of Umbria is hilly and mountainous. It provides spectacular scenery but poor agricultural resources, although good vegetables are grown in the green valleys. White celery, which is considered a great delicacy, comes from Umbria. That is why vegetable dishes such as Celery Italian Style approach the status of a first or second course.

Vegetables in Italy are prepared in many ways—boiled, braised, fried, sautéed, baked, and broiled. This celery dish employs three of the cooking methods, sautéing, braising, and baking.

The Frittata (free-TAH-tah) is common to many regions; however, this recipe is typical of the cooking of Tuscany—traditional, plain, and wholesome. Tuscany, flanked north and east by the Appenine mountains, is a regions of hills, river valleys, and fertile plains. Tuscan cooking has not been influenced by other regions and has retained its peasant style, as in this dish.

The Frittata is a nonfolded omelet, cooked on both sides with vegetables blended into the basic egg mixture. Italians use asparagus, spinach, swiss chard, or artichokes.

Italians usually serve frittatas at the evening meal, the lightest of the day. The main dish, the frittata follows a light soup or plate of cold meat slices. A frittata differs from an omelet as follows:

- an omelet is cooked over high heat; a frittata is cooked over low.
- an omelet is creamy and moist; a frittata is firm and set.
- an omelet is folded; a frittata is open-faced.

SPRINGTIME VEGETABLES WITH NOODLES

Food Category: Vegetable *Low Cost*

- ¼ cup butter
- ½ lb. asparagus
- ½ lb. mushrooms, sliced
- ¼ cup slivered prosciutto or baked ham (optional)
- 1 medium carrot, thinly sliced
- 1 medium zucchini, diced
- 8-oz. package noodles
- 3 green onions, sliced (including tops)
- ½ cup small frozen peas, thawed
- 1 tsp. basil
- ½ tsp. salt
- dash of white pepper
- 1 cup whipping cream
- ¼ cup freshly grated parmesan cheese
- chopped parsley

1. Trim off and discard tough asparagus ends. Cut spears *diagonally* into 1-inch lengths, leaving tips whole.
2. In frying pan over medium-high heat, melt butter. Add asparagus, mushrooms, prosciutto, carrot, and zucchini. Cook for 3 minutes, stirring occasionally. Cover pan. Cook for 1 minute more.
3. Cook noodles until done *al dente*, following package directions. Drain well.
4. To vegetable mixture, add green onions, peas, basil, salt, pepper, and cream. Cook on high heat until liquid boils. Return drained noodles to pan in which they were cooked. Pour vegetable sauce over noodles. Mix gently to coat noodles. Add ¼ cup parmesan cheese and mix again.
5. Turn into warm bowl. Sprinkle with parsley. Serve at once with additional cheese. Serves 6

Recipe Tips

- Clean mushrooms with soft, wet brush. Do not immerse mushrooms in water; they become spongy.
- Crush basil to release the oils.
- Warm bowl by placing in hot water.

CHICKEN CACCIATORE

Food Category: Meat Course *Moderate Cost*

- 2½ lb. frying chicken
- ¼ cup oil
- ½ cup unsifted flour
- 2 cups thinly sliced onion rings
- ½ cup chopped green pepper
- 2 cloves garlic, crushed
- 1-lb. can tomatoes, drained
- 8-oz. can tomato sauce
- 1 cup sliced fresh mushrooms or 1 can sliced mushrooms
- 1 tsp. salt
- ¼ tsp. oregano
- ⅛ tsp. basil
- rice or spaghetti

1. Wash chicken. Pat dry. Add oil to large skillet. *Coat* chicken with flour. Brown quickly. Cover. Cook over medium heat about 15 minutes until tender. Remove chicken.
2. Add onion slices, green pepper, and garlic to skillet. Cook until tender. Stir in remaining ingredients.
3. Remove chicken from bones in large pieces. Discard bones and skin. Add chicken to sauce.
4. Cover tightly. Simmer for 25 to 30 minutes. Serve with rice or spaghetti prepared according to package directions. Serves 6

Recipe Tips

- Pat chicken dry with paper towels after washing. Brown chicken with the skin left on. This enhances the flavor and keeps chicken moist.
- Crush dry basil and oregano to release their oils.
- This dish tastes even better the day after.
- To divide preparation into two days, complete Steps 1 through 3. Cover and refrigerate overnight. Begin with Step 4 the next day, increasing cooking time by about 10 minutes.

This recipe incorporates two of Italy's favorite foods—pasta and vegetables. This type of dish, with its flat, homemade egg noodles, is prepared throughout northern Italy and is given the distinctive flavor of each region by use of the freshest, locally grown vegetables.

The seasonings parsley and basil link this dish with the Italian Riviera in the Ligurian region, a narrow stretch of coastline. The hardy basil plant clings to and survives on the craggy Ligurian slopes overlooking the ocean. Fresh vegetables and herbs have always been major ingredients in the cuisine of Liguria, and people believe this stems from the days when sailors craved fresh produce after their long sea voyages.

Chicken is popular throughout Italy. The best chickens are said to come from Tuscany, one of Italy's larger regions. This dish is like others of Tuscany in that it cooks meat within sauces.

Chicken Cacciatore (cah-cha-TOH-rah) is said to have been created long ago, when a hunter in Tuscany came home to dinner after searching for wild mushrooms. He had not found enough mushrooms to serve by themselves, so his wife threw them into a pot where they had a chicken cooking. The result was the first combination of chicken, mushrooms, and sauce.

STUFFED CHICKEN BREASTS

Food Category: Meat Course   *Moderate Cost*

2 cloves garlic, crushed or finely chopped
3 tbsp. oil
½ lb. lean pork, ground
salt

freshly ground pepper, about 6 twists of the mill
1 tsp. rosemary, crushed
3 large, whole breasts of chicken

2 tbsp. butter
½ cup dry white wine or chicken broth

1. In skillet, *sauté* garlic in oil over medium heat. When garlic is colored lightly, add ground pork, a large pinch of salt, pepper, and rosemary. Stir. Sauté meat for 10 minutes, crumbling with fork as it cooks. With slotted spoon, transfer meat to dish. Allow to cool. Discard all but 2½ to 3 tbsp. fat from skillet.
2. *Fillet* chicken breasts. Sprinkle lightly with salt and pepper. Spread sauteed ground pork on fillets and roll each up tightly. Tie each roll securely with string.
3. Add butter to skillet in which pork was cooked. Turn heat to medium high. When butter foam begins to subside, put in stuffed chicken rolls. Brown well on all sides. Cook for about 2 minutes. When rolls are well browned, transfer them to warm platter. Remove strings. Add wine or broth to skillet. Turn heat to high. Stir and cook until cooking residue is loosened from pan. Turn heat to medium. Continue to cook and stir until mixture is slightly thickened. Pour sauce over chicken rolls. Slice in half. Serve hot.

Serves 6

Recipe Tips

- Crush garlic easily by removing outer skin and pressing clove gently between handle of knife and wooden cutting board.
- A pinch of salt is amount of salt that can be held between thumb and index finger.
- To divide preparation into two days, complete Steps 1 through 2 first day. Store rolls in tightly sealed plastic bag and refrigerate overnight. The next day complete Step 3, increasing cooking time by about 5 minutes.

VEAL SCALLOPINI

Food Category: Meat Course   *High Cost*

¼ cup chopped onion
¼ cup oil
1½ lb. boned veal, cut thin
or
6 boned chicken breasts

¼ cup flour
½ tsp. salt
⅛ tsp. pepper
1 cup mushrooms

8-oz. can tomato sauce
½ tsp. sugar
1 cup beef broth or white wine
rice or spaghetti

1. *Sauté* onions in heated oil. Remove from casserole.
2. Mix salt and pepper with flour. *Coat* veal. *Brown* in oil. Remove to casserole.
3. Put mushrooms in remaining oil and brown lightly. Place on top of veal.
4. Add more oil to make 4 tbsp. Stir in flour left over from coating veal. Brown lightly. Add tomato sauce, sugar, and broth or wine. Cook until slightly thickened. Pour over veal.
5. Bake in 350-degree oven for 1¼ hours or until veal is tender. Cover casserole until the last half hour. Serve with rice or spaghetti prepared according to package directions.

Serves 6

Recipe Tips

- Watch onions carefully when sautéing them. Their high sugar content makes them burn easily.
- Clean mushrooms with soft, wet brush. Do not immerse in water; they become spongy.
- Broth is the liquid that results from simmering meat and bones in water for a long time.
- If pressed for time, use bouillon cubes, one cube per cup of water, to make broth.
- To divide preparation into two days, complete Steps 1 through 4. Cover and refrigerate. Complete Step 5 the following day, increasing cooking time by 5 minutes.

Poultry, including chicken, capon, duck, goose, and turkey, is popular throughout Italy. Northern Italy is well known for its excellent chicken, and breast of chicken, like veal, is a regional specialty.

Stuffed Chicken Breasts might be served in the region of Emilia-Romagna, because of the pork filling. Renowned for its fine pork and pork products such as sausage, Emilia-Romagna is rich in natural resources—fertile soil, pastures, and the well-stocked waters of the Adriatic Sea. As a result, Emilia-Romagna has the most famous cuisine in Italy.

Because grazing land is scarce in Italy, cattle are expensive to raise. So *veal* is more common in Italy then mature beef. This dish, cooked slowly in thick, flavorsome sauces, is representative of the cooking in the Lombardy region. Veal Scallopini (skah-loh-PEE-nee) is a good recipe for American veal, which is less tender than Italian veal. Baking at a low temperature for over an hour ensures a tender result.

CITRUS-ARTICHOKE SALAD

Food Category: Salad *Moderate Cost*

Salad

8-oz. can artichoke hearts
2 oranges, peeled and sectioned
1 grapefruit, peeled and sectioned
1 small red onion
8 cups spinach and romaine

Dressing

¼ cup orange juice
2 tbsp. red wine vinegar
1 tsp. salt
¼ cup oil

1. Separate leaves of spinach and romaine. Wash thoroughly. Pat dry with paper towel. Break into bite-size pieces.
2. Thinly slice red onion. Separate into rings.
3. Drain artichoke hearts. Cut in half.
4. To make dressing, combine ingredients in jar. Shake well. Chill.
5. Just before serving place all ingredients in salad bowl. Shake dressing well. Pour over salad. Toss.
   Serves 6

Recipe Tips

- Do not cut leaves with a knife. The leaves will bruise and wilt quickly.
- Dry leaves carefully so dressing will adhere to them. Wrap leaves loosely in paper towels and gently shake in a plastic bag.
- To divide preparation into two days, complete Steps 1 and 4. Place spinach and romaine in plastic bag with paper towels. Refrigerate along with dressing. Complete Steps 2, 3, and 5 the next day.

GREEN SALAD

Food Category: Salad *Low Cost*

Salad

1 large head of lettuce or of endive, romaine, escarole, or dandelion greens
1 clove garlic

Garlic Croutons

4 slices of white bread
butter
1 tsp. garlic powder

Italian Dressing

3 tbsp. oil
1 tbsp. wine vinegar
1 clove garlic, crushed
¼ tsp. salt
⅛ tsp. pepper

1. Wash lettuce in cold water; remove core; separate leaves; remove bruised ones. Pat leaves dry with paper towel. Tear lettuce into bite-size pieces; put into plastic bag. Chill for 1 hour.
2. To prepare *croutons*, trim crusts. Generously butter both sides of bread. Sprinkle each piece with ¼ tsp. garlic powder. Cut into ½-inch cubes. Bake 10 to 15 minutes in 400-degree oven until golden and crisp.
3. To prepare Italian dressing, place all ingredients in jar. Shake well. Chill. Just before serving, shake well.
4. Prepare salad bowl by gently rubbing with peeled and crushed garlic clove.
5. Just before serving place all ingredients in prepared salad bowl and toss with dressing.
   Serves 6

Recipe Tips

- Crush garlic easily by removing outer skin and pressing clove gently between handle of knife and wooden cutting board.
- To divide preparation into two days, complete Steps 1 through 3 the first day. Refrigerate salad greens and dressing. Cover croutons loosely so they will remain crisp. Begin with Step 4 next.

The Greeks came to the island of Sicily 2,000 yeas ago and were followed by the Romans, Byzantines, Arabs, Normans, and Spaniards. Each group left its mark on the local cuisine and also influenced the cooking on the Italian mainland. Located just three miles off the western coast of southern Italy, Sicily is the largest island in the Mediterranean Sea. The Mediterranean climate produces Europe's best fruits and vegetables, such as the oranges, grapefruit, and artichokes used in this salad. Artichokes, with their stout, globelike, and distinct appearance are used throughout Italy. Italians boil, bake, fry artichokes, and put them on pizza, in pasta sauce, and in salads.

Salad has a special role in the Italian meal. It is served after the main course, signaling the end of the meal and the clearing of the palate for a light dessert. The composition of the salad changes with the seasons, and wild greens are sometimes used.

The excellent olive oil used in Italian salads is a product of northern Tuscany. It gives Tuscan food its unique flavor and aroma. Italian cooks could not imagine cooking without good-quality olive oil, much of which is made locally from freshly picked olives pressed by peasants and villagers.

Bread with salad was originally a peasant-style dinner in the Tuscany region. Traditionally, two- or three-day old bread was soaked in water, squeezed, and added to the salad. In this more modern version, waterlogged bread is replaced by crisp squares of bread called *croutons*.

MARINATED VEGETABLES

Food Category: Salad *Moderate Cost*

- ⅔ cup wine vinegar
- ⅔ cup salad oil
- ¼ cup onion, chopped
- 2 cloves garlic, crushed
- 1 tsp. salt
- 1 tsp. sugar
- 1 tsp dried basil
- 1 tsp dried oregano
- pepper to taste
- 8 oz. fresh mushrooms, halved or quartered
- 1 cup French carrots, whole or halved
- 1 cup cauliflower pieces
- 14-oz. can artichoke hearts, drained and halved
- 1 cup pitted ripe olives, halved
- 1 cup celery slices, ¼ inch thick
- 2 oz. jar sliced pimiento, drained and chopped

1. In saucepan, combine vinegar, oil, onion, garlic, salt, sugar, basil, oregano, and pepper. Bring to boil. Simmer uncovered for 10 minutes.
2. Wash *French carrots* thoroughly. Cook in small amount of boiling water just until *tender-crisp*. Drain.
3. Wash cauliflower. Cook in small amount of boiling water just until tender-crisp. Drain.
4. Combine vegetables in flat *casserole*. Pour hot *marinade* over vegetables; stir gently to coat.
5. Cover tightly; chill several hours. Stir occasionally.
6. Drain vegetables and serve.
   Serves 6

Recipe Tips

- Crush basil and oregano to release oils before adding them to vinegar and oil mixture.
- Clean mushrooms with soft, wet brush. Do not immerse them in water; they become spongy.
- Cook carrots separately from cauliflower so that the cauliflower will remain white.
- You may substitute regular carrots for French carrots. Just halve them and cut in 3-inch lengths.
- Crush garlic easily by removing outer skin and pressing clove gently between handle of knife and wooden cutting board.
- This may be kept in refrigerator for up to 2 weeks. Flavors will improve with standing.
- To divide preparation into two days, complete Steps 2 and 3. Refrigerate covered. Complete Steps 1 and 4 through 6 the next day.

BISCUIT TORTONI

Food Category: Dessert *Moderate Cost*

- 2 cups cold milk
- 2 cups whipping cream
- ¼ cup sugar
- ½ tsp. almond extract
- 2 small pkg. vanilla instant pudding
- ⅔ cup vanilla wafer crumbs

1. Pour milk and cream into large bowl.
2. Add sugar, almond extract, and pudding mix. Combine slowly with rotary beater for at least 1 minute.
3. Pour into 9-inch *springform pan*. Let stand for about 3 minutes.
4. Top with crumbs and freeze overnight.
5. Let stand at room temperature for 15 minutes before serving. Cut into small slices.
   Serves 12.

Recipe Tips

- For fast and easy cleanup, crush vanilla wafers by placing in plastic bag and rolling with rolling pin.
- *Tortoni* may be poured into individual soufflé cups rather than a springform pan. This makes it easier to serve.

In Italy, Marinated Vegetables are often served as *antipasto*, (ann-tee-PAHS-toh). It is served in Italian restaurants or before special meals at home. This dish fits into the style of meals served in Rome, the capital city of Italy, in the Latium region, with its sophisticated dining rooms as well as its neighborhood *trattorias*. The herbs in this marinade are some of Rome's favorites.

During his travels to China in the 13th century, Marco Polo discovered a food similar to modern ice cream. He brought the recipe back, and frozen ice milk was introduced to Europe.

This concoction was improved upon, and in the 18th century, Italians from Naples sold ice cream on the Boulevard des Italiens in Paris, France. Unfortunately, one enterprising gentleman overextended his business and went bankrupt. However, his assistant, named Tortoni, took over the shop, and Tortoni's son was credited for the Biscuit Tortoni (tohr-TOE-neh) so enjoyed by the Italians.

DEEP-FRIED SWEET PASTRY

Food Category: Dessert *Low Cost*

2¼ cups unsifted flour
4 eggs

2 tbsp. milk
confectioners' sugar

⅛ tsp. salt
oil for frying

1. Place 2 cups flour in large bowl. Make *well* in center. Add 2 eggs, plus 2 egg yolks, milk, 1 tbsp. confectioners' sugar, and salt. Using your hands or fork, mix until all flour has been incorporated, and dough will form into rough ball.
2. Sprinkle remaining ¼ cup flour on board. *Knead* for 10 minutes, until extra flour is worked in and dough is smooth and shiny. Refrigerate for 1 hour.
3. On floured board, roll ¼ of dough paper thin. To shape dough follow the steps below and refer to the illustrations (on back):
   (1) With pastry wheel or sharp knife cut dough into strips, 6 or 7 inches long and ½ inch wide.
   (2) Tie strips into loose knots.
4. Heat 4 inches oil to 350 degrees in deep-fat fryer. *Deep-fry* 4 or 5 pastries at a time, for 1 or 2 minutes, just until golden brown. Using slotted spoon or tongs, lift out strips. Drain on paper towels. Sprinkle with confectioners' sugar just before serving. Store loosely covered in a dry place. *Makes 4 dozen.*
Serves 16

Recipe Tips

- A Dutch oven or heavy skillet may be used in place of deep-fat fryer, but there must be room for 4 inches of oil.
- The correct oil temperature is essential. If oil is too cool, foods will absorb it and become greasy. If oil is too hot, foods will burn before they are cooked. Use deep-fat-frying thermometer to check the oil. If you don't have a thermometer, drop a 1-inch cube of bread into hot fat. Time 1 minute. If bread is brown, oil temperature is correct.
- To divide preparation into two days, complete Steps 1 and 2. Cover dough with waxed paper and refrigerate. Begin with Step 3 the next day.

STRAWBERRY FLAVORED GRANITE

Food Category: Dessert *Low Cost*

1 cup water
½ cup sugar (if using frozen berries, use ¼ cup)

2 cups fresh ripe strawberries
2 tbsp. lemon juice

1. Bring water and sugar to boil. Stir until sugar dissolves. Boil for exactly 5 minutes.
2. Remove from heat. Let syrup cool to room temperature.
3. *Puree* strawberries in electric *blender* or force through *sieve* or *food mill*. Stir pureed strawberries and lemon juice into cooled syrup. Pour mixture into divided ice cube tray.
4. Freeze until solid. Remove cubes. Crush in *ice crusher* or blender. Serve immediately. Makes 1½ pints.
Serves 6

Recipe Tips

- Granite is similar to sorbet, which is served between courses to clear the palate.
- If you do not have a blender or an ice crusher, you may be able to use an electric mixer, depending on its strength, to crush ice cubes.
- Serve granite in sherbet dishes or soufflé cups.
- Granite can be crushed and returned to freezer for approximately 15 minutes before it is served.

Variations

- Lemon 2 cups water
          1 cup sugar
          1 cup lemon juice
- Orange 2 cups water
          ¾ cup sugar
          1 cup orange juice
          juice of 1 lemon

Step 1

Step 2

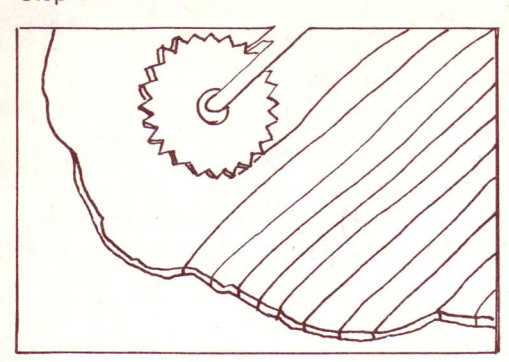

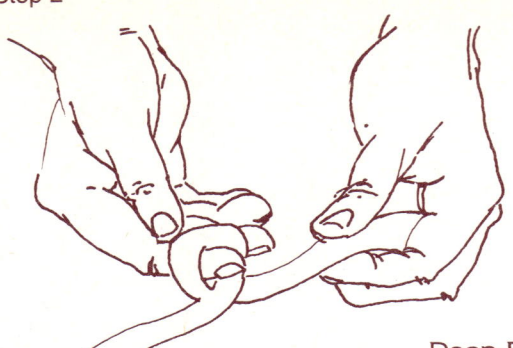

Deep-Fried Sweet Pastry

The Island of Sicily does not have good natural resources because of its mountains and volcanos, yet its cooking has a unique character, flavor, and color. One of Sicily's specialties is dessert. The credit for this goes to the Saracen invaders of Sicily, who introduced pastry delicacies in the 9th century. This dessert is called *cenci* (meaning "tatters" or "rags" in Italian), because the pastry looks ragged when cooked.

Granite (grah-NEE-teh) is a fine, ice-crystal sherbet. As early as A.D. 54, there was mention of some type of flavored ice on the Island of Sicily. Snow was obtained from the mountaintops by runners who relayed the snow down the mountains. It was then flavored with crushed fruit and fruit juices. Much later, granite was invented, and it was sold by Italian vendors in Sicily.

DEEP-FRIED RICE AND CHEESE BALLS*

Food Category: First Course Low Cost

¾ cup rice
1½ cups water
2 eggs
1 cup mozzarella cheese in ½-inch cubes
¾ cup fine, dry bread crumbs
oil for deep-fat frying

1. Bring water to boil.
2. Add rice. Stir to moisten each grain. Cover tightly. Simmer for 20 to 25 minutes. Let stand for 10 minutes. *Do not peek*, or the water will evaporate and rice will burn before it is done.
3. Beat eggs lightly with fork until just combined. Add rice. Stir gently but thoroughly, making sure not to mash rice.
4. Take 1 tbsp. rice mixture. Place cubed *mozzarella* cheese in middle. Top with another tablespoon of rice mixture.
5. Shape into ball. Roll in bread crumbs. Place on waxed paper. Refrigerate for 30 minutes.
6. Heat 4 inches of oil to 350 degrees in deep-fat fryer. *Deep-fry* rice balls, 4 or 5 at a time, for 1 or 2 minutes until golden brown and cheese has melted.
7. Using slotted spoon or tongs, lift out balls. Drain on paper towels. Serve immediately.

Serves 6

Recipe Tips

- *When spaces appear between the grains of rice, it is done.*
- *When rice is prepared ahead it is easier to handle; it will separate into individual grains more readily.*
- *Eggs are essential; they make the ingredients stick together.*
- *A Dutch oven or heavy skillet may be used in place of a deep-fat fryer, but there must be ample room for 4 inches of oil.*
- *The correct oil temperature is essential. If oil is too cool, foods will absorb it and become greasy; if too hot, foods will burn before they are cooked. Use a deep-fat-frying thermometer to check the oil temperature. If you don't have a thermometer, drop a 1-inch cube of bread into hot fat. Time 1 minute. If bread is brown, oil temperature is correct.*
- *To divide preparation into two days, cook rice and refrigerate. The next day the rice will be easier to shape into balls.*

POLENTA WITH SAUSAGE*

Food Category: First Course Moderate Cost

1 lb. Italian sausage
2 tbsp. oil
1 lb. mushrooms, cleaned and sliced
2½ cups canned tomatoes
2½ tsp. salt
⅛ tsp. pepper
1 cup yellow cornmeal
4 cups water
romano cheese

1. Cut sausage casing, remove sausage, and crumble into small pieces with a fork.
2. Heat oil in large skillet. Add sausage and mushrooms. Cook slowly, stirring occasionally, until mushrooms and sausage are lightly browned.
3. Drain excess grease.
4. Slowly stir in tomatoes, 1 tsp. salt, and pepper. Simmer for 20 to 30 minutes.
5. While the mixture is simmering, bring 3 cups water with 1½ tsp. salt to boil. Combine cornmeal and 1 cup cold water. Gradually stir into boiling water, stirring constantly until mixture is thickened.
6. Cover, lower heat, and cook slowly for 10 minutes or longer, until very thick. Transfer cooked cornmeal to warmed platter and top with tomato mixture.
7. Sprinkle with cheese and serve immediately.

Serves 6

Recipe Tips

- *Clean mushrooms with soft, wet brush. Do not immerse mushrooms in water; they become spongy.*
- *Use a fork to break up canned tomatoes.*
- *Cornmeal spatters very easily during cooking. Be careful.*
- *Warm platter by letting stand in hot water. If platter is ovenproof, place in oven for a few minutes at lowest setting.*
- *To divide preparation into two days, complete Steps 1 through 4. Begin with Step 5 the next day after reheating sauce.*

This dish is known as *suppli al telefone*, which means "croquettes on the telephone." This is because when the croquettes are bitten into the melted mozzarella cheese looks like telephone wires.

Rice is grown and eaten mostly in northern Italy. In the Po Valley of the Piedmont region, streams flowing down the mountains are used to irrigate the rice paddies. Since the 1500s, rice grown in Piedmont has been internationally known for its superior quality. Italy still is the largest producer of rice in Europe.

Polenta (poe-LEN-tah) is considered the bread of northern Italy, particularly around Venice in the Veneto region. Venice, on the Adriatic Sea, was once a bustling seaport into which Venetian sailors brought the first maize grains. This changed the traditional wheat Italian polenta to the yellow corn version used here.

Traditionally, polenta was cooked in a deep copper pot. The batter, stirred with a wooden spoon, was considered properly made when the spoon could stand upright in it. When polenta was turned out of a bowl, it retained the shape of the bowl. It was sliced with a tauntly held string.

In many homes, polenta is still made fresh daily. Prepared with cheese, fish sauce, or meat, it can be served as a first course (like rice or spaghetti), as a side dish or as a second course.

LASAGNA*

Food Category: First Course   *High Cost*

- 1 clove garlic, crushed
- 1 onion, finely chopped
- 2 tbsp. oil
- 1 lb. lean ground beef
- ¼ lb. hot Italian sausage, cut in pieces
- 1 tsp. salt
- 28-oz. can Italian tomatoes
  or
- 4 cups peeled, quartered fresh tomatoes
- 6-oz. can tomato paste
- 2 cups water
- ½ tsp. oregano, crushed
- ½ tsp. rosemary, crushed
- ½ lb. lasagna noodles
- 3 quarts water
- 1 tsp. salt
- 1 cup ricotta cheese
- 1 lb. grated mozzarella cheese

1. In large pan, *sauté* garlic and onion in oil until soft. Add ground beef and sausage, stirring until brown. *Drain*. Mix in salt.
2. Crush tomatoes with fork and add to pan with tomato paste, water, oregano, and rosemary.
3. Bring to boil. Lower heat. Simmer for 45 minutes until thick.
4. Cook lasagna noodles in boiling, salted water for 20 to 25 minutes until firm.
5. Drain. Rinse lasagna in cold water. Lay on clean cloth.
6. Lightly grease 13- × 9- × 2-inch pan. Pour thin layer of sauce in bottom. Over it, lay half of the noodles. Cover with ½ remaining sauce, then ½ cheeses. Repeat layers of lasagna noodles, sauce, and cheeses.
7. Bake in 350-degree oven for 30 minutes. Let set for 10 minutes before cutting into squares.

Serves 6

Variations

- White sauce—Use white sauce instead of tomato sauce.
- Cottage cheese—Use cottage cheese instead of ricotta cheese.

CALZONE*

Food Category: First Course   *Moderate Cost*

Dough

- 2 pkgs. dry yeast or 2-cakes of yeast
- 1 pinch sugar
- 1¼ cups warm water
- 3½ cups unsifted flour
- 1 tsp. salt
- ¼ cup oil

Filling

- ½ lb. dry salami
- ¼ cup finely chopped onion
- 1 clove garlic, crushed
- ½ lb. mushrooms, chopped
- ⅓ cup finely chopped green pepper
- 3 tbsp. oil
- 8 oz. can tomato sauce
- 2¼ oz. can sliced olives, drained
- 1 tsp. dry oregano, crushed
- 1 tsp. dry basil, crushed
- ½ tsp. sugar
- ¼ tsp. crushed red pepper
- salt and pepper
- 2⅓ cups shredded mozzarella cheese

1. To prepare dough, sprinkle yeast (which makes bread rise) and sugar (which is food for yeast) into ¼ cup warm water between 105 to 115 degrees (use a *candy thermometer*). Let stand 2 to 3 minutes without stirring. Then stir until yeast and sugar are completely dissolved.
2. Set in *pre-warmed* oven for 3 to 5 minutes.
3. Stir flour and salt together in large bowl. Make a *well* and pour in yeast mixture, 1 cup warm water, and ¼ cup oil. Mix all together into a ball.
4. Place on floured board and, to develop *gluten*, *knead* for 15 minutes.
5. Place in oiled bowl. Cover with oiled waxed paper and damp towel. Let dough rise about 45 minutes until doubled.
6. *Sauté* vegetables in oil until limp. *Drain* excess oil. Add tomato sauce, salami, sliced olives, basil, oregano, garlic, sugar, and red pepper. Reduce heat. Simmer for 5 minutes. Let cool. When ready to assemble, stir in shredded mozzarella cheese. Add salt and pepper to taste.
7. After dough has risen, *punch down* and divide into 4 parts for easy handling. Stretch and roll dough as thin as possible to no more than ⅛ inch thick.

Recipe Tips

- *Crush garlic easily by removing outer skin and pressing clove gently between handle of knife and wooden cutting board.*
- *Crush oregano and rosemary to release oils before adding them to sauce.*
- *Lasagna noodles require a long cooking time because they are large.*
- *If you cook too many lasagna noodles, pat them dry, cut into finger-size pieces, and deep-fat-fry them. Sprinkle with grated parmesan cheese. This makes a tasty, crunch snack.*
- *To divide preparation into two days, complete Steps 1 through 6, cover with plastic wrap and refrigerate overnight. Begin with Step 7 the next day baking approximately 15 minutes more.*

The Calabria region forms the "toe" of Italy, so it is surrounded on three sides by the sea. It is predominately a mountain region with few natural resources. The average family eats little meat, so seafood is an important part of the diet. In the true southern Italian tradition, pasta is also a mainstay of the Calabria diet. Substantial casserole dishes such as Lasagna (lah-ZAHN-ya), combining broad pasta noodles, vegetables, and rich sauces are popular.

---

8. Cut dough into 9-inch rounds. Place rounded teaspoon of filling on one half of round. Roll other half over filling to make half moon. Fold bit of edge up and over. Seal and crimp. Repeat process with remaining dough.
9. Transfer turnovers to greased and cornmeal dusted baking sheet. Poke holes in tops with fork and brush with salad oil.
10. Bake at 475 degrees about 10 minutes, until well browned.
    Four-inch circles make 36 appetizers.
    Serves 18
    Eleven-inch circles make 6 main dish servings.
    Serves 6

Recipe Tips

- *Salt is essential because it controls the growth of the yeast.*
- *Crush garlic easily by removing outer skin and pressing clove gently between handle of knife and wooden cutting board.*
- *Make holes in the tops of filled rounds of dough so steam can escape; otherwise the dough will break.*
- *To divide preparation into two days, complete Steps 1 through 8. Store filled rounds in tightly sealed plastic bag and refrigerate overnight. Begin with Step 9 the next day, baking approximately 2 minutes more.*

Calzone (kahl-TSOH-neh) is a variety of classic pizza and one of the many doughs that Italians either fry or bake. This recipe bakes individually filled circles of dough into crusty turnovers. Small Calzone can be served as appetizers, while larger ones make good lunch or supper dishes.

Calzone is a favorite of the region of Apulia, where wheat is an important crop. Because of the availability of wheat, pasta and savory doughs such as Calzone are popular.

PIZZA*

Food Category: First Course

High Cost

Dough

1 pkg. yeast
1 pinch sugar
½ cup plus 2 tbsp. warm water
1¾ cups unsifted flour
½ tsp. salt
2 tbsp. oil

Toppings

parmesan or romano cheese, grated
tomato sauce
onion, finely chopped
mushrooms, sliced
olives, sliced
ham or sausage
mozzarella cheese, grated

1. To prepare dough, sprinkle yeast and sugar over 2 tbsp. water. Let stand for 2 to 3 minutes without stirring. Then stir until dissolved.
2. Set in *pre-warmed* oven for 3 to 5 minutes.
3. Stir flour and salt together in large bowl. Make a *well* and pour in yeast mixture, ½ cup warm water and 2 tbsp. oil. Mix all together into ball.
4. *Knead* 15 minutes. Let rest for 15 minutes.
5. Place in oiled bowl. Cover with oiled waxed paper. Let rise until dough has doubled in bulk. *Punch down* dough.
6. Grease pizza pan lightly. *Dust* with corn meal. Gently pat the dough into pan, *fluting* edges.
7. *Sauté* onions and mushrooms.
8. If you are using sausage, brown, crumble, and drain it.
9. Place desired toppings on dough in the order listed.
10. Bake about 18 minutes in 425-degree oven. Let stand a few minutes. Slice and serve. Serves 6

Recipe Tips

- The oven must be turned off before placing yeast mixture in it.
- The light coating of corn meal in the pan will make pizza come out easily.
- No amounts for pizza topping ingredients are listed so preferences and items on hand determine how much to use.
- To divide preparation into two days complete Steps 1 through 5. Cover oiled waxed paper with a damp towel and refrigerate overnight. The next day begin with Step 6.

Pizza (PEET-sah) was invented in Naples, which is in the heart of the rich farm land of the Campania region. It is believed that the Neapolitans invented Pizza to use up their leftover bread dough.

There are at least 182 different ways to prepare Pizza today. It is best known in two favorite forms, a Sicilian variety with a thick crust, and a Neapolitan variety with a thin crust. Pizza in Italy is made in special bakeries, but many people regularly make it at home.

The Italian word *pizza* simply means "pie," and some versions of Pizza have double crusts, or the dough is made into individual pies and deep-fried. These varieties are rarely seen outside Italy.

Pizza Neapolitan is the best-known Pizza in the United States. Immigrant Neapolitans first opened pizzerias and introduced the world to their flavorful cheese-and-tomato–topped dough.

NOTES

NOTES

Exploring International Foods

Travel Mexico

Section Seven

INTRODUCTION TO MEXICAN FOODS

¡BIENVENIDOS!

Welcome to Mexico! Your culinary tour of Mexico begins with the roots of Mexican cooking traditions—its Mayan and Aztec Indian heritage. You will learn how traditional Mexican foods were created, and why Mexican cuisine today blends the foods of native Americans and of the Spanish conquistadors and other early settlers.

Reading the recipes will give you a chef's tour through four of Mexico's geographical regions. These 23 recipes were selected from over 2,000 dishes that are representative of Mexico's contrasting culture and geography. Included are classic examples of Mexican appetizers, breads, soups, vegetables, main dishes, and desserts. These foods are not only delicious; they are also practical to prepare outside Mexico.

As you read the recipes and learn the ingredients that are used in Mexican foods, you will begin to understand Mexican cooking style. After you identify on the map the region where each dish is prepared, you will feel as if you have traveled throughout Mexico.

The highlight of your introduction to Mexico will involve your observing the preparation of Flautas (FLOU-tas) and Tacos (TAH-kos). Sampling these demonstration dishes will give you a taste of what you have to look forward to when you cook your own Mexican meal. In this section you will find

- a Mexican food history
- a map of Mexico's regions
- 23 Mexican recipes

17
MEXICAN FOOD HISTORY

The more you know about the history of Mexican food, the better you will understand the influence that food has had on Mexican culture. You will discover that the Mayan (MI-yahn) Indians had an impressive, varied diet. When the Spanish invaded Mexico, they found that dining in the courts of Aztec (AZ-tek) rulers was as highly sophisticated as dining in European castles. The Spanish introduced new foods and cooking techniques to Mexico, and many foods now considered common around the world actually originated with the Mexican Indians.

Much of what we know about the history of Mexican cooking has come from records kept by native Indians and European explorers and from monuments and artifacts discovered in the remains of ancient Indian cities. Early Indians roamed throughout Mexico hunting, gathering wild plants, and fishing for food. The bones of mammoths and the remains of a human from the period 10,000 to 8,000 B.C. indicate that stone-tipped darts and flint knives were used to kill large animals for food and clothing.

As early as 6,000 B.C., some of these Indian nomads settled in central Mexico, discovered how to grow plants for food, and became farmers. A variety of squash, beans, and maize (corn, which was unknown to Europe at this time) gradually became staples in the Indian diet, as did avocados, peppers, and tomatoes.

By 2,500 B.C., hunting had become far less important than farming. In farming villages, Indians used grinding stones to make coarse meal out of maize kernels. They trapped fowl and netted fish, frogs, and tortoises in swamps, rivers, and lakes. Tubers, prickly pears, and other wild fruits were collected.

MAYAN INFLUENCE

The Mayan Indians occupied sites for a continuous period of 2,000 years in what are now Mexico's southern states. Among the first settled peoples in the New World and one of the most accomplished, they developed the New World's most advanced handwriting system and created some of its greatest art and architecture. The Mayas built large cities. They established Dzibilchaltún (ts-eeb-eel-chahl-TOON), which covered at least 31 square miles of the Yucatan peninsula (see Figure 17.1).

The Mayan calendar was as accurate as our own today. It was used by rulers and scholars to plan farming and to direct work in the fields.

Many Mayan agricultural techniques were advanced, even though stone tools and hand labor were all they used. They terraced hillsides for planting, built raised fields on lowlands to prevent flooding, and constructed dams in waterways. These techniques enabled the Mayas to continue farming during the rainy season.

The early Mayas planted many types of crops, thus making good use of the small amount of tropical forest they had cleared. Beans were planted with corn. Bacteria on the bean roots converted nitrogen to a form usable by plants and helped preserve the fertility of the soil. The fertility of the soil would have quickly diminished if just corn alone had been planted.

A diet consisting solely of corn would have been incomplete and unhealthy, so the Mayas added other vegetables and beans, which are rich in protein. This way they were assured of the availability of nutritious food for years. Crops the Mayas cultivated included squash, pumpkins, sweet potatoes, *chili (CHEE-leh)* peppers, tomatoes, *chayote* (chy-OH-teh) pear-shaped squash, avocados, sapote (sah-PO-teh) (marmalade plum), breadfruit (which looks like bread when baked), papayas, and cacao (from which cocoa and chocolate are made). Groves of fruit also were cultivated. Wild fruits, nuts, and seeds were plentiful.

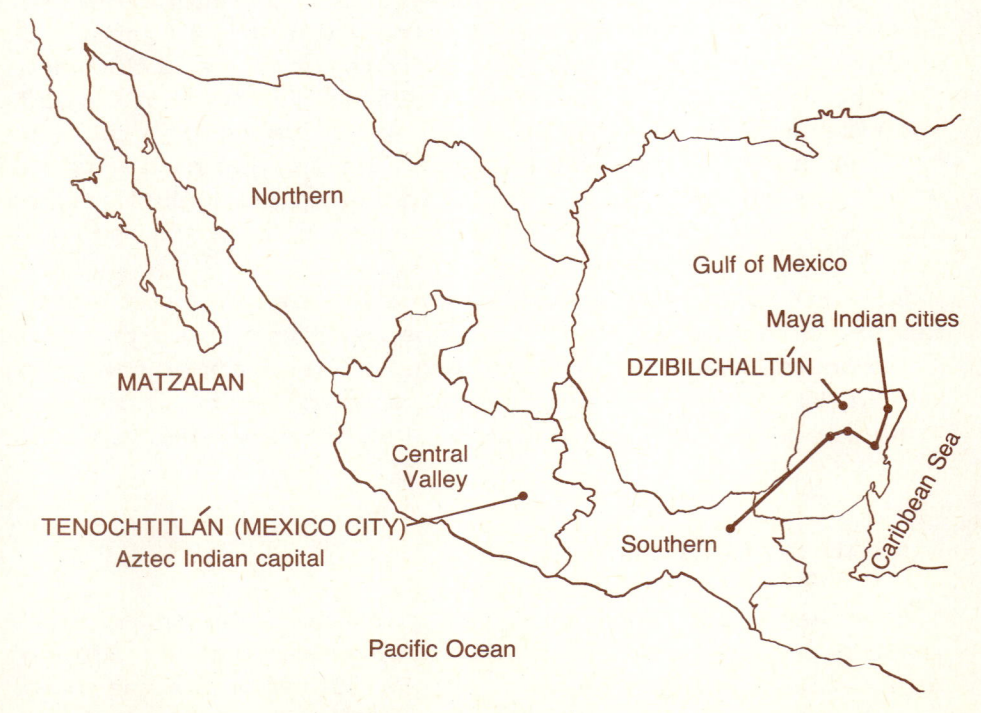

Figure 17.1. Culinary Regions of Mexico

164   Section Seven ● Introduction to Mexican Foods

The ocean provided shellfish, sea turtles, and fish. Meat came from game animals such as deer and birds. The Mayas domesticated turkeys and ducks and cultivated stingless bees. Having no sugar, the Mayas used honey. To keep the bees, they hollowed out a piece of log, sealed the ends with mud, and put a hole in the side to permit the bees to fly in and out.

Mayan families ate their main meal late in the afternoon. It consisted of red or black beans, chili peppers with other vegetables, *tamales*, (tah-MAH-les), spicy stews, roasted meat, fruit, and chocolate. The food was cooked on stone hearths or in ceramic containers. Each household had pottery, gourds, baskets, woven bags, and *metates* (meh-TAH-tehs) and *manos* (MAH-nohs) for grinding maize.

No one knows exactly why the Mayan civilization collapsed. They evolved from a society of farmers to become builders, constructing bigger and better temples. Then, instead of planting different types of crops, they began to plant only corn, the easiest crop to plant and harvest. The few laborers left to manage the fields probably began slashing and burning the landscape just to grow corn. This quickly destroyed the topsoil. The resulting erosion caused widespread famine, one factor that contributed to the severe decline of the Mayan population.

AZTEC INFLUENCE

In 1519, during the time of the European Renaissance, the Spanish explorer Cortés (kor-TEZ) and his crew landed in Mexico. There were a few Mayas left, and several other Indian tribes were scattered throughout Mexico. However, no Indians were as advanced as the Aztecs, who had now established a magnificent civilization. The Aztecs had originally been a wandering Indian group in search of a home. From those humble beginnings arose a tribe of Indians so powerful that they would eventually control many of the seven to nine million natives living in Mexico.

Tenochtitlán, (tee-noche-TEE-tlahn) was the Aztec empire's capital, situated where Mexico City is today. The Spanish had never seen such an elaborate city. The opulent architecture was evident in terraced houses for 200,000 people, with towers, temples, grand palaces, and civic monuments. Buildings were plastered and painted. Entering the city, Cortés saw corn and other vegetables growing in chinampas (floating gardens), and boats loaded with produce heading toward the marketplace.

Even the marketplace surpassed that of the great city of Rome. The Spanish found goods and foods organized into separate groups for trade: dried *maize*, beans, and the grain *amaranth* (am-a-RANTH); salt; turkey and quail; deer and rabbit; ducks and other water birds. There were different types of chili peppers, wild and ordinary tomatoes, and many kinds of fruit—cherries, avocados, plums, *guavas* (yellow and plum-sized), *tuna cactus* and more. Fresh vegetables and greens included onions, thistles, purslane, mixed greens, sorrel, squash, green beans, green maize, and tender maize. Aromatic herbs—maguey syrup (a sweet sap from the maguey, or century, plant, which is fermented to yield *pulque*—POOL-ka), honey, vanilla, and chocolate—were considered special and sold apart from the other produce. Chocolate wasn't the sweet variety with which we are familiar. It was unsweetened and very bitter.

Just as in the shopping malls today, the marketplace was a spot where people could meet, socialize, and discuss the events of the day. There were many prepared foods to eat. Just think, *tortillas* (tor-TEE-yahs) and *tamales* (tah-MAH-les) could be purchased as fast food snacks even then.

Though Cortés had seen the abundance of find food in the marketplace, he was still amazed to discover that Emperor Montezuma (Moctezuma, in Aztec) dined in as much splendor as European royalty. Three hundred dishes were prepared daily for Montezuma, including venison, wild boar, rabbit, chicken, turkey, pheasant, partridge, quail, tame and wild duck, pigeon, and other birds. A typical dinner included 30 different meat dishes, which were kept warm on pottery braziers. As Montezuma walked past the dishes, his aides would tell him the ingredients. He would then select a few dishes and eat lightly, considering what was offered.

Great care was taken in the appearance of the table. Montezuma ate alone, seated on a low stool at an immaculate, cloth-covered table. The table was set with intricately designed red or black earthenware and a large, white linen napkin. Cleanliness was considered very important. Four women would bring a deep gourd of water so that Montezuma could wash his hands before he ate. Plates were held below the gourd to catch the water, and there were fresh towels for him to dry his hands.

Everything was done to make Montezuma comfortable. When he ate, a screen was placed in front of him so that he could dine privately. If it was cold, a large fire was made using fragrantly scented, smokeless tree bark.

Throughout the meal, plates of tortilla bread were brought, and kept covered and hot with spotless white napkins. A frothy chocolate drink made from cacao and corn meal mash was served in a pure gold container. For dessert Montezuma selected from many types of fruit, and he finished his meal by smoking a pipe. The Spanish conquistadors were amazed at the lavish display of food and the civilized manners of the lords of Montezuma's court.

Two years later, in 1521, Cortés conquered the Aztecs, and modern Mexican food history began. Many foods brought from Europe and Asia during the Spanish colonial period were quickly adapted to the Indian diet. Beef, dairy cattle, sheep, pigs, and chickens were shipped to Mexico to be bred for food. Additional imported foods included rice, wheat, citrus fruits, almonds, sugar, onions, garlic, herbs, cinnamon, and other spices. Tortillas began to be made out of wheat as well as corn, and tomatoes and chili peppers were combined with rice to form what became known as Spanish rice.

Before this time, the Aztecs and other Mexican Indians had not used fat or oil for cooking. They boiled, broiled, or steamed their food—or else they ate it raw. Meat was roasted or stewed. However, "new" Spanish cooking techniques greatly influenced Mexico's cuisine. Fat drippings from cooked pork were used to fry meats and other foods. The Spanish taught the Indians to use *lard* when cooking beans. After the beans were simmered in a pot the Indian way, they were mashed and slowly fried in lard until the paste was stiff and dry enough to hold a shape. Today this dish is known as *refried beans*.

Half the modern world's food supply is composed of foods used by the Mexican Indians—a food supply that, for the most part, changed during the Spanish habitation of Mexico. But the Spanish, in their quest for gold, did not recognize the value of the Indians' food. In fact, there was one valuable food Cortés never introduced to Europe. When Cortés destroyed the magnificent city of Tenochtitlán while conquering the Aztecs, he also destroyed what is now thought to be the Aztec's most nutritious food: amaranth. *Amaranth*, a grain, was as important to the Aztecs as corn and beans. It was used in many ways, even popped (like popcorn) with honey to make a sweet treat. The Aztecs combined amaranth with corn in their diet, forming an almost complete protein. For religious reasons, Cortés thought that the way the Aztecs used amaranth was barbaric. So, he forced the Aztecs to stop growing and eating it. Now Western agriculture has rediscovered the benefits of amaranth. Amaranth is thought to contain more protein than wheat and have a higher quality protein than that in soybeans or milk. Amaranth is especially rich in the amino acid lysine, which is lacking in corn, but together they supply the necessary amino acids for quality protein.

The Spanish conquest of Mexico eventually helped spread the influence of Mexican cooking to other parts of the world. European and Asian cuisines were enhanced by the introduction of new ingredients from Mexico, which included beans, corn, potatoes, sweet potatoes, tomatoes, chili peppers, squash, avocados, pineapples, papayas, peanuts, vanilla, and chocolate. Today it would be hard to imagine Italian pasta sauce without Mexico's tomatoes or European desserts without Mexico's vanilla or chocolate.

Although Mexico won independence from Spain in 1821, Spain was not the only European influence on Mexico's cuisine. France and Austria contributed by introducing pasta and baked goods to Mexico's cooking heritage, when France and Austria's archduke, Maximilian, ruled in the 1860s.

Now Mexico is an independent republic with 31 states. Even with the influence of Spain, France, and Austria, Mexican cooking strongly reflects its Indian heritage. Unlike the vanished civilizations of the Middle East and Europe, there are two million descendants of the ancient Mayas, and one million natives who speak the ancient Aztec tongue today. There are Indian groups who speak both Spanish and Indian, and others who speak only one of 90 Indian tongues. All groups are officially Mexican, and all groups remain vitally important to Mexico's food culture.

REGIONAL DIFFERENCES

One factor that has determined the cuisine of Mexico is the land itself. Mexico is a large country, one-fourth the size of the United States. Flavor contrasts within the areas of Mexico are many. Cooking and eating are based on the plant and animal life in each region: the parched wheat and cattle region of the north, the lush agricultural region of the central valley, the Gulf of Mexico's fish and shellfish region in the south, and the tropical fruit region of Yucatán. Mexican dishes vary greatly within these regions, and the cooks in each city and isolated village have their own unique recipes.

In Mexico, two large mountain ranges run from north to south, with valleys and plateaus in between. Crops that flourish in the lowlands usually cannot grow in the mountains because of the altitude. The climate, the terrain, and the altitude of these areas tend to go to extremes—from alpine to tropical, from mountains to plateaus, and from deserts to jungles. This rugged landscape leaves only 15 percent of Mexico's soil suitable for cultivation, with only 8 percent being cultivated (80 percent of the land in the United States can be cultivated). Most of the land must be irrigated. The principal food crops are maize, wheat, rice, and kidney beans.

Differences in agricultural technology range from the modern irrigated fields of the northwestern coast to the age-old slash and burn, single-crop farming that Mayan descendants continue to follow in the south.

MEAL PATTERNS

Some Mexicans in villages along the back roads and mountain trails continue to eat the same foods their Indian ancestors ate. Even in Mexico City, the cultural and industrial center of the country, native food customs remain strong. Conveniences such as wood stoves, charcoal braziers, or more recently, electric hot plates and stoves have not radically changed the foods eaten in Mexico for centuries.

Most Mexicans eat three meals a day with snacks in between. A typical diet includes different forms of tortillas, chili or tomato sauce, beans, and rice. Some Mexicans consider tortillas, soup, and beans as their main foods, occasionally adding some fresh vegetables; most Mexicans, however, have a more varied diet and rely on the fresh foods found in modern grocery stores or markets.

Breakfast for some is early and light and consists of freshly

Table 17.1　Ingredients Common to Mexican Recipes

*avocados	*masa harina (corn flour)	*sour cream
*beans—pink, pinto	nopales	*tomatillos
*beef	*nuts—almonds, pecans,	*tomatoes
chayote	walnuts	*vanilla
*chili peppers—green,	*olives	
red, jalapeño, serrano	*onions	**Seasonings**
*chocolate	*papaya	*chili powder
*cheese—cheddar, jack	*peppers	*cilantro
*corn	plantains	*cinnamon
*fowl	*pork	*cumin
lard	pumpkin seed	*garlic
*lettuce	*rice	saffron

*Foods used in one or more of the Mexican recipes.

baked sweet doughs. Brunch is eaten by those who prefer to eat later in the day. This meal might include fruit, eggs with lightly fried beans, sweet rolls, and perhaps coffee with milk, or it could be sweet tamales with a cup of atole (ah-TOE-lay), a hot chocolate drink.

The most common ingredients in Mexican foods are listed in Table 17.1.

From one to three or four o'clock, all stores and businesses close. It is time for the two-hour main meal called *la comida* (koh-MEE-thah). The entire family gathers, except for those who work too far from home. Those who are too far away either go to a restaurant for la comida or have a light lunch and then eat their main meal after eight o'clock when their workday is finished.

At a formal comida, there may be appetizers such as *guacamole* (guah-kah-MOH-leh) with warm tortillas. The formal comida includes two kinds of soups. There is the *"wet" soup* course and a *"dry" soup* course, which may be pasta or rice. Rice may be served with a fried egg on top or eaten with tortillas and green tomato sauce.

Vegetables are garnished and served as a separate dish before the main course. They are sometimes fried or cooked as a pudding. Vegetables are added to many of the other dishes in the meal, and tomatoes and hot chili peppers form the basis of different sauces. A dish of sauce, which adds flavor to foods, is an important table item.

The main course is served next, and it may be fish, fowl, or meat. A great variety of fish is available along Mexico's 6,000-mile coastline. Ducks, doves, quail, and turkeys are game birds, while the most common meats, though, are beef, lamb, and pork. After the main course, small earthenware bowls of beans and broth are usually served.

La comida usually ends with something sweet for dessert. In addition to cookies, cakes, and *flans* (custards), there are bread puddings, crystallized fruits, sweetmeats (a paste made of fruits, nuts, and thickened milk), and fruits in syrup. Sweet potatoes are used as a base for fruit-flavored sweets. Perhaps the most popular dessert is fresh tropical fruit. Fruits such as strawberries, pineapples, guavas, and coconuts grow abundantly in Mexico.

La cena (SEH-neh) is a light supper served at the end of the day anytime between eight and eleven o'clock. La cena usually includes a few snacks, a bowl of hearty soup, a pastry, and perhaps coffee with milk.

Now turn to the Activities for the Mexico unit and remove Activity 1, Mexican Food History Review. Complete the Mexican Food History Review and give it to your instructor for evaluation.

18
EXPLORING MEXICAN RECIPES

In this chapter, you will use the Mexican recipes provided at the end of the Mexico unit. You will become familiar with Mexican cooking by reading each recipe and completing two related activities. The Mexican recipes are yours to keep when your culinary tour of Mexico is completed.

Complete this chapter by following Steps 1 through 4:

Step 1: Remove the Mexican recipe sheets and cut them apart.

Step 2: Read the Mexican recipes and recipe descriptions. Note that the recipes are labeled in the following categories: Appetizers, Breads, Soups, Vegetables, Main Dishes, and Desserts. For example, the Empanaditas (em-pah-nah-THEE-tahs) recipe is labeled "Food Category: Appetizer." The last five recipes are marked by an asterisk (*). You will read and use them to complete some of the activities, but *not* use them in your menu plans. These recipes are added for you to prepare at home.

To indicate approximately how much the recipe will cost to prepare, each recipe is rated either low cost, moderate cost, or high cost. The cost is based on the prices of the ingredients. The cost of each ingredient may vary because of different seasons and your location. On the back of each recipe is a brief history of each dish and information about the region where the dish is popular.

Step 3: Remove Activity 2, Mexican Recipe Match. Completing this activity will make you aware of recipe histories, names, food categories, and ingredients. Review both sides of each recipe in order to finish this activity. When finished, give your Mexican Recipe Match to your instructor for evaluation.

Step 4: Remove Activity 3, Mexican Map Review. Completing this activity will help you become familiar with the four culinary regions of Mexico and the regions where the recipes are popular. Review the descriptions of the recipes as you do this activity. When finished, give your Mexican Map Review to your instructor for evaluation.

19
MEXICAN RECIPE DEMONSTRATIONS

In this chapter you will get to the heart of Mexican cooking by actually tasting classic Mexican food. Two Mexican recipes will be demonstrated, and you will learn how to prepare them. While the recipes are being demonstrated, be sure to take good notes. The information in your notes will help you prepare the dishes later. The answers to the following questions will add to your knowledge of the recipes. Having the answers explained during the demonstrations and in the recipes will ensure your success.

FLAUTAS DEMONSTRATION

Notes: _____
_____
_____
_____
_____
_____
_____
_____
_____
_____
_____

QUESTIONS ON THE FLAUTAS DEMONSTRATION

1. What ingredient may be substituted for ground beef?

___

2. What procedure must be done as soon as the ground beef is cooked?

___

3. Why is it necessary to add seasonings before adding the flour?

___

4. What indicates that the flour has been absorbed?

___

5. What is an easy method for heating tortillas?

___

6. How many times are tortillas turned?

_____

_____

TACOS DEMONSTRATION

Notes: _____

QUESTIONS ON THE TACOS DEMONSTRATION

1. Why does the recipe say to cook only half the onion?
   _____
   _____
   _____

2. What could be done for a stronger onion flavor?
   _____
   _____
   _____

3. What must you be careful of when frying tortillas?
   _____
   _____
   _____

4. How may tortillas be kept warm after frying?
   _____
   _____
   _____

5. What is an easy method for peeling a tomato?
   _____
   _____
   _____

6. Why is it essential to shred lettuce just before using it?
   _____
   _____
   _____

Section Eight

PLANNING YOUR MEXICAN MEAL

You have already explored Mexico by way of map, history, recipes, and sample tasting. Now your class will prepare a Mexican meal. This meal will be similar in flavor to the native Mexican cuisine that you would find if you were actually in Mexico.

The success of your Mexican meal depends upon the combined effort of all students in each kitchen group. The food should be well prepared and attractively displayed on the buffet. The dining table should be properly set, and the kitchen should be clean. Remember that good table manners enable you to have an enjoyable dining experience.

While working in your assigned kitchen group, you must have your duties clearly in mind to ensure that the Mexican meal is a success. Planning ahead of time for the cooking and evaluation days will give you the confidence necessary to carry out your duties smoothly. Each part of this section is designed to prepare you for both the cooking and evaluation days. In this section you will find

- a guide to help you select your Mexican menu
- guides for Mexican recipe nutrition, convenience, and cost
- directions for setting a buffet and dining table
- seven ways to improve table manners
- a planning form for the cooking and evaluation days

20
SELECTING YOUR MEXICAN MENU

Your meal will be similar to a full comida, which would be served in a Mexican home on special occasions such as a holiday or weekend, when the meal is elaborate.

You will select your menu from recipes in the following food categories: appetizers, breads, soups, vegetables, main dishes, and desserts. Each food category has three recipes. You will choose *one* recipe from each category.

Remember that the recipes marked with an asterisk are for home use only.

After selecting one recipe from each of the food categories, you will have a total of six recipes, one of which you and your kitchen group will prepare.

A brief description of the food categories from which you will choose is as follows:

appetizers   Appetizers are snacks that are eaten throughout the day in Mexico. They can be purchased in marketplaces, bought from street vendors, or made at home and served before la comida or as a light meal.

breads   Both corn- and wheat-flour tortillas are served hot and eaten as bread in Mexico. They are served at the beginning of the meal and are used throughout the meal to scoop up appetizers or beans or to dip into soup.

soups   The variety of soups in Mexico is endless. Soup is a mainstay of the diet. The soups in these recipes are examples of typical "wet" soups—as distinguished from "dry" soups, which are pasta or rice in Mexico. The rice recipe presented here would be served as a "dry" soup and would follow the "wet" soup in a formal meal.

vegetables All Mexican meals include vegetables, especially chili peppers and tomatoes. Fresh vegetables are served as garnishes. Beans are served with every meal and in various ways. Whole beans, cooked in a pot, are served in small bowls after the main course and before the dessert. Refried beans are served at the beginning of the meal with appetizers or anytime during the meal as a basic accompaniment for other dishes.

main courses There is a variety of plain and rich main courses in a Mexican meal. Full comida main courses are usually substantial. They range from fish, *molé* (MOH-leh) dishes, roasted or broiled meats to stews of different types. Lighter dishes, such as *enchiladas* (en-chi-LA-duhs), are served as a main dish of a lunch or supper.

desserts The recipes in this category represent the vast number of sweets available in Mexico, where desserts are very popular.

The dishes from each category add to the appearance, texture, and flavor of the meal, while providing necessary nutrition. As you read the Mexican recipes, decide what you think would make the most appealing combination of dishes for the buffet. Incorporate foods with different colors, flavors, textures, and shapes to add interest to the meal. Be sure not to repeat major ingredients when you select the recipes. For example, if you choose mexican rice for the vegetable, you should not choose a main dish that is served over rice. This way your meal will not become monotonous, with several of the dishes having the same texture and the same taste. Moreover, by not repeating major foods in your menu, your meal will be nutritionally balanced.

When selecting a menu, be adventurous. Choose recipes you have neither tasted nor prepared. Look for ingredients that you have not tried. New taste experiences contribute to the excitement of cooking recipes from other countries. You may be pleasantly surprised, and as a result, you will develop a broader palate. Don't be turned off by unfamiliar or complicated directions. Remember, your kitchen group will prepare only one recipe, so you will have ample time to study it and clear up anything that you do not understand.

Select your menu in these two easy steps:

Step 1: Read the Mexican recipes. After you are familiar with them, proceed to Step 2.

Step 2: Remove Activity 4, Selecting Your Mexican Menu. Complete the activity and give it to your instructor for evaluation. He or she will tell you how the class menu will be selected and how the kitchen group will determine which recipe it will prepare.

21

MEXICAN RECIPES: NUTRITION, CONVENIENCE, AND COST

In this chapter you will learn the nutritional value in your menu. You will learn how to determine if your recipes are convenient to prepare and how much your meal will cost. The knowledge that you gain from completing this part will give you a good background for selecting recipes and planning meals when you are cooking on your own.

NUTRITION

A variety of healthy food is essential to good nutrition. Because people eat not only to enjoy the taste of food but also to remain healthy, it is necessary to consider the nutritional value of your recipes. For example, corn is a grain product and a good source of carbohydrates for energy, but it would be poor nutrition to eat just plain corn all day.

Your body requires more than just energy foods: it needs the nutrients that are found in the four major food groups:

- meat, poultry, fish, eggs, and legumes (dried beans and peas)
- milk products
- fruit and vegetable
- bread and cereal

Eating the recommended amount of food from each group provides the required nutrients needed in your daily diet.

Table 21.1 shows the necessary servings per day from each food group for your age.

Table 21.2 will help you determine the number of servings from these food groups provided by your Mexican meal. The

Table 21.1 Necessary Servings Per Day

Food Group	Servings
Meat/Poultry/Fish/Eggs/Legumes	2
Milk Products	4
Fruit/Vegetable	4
Bread/Cereal	4

completed chart will indicate to you which food group your meal has too much or too little of. If it is low in one group, you simply include food from that group in another meal that day. If it is high in another group, you decrease the amount of food in that group at another meal.

Mexican food is healthful and natural. Food is freshly prepared and includes ingredients from all four food groups. Basic components of a Mexican meal are beans, tortillas, and tomato or chili pepper sauce or both. It is common for a meal to be high in carbohydrates, especially those found in tamales, and tortillas made from corn. The nutritional emphasis is on carbohydrates, not protein. Relatively little complete protein comes from meat. Instead, the Mexican diet combines incomplete protein foods such as dried beans and grains, which supply the necessary amino acids for more complete proteins. The most common protein source is a low-cost combination of beans and corn. When Refried Beans are combined with Corn Tortillas or *tostadas* (fried tortillas), the dish increases in protein nutritional value. This also occurs when beans are combined with rice. Beans supply the essential amino acids missing in grains that are necessary to make a complete protein.

Chili peppers, tomatoes, and *tomatillos* (toh-mah-TEE-yohs) in Mexican cooking add vitamins C and A to the diet. Calcium, a mineral necessary for healthy bones and teeth, is obtained from treated corn. When corn is soaked in lime water to soften it so that it can be ground, it absorbs calcium from the lime water.

Mexican food tends to be high in saturated fats and cholesterol because many foods are fried in lard. The use of polyunsaturated vegetable oil instead of lard would reduce both the saturated fat and cholesterol level in the Mexican diet.

Follow these directions for completing the Food Group Menu Chart.

1. List the recipes your class has selected in the Recipes column on the chart.
2. Read the ingredients of each recipe and check (√) the major food group into which each falls. A recipe may fall into more than one food group. When this occurs, only major ingredients are classified.
3. Total the number of servings in each food group column.
4. Using Table 21.2, write the number of servings still needed to attain the necessary daily food group recommendations.

Table 21.2 Food Group Menu Chart

Food Groups	Meat/Poultry Fish/Eggs/ Legumes	Milk Products	Fruit/ Vegetable	Bread/ Cereal
Daily Necessary Servings*	2	4	4	4
Recipes Appetizer:				
Bread:				
Soup:				
Vegetable:				
Main Course:				
Dessert:				
Totals				
Servings Still Needed				

*for your age group

CONVENIENCE

You will know a recipe is convenient if

- you can easily obtain the ingredients
- you have the necessary equipment to make the dish
- you have adequate time to prepare it

Because some ingredients are too expensive or not available, other ingredients, which still assure the desired results, can be substituted. For example, the *vermicelli* in Vermicelli in Tomato Broth may not be available. However, *spaghettini*, a very thin variety of spaghetti can be broken into pieces and substituted without altering the flavor of the dish.

First, make a list of the equipment needed. Then, check the kitchen to see if all the equipment is there. The correct equipment is essential for the smooth and efficient preparation of your recipe. Carefully read the recipe to determine how much time will be required, and make sure that the recipe fits into your time schedule. Preparing part of the recipe one day and completing it the next will make the dish more convenient to prepare.

The decision to prepare Mexican food may result in some minor inconveniences. You might have to search the grocery store for certain ingredients, such as *masa harina* (MAH-sah ah-REE-nah) or canned tomatillos that you may not be used to buying. You might have to purchase new equipment or figure out how to improvise with what you have in order to prepare a recipe at home. For example, the recipe Refried Beans requires a *Dutch oven* which you might not have. However, you can easily substitute a large, covered saucepan. The heat will transfer more quickly through the thin metal, so you will have to cook the beans at a lower temperature or watch them more carefully. A Mexican wooden bean masher works best for this recipe, but you can substitute an ordinary wooden spoon. You will find that the opportunity to try a new Mexican dish is worth your effort to improvise a special piece of equipment.

Answer the following questions, to help your recipe preparation. Planning ahead will ensure efficiency on preparation day.

1. What recipe ingredients are not available? _____
_____

2. What major pieces of equipment (pans, bowls) will be necessary?
_____
_____

3. What utensils will be necessary? _____
_____

4. What necessary equipment is missing? _____
_____

5. How might you improvise this missing equipment? _____
_____
_____

6. How much time will your recipe take to prepare?

(estimate) _____

7. How do you rate the convenience of your recipe?
Check (√) one:

____ quick and easy

____ somewhat involved

____ difficult but worth the effort

Chapter 21 ● Mexican Recipes: Nutrition, Convenience, and Cost   183

COST

In this activity, each kitchen group will compute the cost of its recipe. Afterwards, you will total the cost of all recipes and find out the cost of the entire meal.

Soon you will be responsible for your own food budget. You will want to keep your food costs within the amount of money you have budgeted. You must know the individual serving cost when you have a certain number of persons to feed within a budget. If a recipe costs $10.00 to prepare and makes ten servings, it costs only $1.00 per serving; however, if that dish made only four servings, the cost would more than double to $2.50 per serving. The cost of the recipe per serving is the meaningful figure.

Study the example of the Mexican Meal Cost Sheet (Figure

SECTION A   Name of Recipe: *Chilaquiles*

(1) Recipe Ingredients	(2) Amount Required	(3) Price Per Item	(4) Amount of Store Container	(5) Cost Computation	(6) Total Ingredient Cost
corn tortillas	2 dozen	.49	1 dozen	2 × .49 = .98	.98
chicken broth (bouillon cubes)	1 cubes	1.09	3.33 ounces (25 cubes)	1.09 ÷ 25 = .043 or .04	.04
jack cheese	2½ cups	2.79	1 pound	2.79 ÷ 5 = .558 or .56; 2.5 × .56 = 1.40	1.40
sour cream	1½ cups	.69	8 ounces	1.5 × .69 = 1.04	1.04
tomatillos	1–10 ounce can	.84	10 ounces	exact amount required (.84)	.84
jalapeno chili peppers	2	1.24	7 ounces	1.24 ÷ 8 = .155 or .16; 2 × .16 = .32	.32

SECTION B ────────────────────▶ Total Recipe Cost: **$4.62**

Total Recipe Cost ÷ Number of Servings = Cost Per Serving

SECTION C ───▶ (**$4.62**) ÷ (**6**) = (**$.77**)

Figure 21.1. Sample Filled-in Activity 5

Chilaquiles

24 tortillas
1 cup chicken broth
2½ cups jack cheese
1½ cups sour cream
1 10 oz. can tomatillos
2 cloves garlic
1 tbsp. cilantro
2 canned jalapeño chili peppers
oil
salt

Figure 21.2. Recipe for Chilaquiles

21.1). The cost per serving of Chilaquiles (chee-la-KEY-less) has been determined. By studying these steps, you will be able to follow the directions for completing your own Mexican Meal Cost Sheet. See how Carlos Ramirez determined the cost of Chilaquiles.

Step 1: Carlos read the recipe to determine what ingredients should be included in figuring the cost of the recipe (see Figure 21.2). Ingredients such as salt, pepper, cornstarch, baking powder, vinegar, vanilla, and most seasonings including chili powder, *cumin*, and *cilantro* (si-LAHN-tro) were on hand in the kitchen, so it was not necessary to include small amounts of these items when figuring per serving cost. Carlos decided that the cost of the salt and cilantro did not have to be included. He recorded the remaining ingredients for Chilaquiles in Column 1 of the Mexican Meal Cost Sheet.

Step 2: Carlos wrote the amount of each ingredient he needed in Column 2.

Step 3: Carlos took the Mexican Meal Cost Sheet to the grocery store. He listed the price the store charged for each item in Column 3, and then bought the quantity of each ingredient closest to the amount he needed.

Step 4: Carlos listed the amount of the item's store container in Column 4. Stores sell items in different measure-

Table 21.3 Table of Weights and Measures

3 teaspoons	1 tablespoon
4 tablespoons	¼ cup
5⅓ tablespoons	⅓ cup
8 tablespoons	½ cup
16 tablespoons	1 cup or 8 ounces
2 cups	1 pint
2 pints	1 quart
4 cups	1 quart
4 quarts	1 gallon
16 ounces	1 pound

ments, weights, and quantities, depending on the item itself. Pints, quarts, gallons, ounces, pounds, bunches, or "per each" are common quantity terms.

Step 5: Carlos computed the cost of each ingredient in Column 5. When necessary, he referred to the Table of Weights and Measures or to the Table of Equivalent Amounts (see Tables 21.3 and 21.4).

Table 21.4 Equivalent Amounts (Approximate)

Item	Common Weights or Units	Equivalence in Cups or Spoons
Bananas	1 pound (2 large, 3 medium, 4 small)	2 cups sliced
Beans, dry (pink, pinto, etc.)	1 pound (2½ cups) raw 2/5 pound (1 cup) raw	5 to 7 cups cooked 2 to 3 cups cooked
Bread Crumbs	3 to 4 slices dried bread 1 slice fresh bread	1 cup fine dry crumbs ½ cup fresh crumbs
Butter	1 pound (4 sticks) 1 stick	2 cups ½ cup
Carrots	1 pound (6 medium)	2 cups sliced
Cheese, freshly grated hard	1 pound 1 pound	5 cups 4 cups
Chicken Bouillon (for broth)	3.33-ounce package (25 cubes) 1 cube	25 cups with water 1 cup with water
Chocolate	8-ounce box	8 squares
Corn Meal	1 cup uncooked	4 cups cooked
Flour, corn (masa harina) or wheat	1 pound	4 cups unsifted
Greens, salad	1 serving 1 head or 1 bunch (4 servings)	2 cups loosely packed 8 cups loosely packed
Nuts, almonds, pine nuts, walnuts	8 ounces	2 cups
Olives	16-ounce can	1¼ cups
Onions, dry	1 pound (3 large, 4 medium, 5 small)	3 cups
green	1 bunch with tops (12 to 15)	⅓ cup
Peas, frozen	10 ounces	2 cups cooked
Peppers, bell	1 pound (3 to 6 small) ¼ pound	4 cups chopped 1 cup chopped
Jalapeño chili	7-ounce can (8 large)	1 cup chopped
Serrano chili	7-ounce can (10 large)	1 cup chopped

Table 21.4 (Continued)

Item	Common Weights or Units	Equivalence in Cups or Spoons
Raisins	4 ounces	¾ cup
Rice	½ pound (1 cup) raw	3 cups cooked
Shortening	1 pound	2 cups
Sour Cream	8 ounces	1 cup
Sugar, granulated confectioners'	1 pound 1 pound, sifted	2 cups 4¼ cups
Tomatillos	10 ounces	¾ cup
Tomatoes, fresh	1 pound (3 medium, 4 small)	1½ cups peeled and chopped
Tomato Paste or Puree	6 ounces	½ cup
Tomato Sauce	8 ounces	1 cup
Vermicelli	4 ounces (2 cups) uncooked	4 cups cooked
Zucchini	1 pound (6 small, 4 medium) 1 medium	3½ cups sliced 1 cup

The Tables of 21.3 and 21.4 will help you figure the cost of the ingredients in a recipe. To use the tables, you need to know the amount of each ingredient required for your recipe. Here are two examples:

1. Suppose your recipe calls for 7 tablespoons of oil and you want to figure the cost. Table 21.3 shows that 16 tablespoons equal 1 cup, and 4 cups equal 1 quart. Multiply 4 × 16, which is 64—the number of tablespoons in 1 quart. Next, divide the current market price for 1 quart of oil by the number of tablespoons in 1 quart (64). This gives you the price per tablespoon: $1.84 ÷ 64 = $.028, which is approximately 3 cents per tablespoon. Finally, 7 × $.03 = $.21, which is 21 cents, the cost of 7 tablespoons of oil.
2. Your recipe calls for ½ cup of butter, and you want to figure the cost. Table 21.4 tells you that 4 sticks equal 1 pound of butter, and 1 stick equals ½ cup butter. Divide the current market price for one pound of butter by 4: $1.89 ÷ 4 = $.471, or 47 cents, the cost of ½ cup of butter.

Figure 21.3 shows an explanation of the computation Carlos did in Column 5, using both tables.

Step 6: In column 6, Carlos recorded the answers he had computed in Column five.

Now you are ready to figure the cost of your recipe. Remove Activity 5, Mexican Meal Cost Sheet.

Cost Analysis

1. Corn tortillas
   Store quantity .... 1 dozen
   Store cost (in dollars) .... .49
   Amount required (2 dozen) × cost for one (.49) = Cost for ingredient (.98)
2. Chicken Broth (bouillon cube)
   Store quantity .... 3.33-ounce package (25 cubes)
   Store cost (in dollars) 1.09
   Cost per cube .... 1.09 divided by 25 = .043 or .04
   Amount required (1 cube at .04) = Cost for ingredient (.04)
3. Jack Cheese
   Store quantity .... 1 pound
   Store cost (in dollars) 2.79
   Cost per cup .... 2.79 divided by 5 = .558 or .56
   Amount required (2½ cups) × cost for one (.56) = Cost for ingredient (1.40)
   In Table 21.4, Carlos found that 5 cups = 1 pound of freshly grated cheese.
4. Sour cream
   Store quantity .... 8 ounces
   Store cost (in dollars) .... .69
   Cost per cup .... .69
   Amount required (1½ cups) × cost for one (.69) = Cost for ingredient (1.04)
   In Table 21.3, Carlos found 8 ounces = 1 cup.
5. Tomatillos
   Store quantity .... 10 ounces
   Store cost (in dollars) .... .84
   Cost per can .... .84
   Amount required (10 ounces at .84) = Cost for ingredient (.84)
6. Jalapeño chili peppers
   Store quantity .... 7 ounces
   Store cost (in dollars) 1.24
   Cost per pepper .... 1.24 divided by 8 = .155 or .16
   Amount Required (2 jalapeño chili peppers) × cost for one (.16) = Cost for ingredient (.32)
   In Table 21.4, Carlos found a 7-ounce can of jalapeño chili peppers contained 8 peppers.

Note: All costs should be approximate. When a price per unit comes out unevenly, round up (as stores do) to the nearest cent.

Figure 21.3. Recipe Cost Analysis

Follow the directions given here to complete this activity. Refer to the example of Carlos Ramirez if you need help. Remember, the recipe cost you compute should be *approximate*. Current market prices should be used to determine the cost of your recipes. You can read grocery store advertisements or go to the market to find out current prices.

First, fill in the name of the recipe your kitchen group will prepare in the space provided. Then do as follows:

Section A

Column 1: Determine what ingredients should be figured in the cost of the recipe. List each of these ingredients.
Column 2: List the amount of the ingredient your recipe requires.
Column 3: List the price of the item.
Column 4: List the amount of ingredient in store container.

Column 5: Show your computation of the cost per ingredient.
Column 6: List the cost of each ingredient.

Section B

Add the cost of each ingredient in Column 6 to get the total cost of the recipe. Write that figure in Section B.

Section C

Divide the total cost of the recipe by the number of persons it serves to determine the cost per serving. Write these figures in Section C.

Section D

Column 1: List the recipes prepared by other kitchen groups.
Column 2: List the total cost of each recipe.
Column 3: List the cost per serving of each recipe.

Section E

Add the cost of each recipe in Column 2 to get the cost of the total meal. Write that figure in Column 2. Add all of the recipe costs for each serving in Column 3 to determine the total cost of the meal per serving. Write that figure in Column 3.

Give your completed Mexican Meal Cost Sheet to your instructor for evaluation.

22

TABLE SETTINGS AND TABLE MANNERS

BUFFET SETTINGS

It is important to know how to set the buffet and dining tables properly when you serve your Mexican meal on evaluation day. If you are the host or hostess, setting the tables is one of your duties. You will place the dish your kitchen group prepares on the buffet table and set your kitchen group's dining table. Even if you are not the host or hostess, it is every kitchen group member's responsibility to make sure that the buffet and dining tables are set properly. A properly set table adds to the enjoyment of the meal.

Serving a meal buffet-style is extremely efficient for entertaining. A buffet enables a large group of people to serve themselves easily in a short period of time. This is particularly important at school.

Boldly colored Mexican handicrafts or bright flowers in a folk pottery vase will add a note of festivity to the table and contribute to the spirit of the meal. You might use one or more of the following: a brilliantly colored, handloomed or embroidered tablecloth, baskets of various sizes and shapes and lacquerware trays to hold serving containers, cut tinware, *paper maché piñatas*, or earthenware bowls with a geometric design.

The correct placement of the food is important. Everything should be organized to assure ease in serving. The foods for each course are placed next to each other on the table, in the order in which you wish them to be selected. The foods for the Mexican meal designed for your class are placed on the buffet table and served in the following order:

- Appetizers
- Main Dish
- Vegetable
- Breads
- Soup
- Desserts

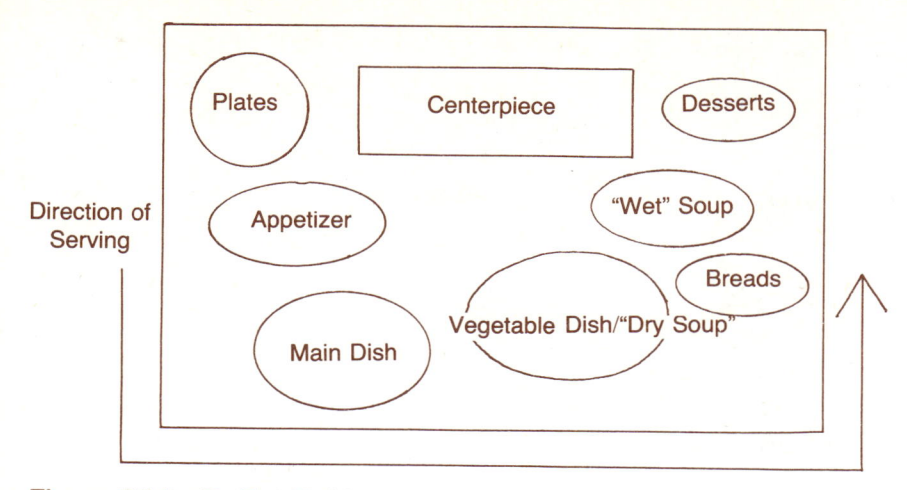

Figure 22.1. Buffet Table

Figure 22.1 shows a correctly set buffet table for your Mexican meal.

It is easier for you to carry and fill your plate if you pick up the soup near the end of the buffet. This way, the soup will be eaten soon after it is served and still be warm.

DINING TABLE SETTINGS

How you set the dining table in your classroom depends on the table equipment available. The following directions tell how a

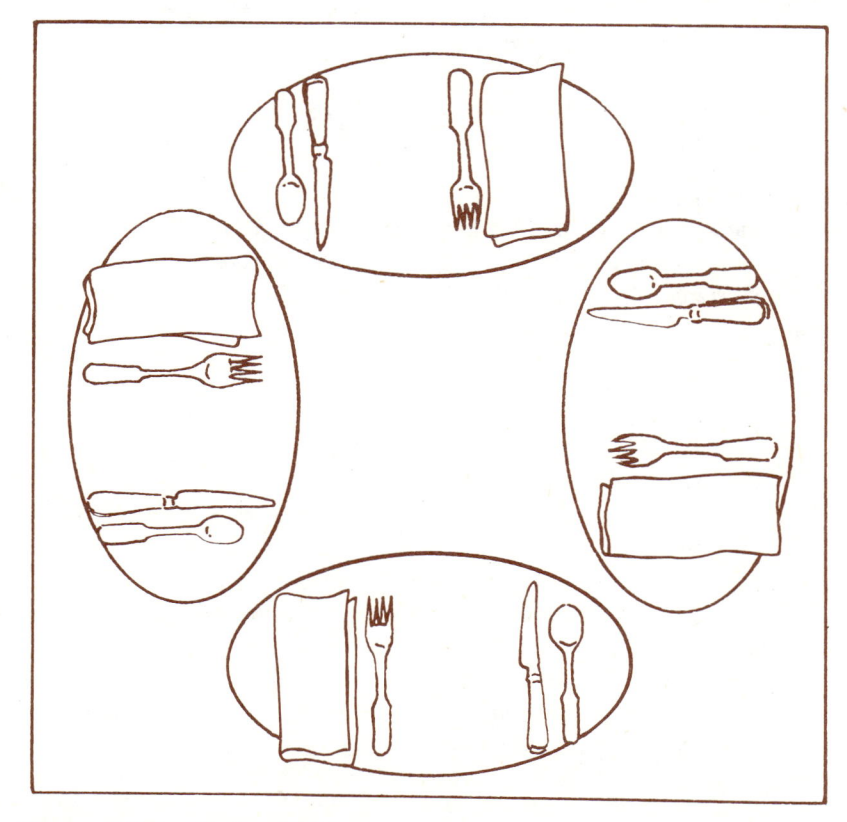

Figure 22.2. Dining Table

Chapter 22 • Table Settings and Table Manners   191

Figure 22.3. Dining Table Placemat

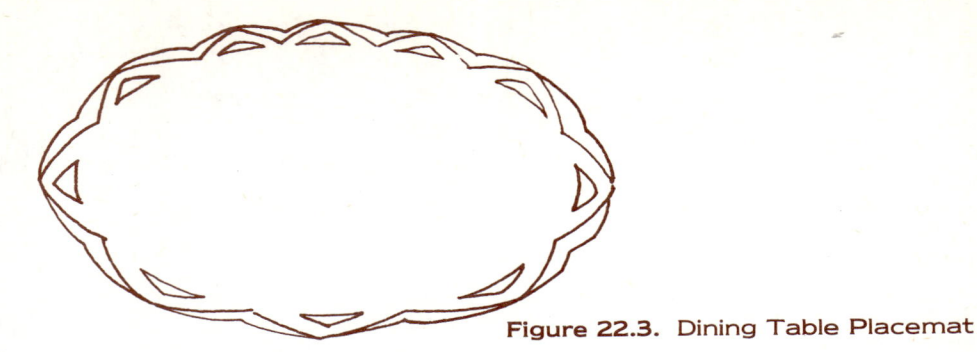

basic table should be set. Refer to Figure 22.2 as you read the instructions.

1. The napkin, plate, and flatware should be placed one inch from the edge of the placemat. If you have trouble judging an inch, use your thumb as a ruler. From the tip of your thumb to the first joint is approximately one inch.
2. If you are serving buffet style, the plates will be on the buffet table. The utensils must be correctly positioned on the dining table so that there will be room for the plate after it has been filled from the buffet. To set the table properly, use one plate as a guide to position the utensils properly.
3. The knife is placed to the right of the plate, with the sharp edge facing the plate.
4. The spoon is placed next to the knife.
5. The waterglass is placed at the tip of the knife.
6. The fork is placed to the left of the plate, with the tines facing up.
7. The napkin is placed beside the fork and folded so that it opens like a book.

Now that you are familiar with the way to set a dining table, draw a place setting on the placemat in Figure 22.3. Include the table equipment that you have available for your kitchen group. The completed drawing will remind you how the table should be set for your Mexican meal.

TABLE MANNERS

Good table manners allow you and your companions to have a pleasant mealtime experience. Your concern for the pleasure of others at the table is obvious from your good manners. Be aware of good table manners and practice them while eating at all times—not just in the classroom. Eventually good manners will become second nature.

After your meal is finished, you will evaluate the manners you observed during the meal with your kitchen group. Here are some suggestions for good table manners.

1. Make sure you are well-groomed before you serve yourself at the buffet table. Check that your hands and finger-

nails are clean and your hair and clothes are neat.

2. After you have served yourself, put your plate at your table setting, then sit down from the left side of your chair.
3. Unfold your napkin when the host or hostess at your table does. Do not shake it open. A small napkin may be opened completely, while a large one may be left folded in half.
4. Begin eating when your host or hostess does. Eat slowly, one piece of food at a time. Do not talk with your mouth full; take small bites that can be easily swallowed, so that you will be able to talk. Chew your food quietly with your mouth closed.
5. Sit upright when you eat. Keep your arms off the table and your hands away from your face and hair. Do not play with anything on the table.
6. It is the responsibility of the host or hostess to keep the conversation moving, while making sure everyone is included. Each person, however, should contribute to the conversation. Listen to others and acknowledge what they say.
7. When you have finished eating, place your knife (carving end well in the center of the plate) and fork (tines up) across the center of your plate, parallel to each other. When everyone has finished eating, the host or hostess will put his or her napkin on the table. This signals that the meal is completed. Place your napkin on the table without refolding or crumpling it. Return it, loosely gathered, to its original place to the left of the plate. If you have to get up during the meal, put your napkin on your chair. If you put it on the table, it may get in the way of the person sitting next to you. Also, if your napkin is messy, it isn't an attractive sight for anyone to see while eating.

23

YOUR MEXICAN MEAL PLANNING FORM

You will use your Mexican Meal Planning Form during the cooking and evaluation days. On the cooking day you will prepare as much of the recipe as possible. On evaluation day, you will finish preparing the recipe, set the dining table, arrange the food on the buffet, serve yourself, eat, and write an evaluation of your recipe. The planning form has a time schedule to follow, so you will easily be able to complete all your responsibilities on both days. If you do run behind, the time schedule on your planning form lets you know what still must be completed.

The success of both the cooking and evaluation days depends upon the ability of the kitchen group members to work together to ensure that all the duties are completed correctly. You are expected to help other students in your kitchen group if you finish your job duties early. Your completed planning form will have the names and duties of the members of your kitchen group, so you will know how you can help each of them. For example, if you, as the host or hostess, finish your assigned duties early and see that the cook has not completed the recipe, you can offer to help. You will know how to help because you have read the recipe and are familiar with the ingredients. Carefully check to see that the place settings are correct on the dining table (refer to Chapter 22). Be aware of all of your kitchen group's duties, and if you see something has not been done right, alert the person who has that job responsibility and offer to help if you can.

HOW TO COMPLETE YOUR PLANNING FORM

Remove Activity 6, Mexican Meal Planning Form. Figure 23.1 shows a sample filled-in Mexican Meal Planning Form. Use this

Class Menu (1) Chilaquiles (2) Flour Tortillas (3) Corn Soup
(Your Kitchen's Recipe)
(4) Refried Beans (5) Chicken Molé (6) Flan

Name	Kitchen Job	Preparation Duties	Cleanup Duties
Bob Iversen	Cook	Prepare the recipe; prepare food for serving	Check kitchen (canisters, cupboards, drawers, counters) for cleanliness and order
Jennifer Chin	Assistant Cook	Assist cook	Wash equipment; scour sink
Carlos Ramirez	Host or Hostess	Obtain supplies needed; set table/set buffet	Clear table; clean table and chairs
Mary Hughes	General Assistant 1	Assume duties of anyone absent; assist where needed	Dry dishes
Diana Stoltz	General Assistant 2	Do weekly duty (see instructor); turn in evaluations; assist where needed	Put dishes away; clean range

Recipe Ingredients not in the Kitchen: 2 dozen tortillas, oil for frying, 1 cup chicken broth, 2½ cups jack cheese, 1½ cups sour cream, 1-10 oz. can tomatillos, 2 cloves, 1 teaspoon cilantro, 2 canned jalapeño chili peppers.

Equipment not in the Kitchen: blender

Cooking-Day Time Schedule		Evaluation-Day Time Schedule	
Time	Duty	Time	Duty
8:00-8:05	Read Recipe	8:00-8:05	Read Recipe
8:05-8:20	cut tortillas in ½" strips and leave out to dry overnight; crush garlic.	8:05-8:20	Fry tortilla strips, drain. Heat salsa, broth, strips, cheese, sour cream. Broil.
8:20-8:40	blend with tomatillos, cilantro, peppers, and salt. Grate cheese. Refrigerate.	8:20-8:35	Serve Yourself and Eat
		8:35-8:40	Cleanup: check kitchen
8:40-8:50	Cleanup: check kitchen	8:40-8:50	Written Evaluation: Refer to Mexican Sample Activity 7.

Figure 23.1. Sample Filled-in Activity 6

illustration as a guide for completing Activity 6. Use the front of Activity 6 for a five-member kitchen group and the back for a four-member kitchen group.

Follow these directions when completing Activity 6.

Section A

Write your name, class period, kitchen number, and date due. Write the names of each recipe your class will prepare. List your kitchen group's recipe first.

Section B

Write the names of each kitchen group member next to the appropriate kitchen job.

Section C

List recipe ingredients not in the kitchen.

Carefully read the recipe your kitchen group will prepare, and determine what ingredients will have to be obtained from outside your assigned kitchen.

Once you have determined which ingredients are not in your kitchen, list those ingredients and the amounts you will need. This will enable your teacher to know what has to be purchased from the grocery store or obtained from another storage area.

Each kitchen will have some staples such as salt, pepper, flour, sugar, baking powder, and baking soda. Check to see what staples are available in your kitchen. List these staples below:

Staples in the Kitchen

1. _____   4. _____   7. _____

2. _____   5. _____   8. _____

3. _____   6. _____   9. _____

List equipment not in the kitchen in this space. Refer to Figure 23.1. The missing equipment will be placed in the supply area ready for your kitchen group's use at the beginning of your cooking day.

Section D

Devise a time schedule for all duties assigned to you on *cooking day*.

- Write the time you allot to read the recipe on cooking day.
- Write the time you allot for preparation duties assigned to you for cooking day. Write a few notes that will help you perform these duties.
- Write the time you allot for cleanup duties. Write your cleanup duty assignments.

Section E

Devise a time schedule for all duties assigned to you on *evaluation day*. A time schedule will help you accomplish every duty.

- Write the time you allot to read the recipe on evaluation day.

- Write the time you allot for preparation duties assigned to you for evaluation day. Include the time for final food preparation and setting the buffet and dining table. Write a few notes that will help you perform these duties.
- Write the time you allot to serve yourself and eat.
- Write the time you allot for cleanup duties. Write your cleanup duty assignments.
- Write the time you allot for the written evaluation.

Give your completed Mexican Menu Planning Form to your instructor for evaluation.

ARE YOU READY?

The success of your dish depends on your following recipe directions exactly and on your ability to complete your duties on time. On cooking day, use your completed Mexican Meal Planning Form to guide you through your duties and time schedule. All the duties must be finished and as much of the recipe prepared as possible, so that everything can be completed on evaluation day.

Before you start your duties, a quick review is necessary. Read the following questions. If you answer no to any of these questions, check your notes or any other source of information you have for help.

1. Are you familiar with your kitchen group's recipe?
2. Do you know what the cooking terms mean in your recipe?
3. Do you know your kitchen job assignment?
4. Do you know your preparation duties?
5. Do you know your cleanup duties?
6. Are you aware of your time schedule?
7. Do you know your co-workers' duties?
8. Are you prepared to help your co-workers if you finish your duties early?
9. Do you know where the equipment is located in the kitchen so that preparation and cleanup will be efficient?

When you have answered yes to all the questions, you are ready to begin your cooking day duties. Enjoy your experience with Mexico's cuisine.

¡QUÉ SE DIVIERTAN!

Section Nine

EVALUATING YOUR MEXICAN MEAL

Whether you are evaluating a trip you have taken, a movie you have seen, or a meal you have helped prepare, you should always be aware of what did not meet your expectations. Your judgments and observations are important.

Consider the following questions concerning your Mexican meal:

- Did your kitchen group prepare a dish of the quality and taste you expected? How did the dish vary from your expectations?
- After tasting the dish, what changes would you suggest in the ingredients for the next time?
- How would you rate the appearance, texture, and flavor of all the dishes?
- What one dish did you especially enjoy? Give your reasons for this choice.

Answers to these questions will help in your evaluation of the foods that were prepared by you and your class. Remember, constructive criticism is the key to becoming a better cook, and an honest evaluation will improve your cooking in the future. In this section you will find:

- a sample Mexican Product Evaluation Form
- a Mexican Product Evaluation Form for you to complete

24

MEXICAN PRODUCT EVALUATION

Three criteria will be used to evaluate the food your class has prepared. These are appearance, texture, and flavor.

Appearance

Appearance is the color, size, and shape of the product. Mexican cooking is attractive and colorful. The Mexican cook combines ingredients to enhance their color. For example, flour tortillas will have a good appearance if they all are approximately the same size, thin, fairly round, and have golden brown blisters. The vegetable combination of red bell peppers, corn, and green squash makes a festive statement. If a product looks so attractive to you that you can hardly wait to taste it, it should rate high in appearance.

Texture

The texture of a product is described as crisp, crunchy, flaky, moist, dry, tender, light, soft, or hard. A variety of contrasting textures in one dish is appealing. For example, Empanaditas (em-pah-nah-THEE-tahs) have a tender pastry crust enclosing a filling of crumbly meat, plump raisins, and crunchy almonds, moistened with a tomato sauce, a wonderful combination of textures. A dish with pleasing texture should earn a high rating.

Flavor

Flavor is a blend of taste and aroma and can be described as salty, sweet, sour, bitter, bland, delicate, or rich. The aroma of food influences its flavor. For example, much of the flavor of Chicken Molé comes from the aroma of its ingredients. *Molé,* (a coarse sauce) is a concoction of ingredients including almonds, tortillas, and chocolate. As with other Mexican sauces, one taste does not predominate. There is a pleasing blend of sharp flavors.

True Mexican cuisine depends on the use of native cooking techniques to retain the authentic flavor of the dish. Some of the original recipes for molé call for first frying or toasting the basic ingredients individually over high heat. This is thought to bring out the true flavor of the sauce. Better flavor is thought to be retained by grinding the nuts, seeds, spices, chili peppers and tortillas for the sauce on a *metate* instead of using a blender. Today, even though you may use different processes and equipment in your Mexican cooking, the necessary character of the dish is not lost if the preparation techniques of the recipe are followed accurately.

If the appearance, texture, or flavor of a particular dish is not what you think it should be, try to determine what caused the disappointment. Improper cooking techniques negatively affect a recipe. For example, when almonds and other ingredients for Chicken Molé are combined in the blender, the sauce sometimes turns out frothy and loses its coarse texture. To avoid this, add just a drop or two of liquid at a time and do not overblend. Turn the blender on and off at short intervals so you can look at the sauce. Blend only until it is almost smooth.

Evaluating the Mexican dish you have made will help you improve it the next time you make it. By altering the ingredients, you can create a different, but just as pleasing, dish. Your sight, taste, and imagination will provide you with clues on what to add or eliminate. Figure 24.1 is an example of a recipe for Chilaquiles which can be altered with the following variations.

By applying one or a combination of the following ideas, you change the flavor of Chilaquiles.

1. Add 2 cups cooked and shredded chicken or turkey.
2. Add 2 cups cooked, diced ham.
3. Add 2 cups refried beans.
4. Use 2 *chorizos* (sausages), crumbled and fried for a garnish.
5. Use ⅓ chopped onion for a garnish.
6. Use 2 limes cut in wedges for a garnish.
7. Substitute 1½ cups heavy whipping cream with 3 tbsp. buttermilk for sour cream.
8. Substitute ¼ tsp. cumin seeds for cilantro.

Chilaquiles

24 tortillas
1 cup chicken broth
2½ cups jack cheese
1½ cups sour cream
1 10 oz. can tomatillos
2 cloves garlic
1 tbsp. cilantro
2 canned jalapeño chili peppers
 oil
 salt

Figure 24.1. Chilaquiles Recipe

9. Substitute 2 serrano chili peppers for jalapeño (hah-lah-PEH-nyoh) peppers.
10. Substitute 2½ cups mild cheddar for jack cheese.

EVALUATION FORM

Evaluation forms are used to help improve your cooking. Study the example of a completed evaluation form for Carlos Ramirez (see Figure 24.2).

Note that Carlos wrote the names of the Mexican recipes his class prepared. He evaluated the foods by indicating in the appropriate column his opinion of their appearance, texture, and flavor. He then suggested a change in the ingredients for the dish he helped prepare. Next, he discussed his questions concerning the preparation of the recipe with his kitchen group and checked the appropriate space for the answers. After doing this, Carlos found out why his dish did not turn out as well as he had expected. He then wrote a paragraph telling what was

---

Write the names of the products that will be evaluated, and check (✓) the space that best describes the product: E = Excellent, G = Good, P = Poor.

	Appearance			Texture			Flavor		
	E	G	P	E	G	P	E	G	P
1. Chilaquiles	✓				✓			✓	
2. Flour Tortillas	✓			✓			✓		
3. Corn Soup		✓		✓				✓	
4. Refried Beans		✓		✓			✓		
5. Chicken Molé	✓			✓			✓		
6. Flan	✓			✓			✓		
7.									
8.									

Write the name of the recipe your kitchen group prepared: *Chilaquiles*
Describe how you would change the ingredients of your recipe to make a different product: *I would omit the jack cheese and sour cream. I would combine 3 cups cheddar cheese and 3 cups cooked and diced chicken and using 2 cups refried beans, alternate with strips, sauce and broth and bake.*

Figure 24.2. Sample Filled-in Activity 7 (Continued)

Answer these questions about your recipe preparation. Check (√) the appropriate space.

	Yes	No
1. Were the ingredient amounts measured correctly?	√	
2. Were the proper utensils used for the measuring?	√	
3. Were the correct techniques used to prepare the ingredients?		√
4. Were the ingredients added in the right order?	√	
5. Was the correct size cookware used?	√	
6. Was the cookware prepared correctly?	√	
7. If the oven was used, was it preheated?	√	

Write a paragraph that explains what contributed to the product's success and what could have been done to improve the product:

We checked the oil with a deep-fat frying thermometer to be sure it was 350° before we fried the tortilla chips. However, we left the strips in the oil too long and they became too crisp and dry. As a result, they absorbed too much liquid from the sauce and broth. We should have watched them closely and fried them only until they were pale gold. Even so the flavor combination was good.

Describe the good table manners that made the Mexican meal more enjoyable for your kitchen group:

I was glad my kitchen remembered to put their napkins to the left of their plates after eating. It made my job, helping Diana clean up the table, a lot easier. I did not have to look for napkins on the floor or stuffed into a glass.

Figure 24.2 (Continued)

successful about the dish and how it should be prepared the next time to ensure the best results. Finally, after a discussion with his kitchen group, Carlos described the good table manners that made the Mexican meal with the group members pleasant and enjoyable.

Remove Activity 7, the Mexican Product Evaluation Form. Use the sample Figure 24.2 to complete Activity 7 and give it to your instructor for evaluation.

Name _____ Class Period _____ Kitchen Number _____ Date Due _____

Activity 1 MEXICAN FOOD HISTORY REVIEW

Test your knowledge of Mexican Food History by completing the following sentences with the proper word or words. Place your answer in the answer column at the right.

Answers

1. Nomads settled in central Mexico as early as 6,000 B.C. and learned to grow __?__, __?__, and __?__ for food.

   1. _____
   _____
   _____

2. By 2500 B.C. Indians of central Mexico were using grinding stones to make meal out of maize, which is __?__.

   2. _____

3. Mayan farming was planned by using a __?__ as accurate as our own.

   3. _____

4. Mayan farmers terraced hillsides, built raised fields on lowlands, and diverted water with dams, using only stone tools and __?__ labor.

   4. _____

5. The __?__ had established a powerful Indian empire in Mexico when Cortés invaded.

   5. _____

6. Prepared foods such as __?__ and __?__ could be purchased in the Aztecs' marketplace.

   6. _____
   _____

7. The Aztec emperor, __?__, enjoyed luxurious dining in his opulent palace.

   7. _____

8. During the Spanish colonization of Mexico, new foods including __?__ for tortillas and __?__ for dairy products were introduced into the diet of the Indians.

   8. _____
   _____

9. After the Spanish conquered the Aztecs, Indian food began to be __?__ using the fat drippings from cooked pork.

   9. _____

10. Mexico is one-fourth of the size of the United States, but only __?__ percent of its land can be cultivated, as opposed to 80 percent of the land in the United States.

    10. _____

11. La __?__ is the two-hour, main meal of the day.

    11. _____

12. At a formal comida, __?__ may be served as an appetizer with warm tortillas.

    12. _____

13. In Mexico, "dry" soups may be __?__ or __?__.

    13. _____
    _____

14. Sauces made from __?__ or __?__ __?__ are an important part of a Mexican meal.

    14. _____
    _____
    _____

15. Fresh __?__ __?__, which grows abundantly in Mexico, makes a popular dessert.

    15. _____

Name _____ Class Period _____ Kitchen Number _____ Date Due _____

Activity 2 MEXICAN RECIPE MATCH

This activity will test your knowledge of popular and classic Mexican cooking. In the space provided in the answer column at the right of each definition in Column 2, print the letter of the phrase in Column 1 that matches the definition.

Column 1	Column 2	Answers
a. Queso	1. The way the Spanish taught the Aztecs to prepare beans	1. _____
b. Refried	2. Common Mexican baked roll	2. _____
c. Bolillos	3. The Spanish word for cheese	3. _____
d. Tomato	4. First cultivated by Indians	4. _____
e. Soup	5. A dish made with leftover tortillas	5. _____
f. Rice	6. A corn tortilla dish	6. _____
g. Corn Tortillas	7. Fruit/vegetable commonly eaten cooked	7. _____
h. Guacamole	8. A classic custard dessert	8. _____
i. Zucchini	9. Word means "snack" in Mexico	9. _____
j. Empanaditas	10. Sometimes called "bride's cookies"	10. _____
k. Flour Tortillas	11. Flute-shaped wheat- or corn-flour tortilla snack	11. _____
l. Corn	12. Mexico's most important food	12. _____
m. Enchiladas	13. A staple dish in the Mexican diet	13. _____
n. Tamales	14. Small baked or fried pastry turnover	14. _____
o. Flautas	15. The ancient, flat "bread" of Mexico	15. _____
p. Bunuelo	16. Rolled wheat flour tortilla snack	16. _____
q. Flan	17. Steamed in a corn husk or banana leaf	17. _____
r. Mexican Wedding Cakes	18. Fried sweet bread	18. _____
s. Taco	19. Aztec chili sauce	19. _____
t. Chilaquiles	20. A variety of squash, a basic food for thousands of years	20. _____
u. Tomatillos	21. Flat bread made of wheat flour	21. _____
v. Molé	22. One way avocados are prepared	22. _____
w. Burritos	23. Became a grain food after the Spanish arrived	23. _____

Name _____ Class Period _____ Kitchen Number _____ Date Due _____

Activity 3 MEXICAN MAP REVIEW

To complete this activity, match the recipe with the culinary region for which it is known. Write the letter of the recipe on the lines provided within each region of the map. For example, the first recipe is Empanaditas. After reading the recipe for Empanaditas, you know it is identified with the southern region. The letter "a" is written on the line in the southern region as an example.

Recipes

a. Empanaditas
b. Nachos Con Queso
c. Totopos with Guacamole
d. Bolillos
e. Corn Tortillas
f. Flour Tortillas
g. Corn Soup
h. Meatball Soup
i. Vermicelli in Tomato Broth
j. Mexican Rice
k. Refried Beans
l. Zucchini with Corn and Peppers
m. Chicken Molé
n. Enchiladas
o. Pork Stew with Tomatillos
p. Buñuelos
q. Flan
r. Mexican Wedding Cakes
s. Chilaquiles
t. Deep-Fried Meat Burritos
u. Flautas
v. Tacos
w. Tamale Pie

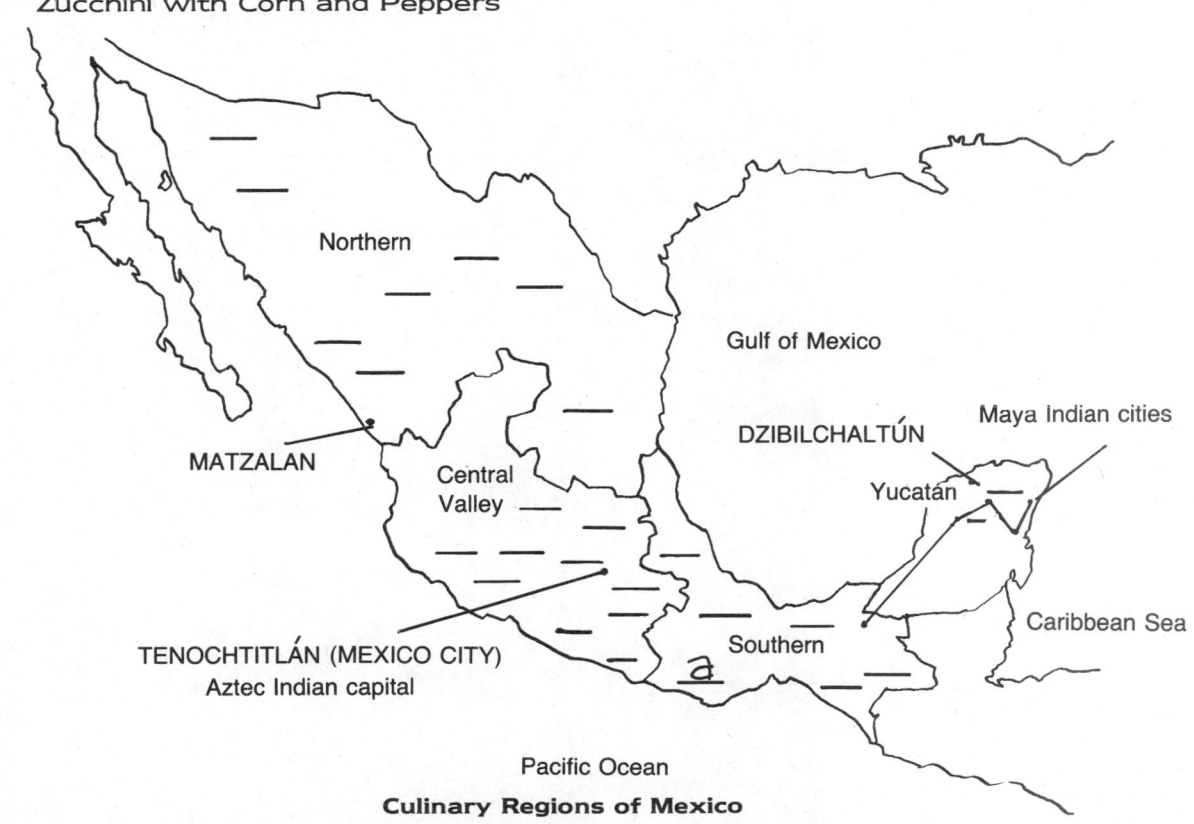

Culinary Regions of Mexico

Name _____ Class Period _____ Kitchen Number _____ Date Due _____

Activity 4   SELECTING YOUR MEXICAN MENU

By completing this activity, you will have a better understanding of the Mexican recipes. This will make choosing your menu easier.

Place a check mark (√) in the appropriate column(s) to complete the following activity.	APPE-TIZERS			BREADS			SOUPS			VEGE-TABLES			MAIN COURSES			DESSERT		
	Empanaditas	Nachos con Queso	Totopos con Guacamole	Bolillos	Corn Tortillas	Flour Tortillas	Corn Soup	Meatball Soup	Vermicelli in Tomato Broth	Mexican Rice	Refried Beans	Zucchini with Corn and Peppers	Chicken Molé	Enchiladas	Pork Stew with Tomatillos	Buñuelos	Flan	Mexican Wedding Cakes
1. The recipes that use cooking techniques you have not tried.																		
2. The recipes that have unfamiliar ingredients.																		
3. The recipes that you have tasted before.																		
4. The recipes that you have tasted and would like to taste again.																		
5. The recipes that you have not tasted but would like to taste.																		
6. The appetizer recipe that would be your first choice to taste.																		
7. The bread recipe that would be your first choice to taste.																		
8. The soup recipe that would be your first choice to taste.																		
9. The vegetable recipe that would be your first choice to taste.																		
10. The main dish recipe that would be your first choice to taste.																		
11. The dessert recipe that would be your first choice to taste.																		

(Continued)

Activity 4 (Continued)

You have now selected the dishes you would like to taste. Will your choices provide a variety in color, shape, texture, and flavor? After carefully considering this question and making any changes, write your recipe selections for the menu you would like your class to prepare.

Appetizer _____   Vegetable _____

Bread _____   Main Dish _____

Soup _____   Dessert _____

Name _____ Class Period _____ Kitchen Number _____ Date Due _____

Activity 5 MEXICAN MEAL COST SHEET

SECTION A Name of Recipe:

(1) Recipe Ingredients	(2) Amount Required	(3) Price Per Item	(4) Amount of Store Container	(5) Cost Computation	(6) Total Ingredient Cost

SECTION B ⟶ Total Recipe Cost: _____

SECTION C Total Recipe Cost ÷ Number of Servings = Cost Per Serving
⟶ (_____) ÷ (_____) = (_____)

SECTION D

Final Class Meal Cost		
(1) Recipe	(2) Recipe Cost	(3) Cost Per Serving
Appetizer:		
Bread:		
Soup:		
Vegetable:		
Main Dish:		
Dessert:		
SECTION E TOTALS: Meal Cost:		Meal Cost Per Serving:

Name _____ Class Period _____ Kitchen Number _____ Date Due _____

Activity 6   MEXICAN MEAL PLANNING FORM (FOUR-MEMBER KITCHEN)

Class Menu   (1) _____ (2) _____ (3) _____
(Your Kitchen's Recipe)
             (4) _____ (5) _____ (6) _____

Name	Kitchen Job	Preparation Duties	Cleanup Duties
	Cook	Prepare the recipe; prepare food for serving	Check kitchen (canisters, cupboards, drawers, counters, etc.) for cleanliness and order
	Assistant Cook	Assist cook	Wash dishes; scour sink
	Host or Hostess	Obtain supplies needed; set table/set buffet; do weekly duty (see instructor)	Clear table; clean table and chairs
	General Assistant	Assume duties of anyone absent; turn in evaluation; assist where needed	Dry dishes; put dishes away

Recipe Ingredients not in the Kitchen: _____

_____

Equipment not in the Kitchen: _____

| Cooking-Day Time Schedule || Evaluation-Day Time Schedule ||
Time	Duty	Time	Duty
_____	Read Recipe	_____	Read Recipe
_____	_____	_____	_____
_____	_____	_____	_____
_____	_____	_____	Serve Yourself and Eat
_____	_____	_____	Cleanup: _____
_____	Cleanup: _____		Written Evaluation: Refer to Activity 7.

Activity 6 ● Mexican Meal Planning Form (Four-Member Kitchen)   213

Name _____ Class Period _____ Kitchen Number _____ Date Due _____

Activity 6 MEXICAN MEAL PLANNING FORM (FIVE-MEMBER KITCHEN)

Class Menu (1) _____ (2) _____ (3) _____
(Your Kitchen's Recipe)
(4) _____ (5) _____ (6) _____

Name	Kitchen Job	Preparation Duties	Cleanup Duties
	Cook	Prepare the recipe; prepare food for serving	Check kitchen (canisters, cupboards, drawers, counters, etc.) for cleanliness and order
	Assistant Cook	Assist cook	Wash equipment; scour sink
	Host or Hostess	Obtain supplies needed; set table/set buffet	Clear table; clean table and chairs
	General Assistant 1	Assume duties of anyone absent; assist where needed	Dry dishes
	General Assistant 2	Do weekly duty (see instructor); turn in evaluations; assist where needed	Put dishes away; clean range

Recipe Ingredients not in the Kitchen: _____

Equipment not in the Kitchen: _____

Cooking-Day Time Schedule		Evaluation-Day Time Schedule	
Time	Duty	Time	Duty
_____	Read Recipe	_____	Read Recipe
_____	_____	_____	_____
_____	_____	_____	_____
_____	_____	_____	Serve Yourself and Eat
_____	_____	_____	Cleanup: _____
_____	Cleanup: _____		Written Evaluation: Refer to Activity 7.

Name _____ Class Period _____ Kitchen Number _____ Date Due _____

Activity 7 MEXICAN PRODUCT EVALUATION FORM

Write the names of the products that will be evaluated, and check (√) the space that best describes the product: E = Excellent, G = Good, P = Poor.

	Appearance			Texture			Flavor		
	E	G	P	E	G	P	E	G	P
1.									
2.									
3.									
4.									
5.									
6.									
7.									
8.									

Write the name of the recipe your kitchen prepared: _____

Describe how you would change the ingredients of your recipe to make a different product:

_____
_____
_____
_____

Answer these questions about your recipe preparation. Check (√) the appropriate space.

	Yes	No
1. Were the ingredient amounts measured correctly?		
2. Were the proper utensils used for measuring?		
3. Were the correct techniques used to prepare the ingredients?		
4. Were the ingredients added in the right order?		
5. Was the correct size cookware used?		
6. Was the cookware prepared correctly?		
7. If the oven was used, was it preheated?		

Activity 7 (Continued)

Write a paragraph that explains:
1. What contributed to the product's success?
2. What could have been done to improve the product?

_____

_____

_____

_____

_____

_____

Describe the good table manners that made the meal more enjoyable for your kitchen group:

_____

_____

_____

_____

_____

EMPANADITAS

Food Category: Appetizer   *High Cost*

Filling

- ½ lb. lean ground beef
- ½ lb. lean ground pork
- 1 large clove garlic, minced
- ½ cup tomato sauce
- ½ cup seedless raisins
- ¼ cup apple juice
- 2 tsp. ground cinnamon
- 1 tsp. salt
- ½ tsp. ground cloves
- 2 tbsp. vinegar
- 1 tbsp. sugar
- ¾ cup slivered almonds
- 1 tbsp. water

Pastry

- 2 cups flour
- ¼ tsp. salt
- ⅔ cup + 2 tbsp. shortening

1. In a frying pan, cook meat, stirring often, until brown. *Drain* excess fat.
2. Stir in garlic, tomato sauce, raisins, apple juice, cinnamon, salt, cloves, vinegar, and sugar.
3. Cook uncovered over medium heat until most of liquid has evaporated (about 20 minutes). Add almonds. Cool.
4. For pastry, sift flour and salt together. *Cut in* shortening until size of small peas. Add ice water 1 tbsp. at a time. Toss gently with fork to mix. Shape into ball. Chill for 20 minutes.
5. Roll out until ⅛ inch thick. Cut out 3-inch circles.
6. To fill, follow steps and refer to illustrations (on back):

(1) Place 1 tbsp. filling on one side of each pastry round.
(2) Moisten edges of pastry with water. Fold over. Seal by pressing edges with fork.

7. Bake in 400-degree oven for 15 to 20 minutes or until brown. *Makes 3½ dozen.*

Recipe Tips

- *Lean ground beef may be substituted for the pork.*
- *Pork must be cooked until done. Internal temperature must reach 140 degrees to destroy trichinae.*
- *Do not cut in shortening too much. The dough will be sticky and difficult to handle.*
- *Freeze pastry for 10 minutes to chill quickly.*
- *Serve as main course by increasing size of pastry circle to 4 or 5 inches and amount of filling by 3 tbsp.*

NACHOS CON QUESO

Food Category: Appetizer   *Moderate Cost*

- 1 pkg. corn tortillas
- oil for frying
- 2 cups grated jack cheese
- 5 canned, pickled jalapeño chilis, stemmed and sliced
- lime wedges

1. Leave tortillas out of package overnight.
2. Cut each tortilla into 8 equal pie-shaped pieces.
3. Pour ¼ inch of oil in heavy frying pan. Heat oil to 375 degrees. Fry 8 tortilla pieces 2 to 3 minutes. *Drain* on paper towels. Repeat process until all are done.
4. Spread chips close together on baking sheet. Sprinkle cheese on top. Place chili pieces over cheese. Broil until cheese melts. Serve immediately with lime wedges.

Serves 6

Recipe Tips

- *The correct oil temperature is essential. If oil is too cool, foods will absorb it and become greasy; If too hot, foods will burn before they are cooked. Use a deep-fat-frying thermometer to check the oil temperature. If you don't have a thermometer, drop a 1-inch cube of bread into hot fat. Time 1 minute. If bread is brown, oil temperature is correct.*
- *Don't fry chips too long. Chips should be crisp but chewy.*

- To divide preparation time into two days, complete Steps 1 through 4, wrapping pastry in waxed paper and refrigerating overnight. The next day let pastry stand at room temperature ½ hour. Then begin with Step 5.

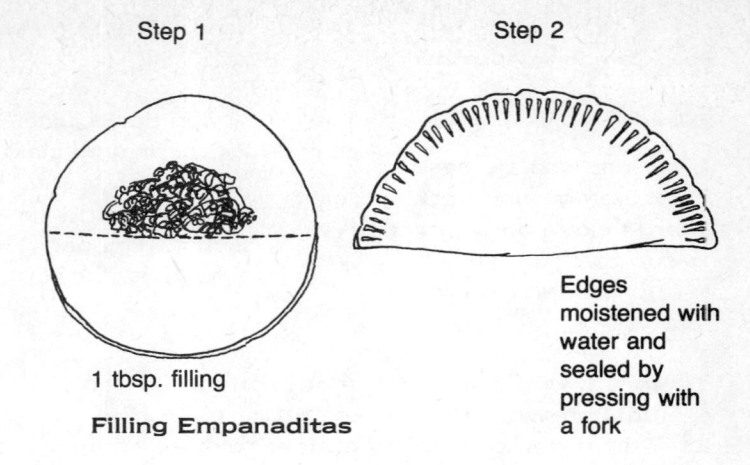

Step 1

1 tbsp. filling

Filling Empanaditas

Step 2

Edges moistened with water and sealed by pressing with a fork

Empanaditas (em-pah-nah-THEE-tahs) are just one of many between-meal snacks that Mexicans enjoy. This version comes from a fertile basin near El Chichon, an active volcano in southern Mexico. It is elegant enough to serve at wedding receptions.

Fillings for Empanaditas may include one major ingredient, such as chicken, potatoes, tuna, or dry cheese, or they may be delicious concoctions with chicken, hot chilis, tomatoes, zucchini, and carrots all together. Varieties of sweet Empanaditas include those filled with custard, jam, preserves, guava paste, or pumpkin. The tops are then sprinkled with *granulated sugar* before baking.

Cooking methods vary. Some recipes call for frying Empanaditas because many Mexican homes do not have ovens.

Nachos con Queso (NAH-chos kohn KEH-soh) are made with fried tortilla chips and cheese. *Queso* is the Spanish word for cheese. Mexico City obtains much of its dairy products from El Bajio, the largest of the seven valleys that make up the vast central plateau—one of Mexico's most fertile agricultural regions.

Chilis are air-pollinated, and there are many varieties grown in Mexico. Fresh jalapeño chilis have a sharp flavor and are used extensively. Sometimes jalapeño chilis are cut into strips and fried, or cooked and blended with other ingredients into a sauce. Pickled jalapeño chilis are widely used as an additional seasoning on the Mexican meal table.

Nachos con Queso are best served in the container in which they are broiled. Guests use their fingers to pull apart the individual chips in order to eat them.

TOTOPOS CON GUACAMOLE

Food Category: Appetizer *Moderate Cost*

Totopos

6 dry corn tortillas
oil for frying

Guacamole

2 large ripe avocados
2 to 3 tbsp. lemon juice

1 clove garlic, minced
3 tbsp. minced onion
1 tomato, chopped

¼ tsp. salt
2 drops Tabasco sauce

1. Leave tortillas out of package overnight.
2. Cut each tortilla in 6 equal pie-shaped pieces.
3. Pour 1 inch of oil in heavy frying pan. Heat oil to 375 degrees.
4. Fry and stir tortilla pieces, a few at a time, until golden and crisp. *Drain* on paper towels. Serve warm for dipping into guacamole or refried beans.
5. Cut avocados in half.
6. Remove pits. Scoop out pulp.
7. Mash coarsely with fork while *blending* in lemon juice.
8. Add salt, Tabasco sauce, onion, and garlic. Mix well.
9. Stir in tomato. Serve immediately with totopos for dipping.

Serves 6

Recipe Tips

- *Crisp vegetable sticks such as jicama make good dippers for guacamole.*
- *The correct oil temperature is essential. If oil is too cool, foods will absorb it and become greasy; if too hot, foods will burn before they are cooked. Use a deep-fat-frying thermometer to check the oil temperature. If you don't have a thermometer, drop a 1-inch cube of bread into hot fat. Time 1 minute. If bread is brown, oil temperature is correct.*

BOLILLOS

Food Category: Bread *Low Cost*

2 cups water
1½ tbsp. sugar
1 tbsp. salt

2 tbsp. butter or margarine
1 pkg. dry yeast
6 cups (approximately) all-purpose flour

1 tsp. cornstarch dissolved in ½ cup water
3 tbsp. shortening for greasing bowl and baking sheets

1. Combine water, sugar, salt, and butter in sauce pan. Stir over low heat. Temperature should be 105 to 115 degrees on *candy thermometer*. Pour into large warmed bowl.
2. Add yeast. Stir until dissolved. Gradually beat in 5 cups flour to form dough.
3. *Turn* dough onto lightly floured board. *Knead* 10 minutes or until dough is smooth. Add more flour if needed to keep dough from sticking.
4. Place in greased bowl. Turn dough over so that top gets greased. Cover bowl with waxed paper. Let dough rise in warm place until it has almost doubled, about 1½ hours.
5. *Punch down* dough to release air bubbles. Turn onto lightly floured board. Cut into 16 equal pieces. Form each piece into smooth ball.
6. Gently roll ball into 4-inch oblong.
7. Place rolls 2 inches apart on greased baking sheets. Cover with waxed paper.
8. Let rolls rise about 35 minutes or until almost double in size.
9. In pan, heat cornstarch and water to boiling. Cool slightly. Brush each roll with cornstarch mixture. With sharp knife, cut a slash ¾ inch deep about 2 inches long on top of each roll.
10. Bake in 375-degree oven for 35 to 40 minutes. When done, the rolls will be golden brown and sound hollow when tapped. Cool on wire racks and wrap tightly in plastic wrap to store. *Makes 16 rolls.*

Totopos con Guacamole (toh-TOH-pohs kohn guah-kah-MOH-leh) is a Mexican "chip and dip." Totopos are corn tortilla chips that are used as dippers for salsas, guacamole, and other appetizers. You should use leftover tortillas for crisp totopos, because fresh ones absorb too much oil. This is a delicious way the Mexicans make good use of dry tortillas.

The avocado is an ancient (and still favorite) fruit in Mexico. Varieties of enormous avocados can be seen growing in lush tropical groves near the southern coast of the Gulf of Mexico. Avocados are used in guacamole, salads, soups, stews, or eaten out-of-hand with lime or salt.

There are many variations of guacamole. A favorite one in Mexico is made by adding minced hot chili peppers, chopped cilantro leaves, and tomatillos. Guacamole can be served as a dip or spread on tortillas and rolled up. It is also excellent with refried beans.

Recipe Tips

- Warm bowl by placing it in hot water.
- An easy way to divide dough into 16 pieces is to cut dough into 4 equal pieces. Then cut each piece into 4 equal pieces again.
- To divide preparation time into three days, complete Steps 1 through 4 and refrigerate. Complete Steps 5 through 8 the next day and refrigerate. Begin with Step 9 the following day.

Bolillos (boh-LEE-yohs) have a crisp outer crust, like French rolls, but are softer and sweeter inside. The Spanish brought wheat breads of this type to Mexico. They became more popular during the French occupation in 1863.

Today Bolillos are frequently served in Mexican restaurants and can be purchased in bakeries, which make a variety of breads and pastries fresh daily. This recipe came from a village in northern Mexico in the center of an extensive farming, ranching, and citrus-growing area.

Bolillos make delicious dinner or breakfast rolls. They can also be split and used for sandwiches. Bolillos taste best when taken freshly baked and piping hot from the oven and spread with plenty of butter. They also can be reheated in the oven to become crisp again.

CORN TORTILLAS

Food Category: Bread *Low Cost*

2 cups masa harina (corn flour)

1⅓ cups (approx.) warm water

1. In a bowl, mix *masa harina* with just enough warm water to make dough hold together well. Shape into smooth ball.
2. Divide into 12 equal pieces. Roll each piece into ball.
3. Flatten each dough ball slightly and place it between two damp cloths.
4. With light, even strokes of the rolling pin, roll cloth-covered dough outward in all directions until it is about 6 inches in diameter. Carefully remove cloths from dough.
5. Trim tortilla to round shape, if necessary, and place between two squares of waxed paper. Repeat process until all dough balls are rolled.
6. Place heavy, ungreased frying pan on medium heat.
7. To cook tortillas, carefully peel off top piece of waxed paper. Turn tortilla over, paper side up. Place in preheated frying pan. As tortilla becomes warm, peel off remaining paper.
8. Cook for about 1½ minutes, turning frequently, until tortilla looks dry and is lightly flecked with brown. It will puff up briefly and should be soft. Repeat this process for all dough. Serve warm. Makes 1 dozen 6-inch tortillas.

Recipe Tips

- *The moisture content of flour varies. Consider this when adding water.*
- *A cast-iron griddle works well for cooking tortillas.*
- *Tortillas should be stored in a tightly sealed plastic bag in the refrigerator.*

FLOUR TORTILLAS

Food Category: Bread *Low Cost*

4 cups flour
1½ tsp. salt

½ cup shortening
1 cup plus 2 tbsp. cool water

1. In a large bowl, mix salt into flour. *Cut in* shortening.
2. Add water all at once. Mix well.
3. Place dough on lightly floured board. *Knead* until smooth.
4. Return dough to bowl. Cover with waxed paper. Let stand for 1½ hours.
5. Return dough to lightly floured board. Divide into 16 equal pieces. With well-floured rolling pin, roll each piece outward in all directions until a very thin 6-inch circle is formed.
6. Heat heavy, ungreased frying pan on medium high.
7. Place tortilla in hot frying pan about ½ minute on each side. Repeat this process with all dough. Serve warm. *Makes 16 tortillas.*

Recipe Tips

- *The moisture content of flour varies. Consider this when adding water.*
- *To divide preparation time into two days, complete Steps 1 through 4 and refrigerate. Start with Step 5 the next day.*

Flat, maize *tortillas* (tor-TEE-yahs) have been the "bread" of Mexico since ancient Indian times. Maize was first cultivated from primitive, coarse grass that grew ears one-inch long, each wrapped in its individual husk.

Mexicans either buy tortillas or make them at home daily, so they are always fresh. Some tortillas are now made commercially by machine. But in rural villages and Indian huts of the south, tortillas are still shaped by hand and cooked on a steel sheet over an open flame. This method is almost the same as that used over a thousand years ago.

Tortillas are the most versatile of breads. The warm, cooked tortilla can be eaten plain, or it can be combined with other food and stacked, folded, or rolled. Tortillas can also be cut into pieces and used to scoop up other foods. They can be crisply fried in oil or rewarmed on an ungreased griddle. Frying is also a good way to use leftover tortillas, which are the basis for Totopos and Chilaquiles. One of the best features of tortillas is that they can be cooked on any heat source and do not require an oven.

The Spaniards introduced wheat flour to the Aztecs, and *tortillas* (tor-TEE-yahs) began to be made out of wheat as well as corn. Flour Tortillas have a milder flavor than Corn Tortillas, so they work well in Mexican dishes that are seasoned more subtly.

Today the flat, irrigated land of the north is Mexico's most important wheat-growing region—the major source of flour for tortillas. Tortillas can be purchased in several sizes, from 4-inch rounds for snacks to an enormous—almost transparent—18-inch size. The large ones are buttered before serving and folded to keep the melted butter inside.

To keep tortillas hot and moist as they finish cooking, wrap them in a foil packet and place them in the oven. When serving, wrap tortillas in a napkin to keep them warm and soft.

CORN SOUP

Food Category: Soup *Low Cost*

2 tbsp. butter
1 tsp. chili powder
2 cups green bell pepper, seeded and diced

2 12-oz. cans corn with chopped red and green bell peppers, drained
1 small, dry, whole hot chili pepper

6 cups chicken broth
1 cup whipping cream
¼ tsp. salt

1. Melt butter in large saucepan.
2. Stir in chili powder and green bell pepper.
3. Cook uncovered over medium heat for 3 minutes, stirring constantly.
4. Add corn and broth. Bring to boil. Reduce heat. Simmer for 3 minutes. Remove whole chili pepper.
5. Whip cream with ¼ tsp. salt until stiff. Pour soup into large, warmed serving dish. Place whipped cream on top. Stir slightly.
6. Ladle mixture from bottom of dish into warmed bowls.

Serves 6

Recipe Tips

- *Chicken bouillon cubes (one cube per cup of water) may be substituted for the chicken broth.*
- *Warm bowls by placing in hot water.*

MEATBALL SOUP

Food Category: Soup *Moderate Cost*

1 lb. lean ground beef
1 small onion, minced
1 cup soft bread crumbs
⅓ cup pine nuts (optional)
1 egg, slightly beaten

⅓ cup milk
1 tsp. salt
½ tsp. thyme
¼ tsp. nutmeg
2 qt. beef broth

1 bay leaf
⅓ cup apple juice
serrano chilis, chopped
lime wedges

1. In a bowl, mix beef, onion, bread crumbs, and pine nuts.
2. In another bowl, combine egg, milk, salt, thyme, and nutmeg. Stir into meat mixture. Mix well.
3. In a large saucepan, heat broth with bay leaf.
4. Shape meat mixture into 18 small balls. Gently place meatballs in broth. Cook covered for 25 to 30 minutes.
5. Remove bay leaf.
6. Just before serving, stir in apple juice. Serve in warmed bowls with chopped *serrano chilis* and lime wedges as a garnish.

Serves 6

Recipe Tips

- *Beef bouillon cubes (one cube per cup of water) may be substituted for beef broth.*
- *Warm bowls by placing them in hot water.*
- *Jalapeño chilis may be substituted for serrano chilis.*

The Indians learned to grow corn thousands of years ago, and it is still Mexico's most important food.

This soup is an enjoyable dish to present at the table. Put the whipped cream on top of the hot soup just before serving it. The cream will melt, giving the soup a rich, creamy taste. Another version using milk as a base is poured into bowls over fresh, chopped chilis and crumbled cream cheese.

Mexico is famous for its good soups. Corn Soup, with its blend of sweet mild peppers, corn, and cream, is popular all over Mexico. This version is a favorite in the north.

This recipe for Meatball Soup is from Lake Chapala, which, surrounded by mountains in Mexico's central resort region, is Mexico's largest lake. Meatball Soup is an example of the many hearty soups that are staples in the Mexican diet and meals in themselves when served with tortillas.

The *serrano chilis* called for in the salsa are smaller and slimmer than the jalapeño variety and are very hot. They can be purchased canned, and sometimes fresh, in the United States. You can expand your creative cooking skill by experimenting with the different varieties of chili peppers available in your area.

VERMICELLI IN TOMATO BROTH

Food Category: Soup   *Low Cost*

- 4 tbsp. oil
- 4 oz. very fine coiled vermicelli
- ¾ lb. very ripe tomatoes
- 1 clove garlic, minced
- ¼ medium onion, chopped
- 3 cups chicken broth
- 4 cups water
- 2 sprigs parsley

1. In a large frying pan, heat oil very hot.
2. Add whole bundles of coiled *vermicelli*. Fry until golden brown, stirring constantly.
3. *Drain* all but 2 tbsp. oil.
4. *Blend* unpeeled tomatoes with garlic and onion until smooth. Add to fried vermicelli.
5. Continue cooking over high heat, stirring and scraping bottom of pan, until the mixture is almost dry.
6. Add broth, water, and parsley. Bring to boil. Lower heat. *Simmer* until pasta is soft (about 20 minutes). Adjust seasoning. Serve in warmed bowls.

Serves 6

Recipe Tips
- Chicken bouillon cubes (one cube per cup of water) may be substituted for the chicken broth.
- Warm bowls by placing in hot water.

MEXICAN RICE

Food Category: Vegetable   *Low Cost*

- 1 cup uncooked rice
- 1 tbsp. oil
- 1 small onion, minced
- ½ clove garlic, minced
- ½ cup tomato sauce
- 1 tsp. salt
- 2 cups warm water
- 1 cup frozen peas
- 2 carrots, thinly sliced
- 1 egg, hard-cooked
- 1 red pimiento

1. Heat oil in frying pan on medium heat until hot. Add rice and *sauté* until light brown. Stir occasionally.
2. Add onion, garlic, tomato sauce, and salt. Stir to blend.
3. Add warm water and carrots. Cover tightly. Bring mixture to boil. Add peas. Turn heat very low. *Simmer* for 20 minutes. *Do not peek*.
4. Place rice in warmed bowl. Serve *garnished* with egg slices and *pimiento*.

Serves 6

Recipe Tips
- Do not peek *while rice is cooking*. The liquid will evaporate and the rice will burn.
- When spaces appear between the grains of rice, it is done.
- Warm serving bowl by placing in hot water.

Vermicelli in Tomato Broth is a typical yet satisfying soup that most Mexican families enjoy everyday. It is traditionally served with a separate dish of salsa for additional seasoning and sometimes a cut lime for the sour juice. This soup is economical because it does not contain meat and is easy to prepare because it requires only a few simple ingredients.

The combination of tomatoes and vermicelli blends Mexico's Indian and, surprisingly, French heritage. The early Indians cultivated many vegetables, but one of their greatest achievements was the successful cultivation of the tomato around A.D. 700. Pasta has been used in Mexican cooking since the short French occupation in the early 1860s. French tastes by that time had been influenced by the Italian background of the French queen, Catherine dé Medici. Today, both tomatoes and wheat for pasta flour are grown commercially in Mexico north of Mazatlan in the irrigated, agricultural area along the otherwise scrublike, desert coastline.

Rice became a staple of the Mexican diet after being introduced by the Spanish in the 16th century. The Aztec Indians quickly learned to combine tomatoes and onions with rice for this flavorful dish.

Today rice is grown in the irrigated region near Matzalan in northern Mexico. Here, cultivation has become mechanized; on smaller farms in inland hills, rice fields are still tilled by ox-drawn plows.

In Mexico, this dish is considered one of the "dry" soups and is served after the regular "wet" soup in a full-course meal. "Dry" soups are called *sopa seca* on a Mexican menu, and Mexican Rice is called *sopa seca de arroz*. Tourists sometimes confuse sopa seca with the more familiar wet soups. The addition of shrimp, ham, or another meat to this recipe would make it a main-course dish.

REFRIED BEANS

Food Category: Vegetable *Low Cost*

1 cup pinto beans
6 tbsp. oil
¼ medium onion, finely chopped
jack cheese, grated

1. Place beans in *Dutch* oven. Wash thoroughly. *Drain.* Cover with water.
2. Soak overnight.
3. Bring beans and water to boil. Cover. Simmer for about 3 hours, adding more water as necessary until beans are tender.
4. In a heavy frying pan, heat oil. *Sauté* onion without browning until limp.
5. Add 1 cup beans and their broth. Mash well. Cook over high heat.
6. Gradually add remainder of beans. Continue to mash and stir as beans cook until you have a coarse *puree*. When puree begins to dry out and sizzle at edges, it is ready to serve. Place in warmed bowl. Serve with grated cheese for topping.

Serves 6

Recipe Tips

- Pinto beans and pink beans are generally used for Mexican dishes because they are bland and provide a good base for heavy spicing.
- To wash beans, cover them with cold water, then pour it off. Repeat process until the water remains clear. Remove any floating beans or other foreign particles.
- Beans increase size as they cook. Be sure to use a large pan for cooking.
- Warm serving bowl by placing in hot water.
- To divide preparation time into three days, complete Steps 1 and 2. Complete Step 3 the next day. Cover and refrigerate. Begin with Step 4 the following day.

ZUCCHINI WITH CORN AND PEPPERS

Food Category: Vegetable *Low Cost*

3 tbsp. bacon grease
1 lb. zucchini, cut into ½-inch cubes
1 10-oz. pkg. frozen corn
1 red bell pepper, seeded and chopped
1 medium onion, chopped
2 cloves garlic, minced
salt
pepper

1. In a frying pan, melt bacon grease.
2. Add zucchini, thawed corn, bell pepper, onion, and garlic.
3. Cook for about 5 minutes, stirring often, until most vegetable liquid has evaporated and vegetables are *tender-crisp*. Add salt and pepper to taste.
4. Serve in warmed bowl.

Serves 6

Recipe Tips

- Bacon grease is a staple in many kitchens. It should be refrigerated to prevent it from becoming rancid.
- Zucchini becomes mushy if overcooked.
- Warm serving bowl by placing in hot water.

Beans are widely used in Mexican cooking—as appetizers, snacks, even as breakfast food. In Spanish, *re* sometimes means "thoroughly," so these beans were never meant to be fried twice. When Refried Beans are prepared as a vegetable dish (they are not usually served alone), they are served with a *garnish* of cheese or sauce.

The Aztec Indians of central Mexico cultivated and adapted different types of beans to the various climates of Mexico. There were white, black, yellow, red, brown, pink, and speckled beans. The Aztecs either boiled them in soups and stews or mashed and mixed the beans with chili peppers or other flavorings.

After the Spaniards arrived in Mexico, they showed the Aztecs how to fry mashed beans with lard made from the drippings of cooked pork; this resulted in Refried Beans.

Squash and corn have been combined in Mexico City and the central region for thousands of years. The use, in this recipe, of the red bell pepper (a common pepper in the United States) makes a colorful, festive Mexican dish.

Retail food markets in Mexico City are operated by the city and are not open-air but are roofed-over. There are also modern supermarkets such as those common in the United States. However, it is still the custom in Mexico to shop and bargain for the best food and vegetables at wholesale markets. Not only is the food fresher but the merchants are willing to haggle over prices.

CHICKEN MOLÉ

Food Category: Main Dish *Moderate Cost*

Chicken
1 2½ lb. chicken
1 onion, sliced
2 cloves garlic, minced
water
2 tbsp. cilantro

Molé
2 tbsp. chili powder
20 whole blanched almonds
¼ cup diced green-tipped banana
1 tsp. cinnamon
1 tsp. salt
2 corn tortillas, torn in pieces
2 tbsp. sesame seeds
6 tbsp. butter
1 oz. semi-sweet chocolate
⅓ cup chicken broth

Toppings to choose from:
2 medium tomatoes, chopped
1 bunch parsley, chopped
4 green onions, thinly sliced
1 bunch radishes, thinly sliced
1 small can green chilis, chopped
3 limes, cut in wedges
¼ cup sesame seed

Rice
3 cups water
1½ cups rice
½ tsp. salt

1. Cut chicken into pieces.
2. Place in *Dutch oven* with onion and garlic. Cover with water. Cook covered for about 45 minutes or until done.
3. Lift chicken from broth. Cool slightly. Remove meat from bones in large pieces.
4. *Strain* broth and reserve. Discard onion and garlic.
5. Skim off fat and discard.
6. Measure broth. Add water to make 3 cups. Measure ⅓ cup of broth and place by sauce ingredients.
7. Place chili powder, almonds, banana, cinnamon, salt, tortillas, and sesame seeds in blender. Whirl ingredients. Add enough chicken broth, a drop at a time, to blend smoothly.
8. Pour sauce into Dutch oven. Add remaining broth, butter, and chocolate.
9. Simmer over medium heat. Stir constantly. Add chicken. Heat through.
10. Prepare rice. Bring water to boil. Add rice.

ENCHILADAS

Food Category: Main Dish *High Cost*

1 lb. ground beef
1 medium onion, chopped
½ tsp. salt
12 corn tortillas
1 cup cheddar cheese, grated
1 5¾-oz. can chopped black olives
1 16-oz. can enchilada sauce
oil for frying

1. In a frying pan, cook beef and onion until done. Add salt. *Drain* excess grease.
2. In another frying pan, heat ¼ inch of oil until hot. Fry tortillas briefly on both sides until soft. Stack fried tortillas between sheets of paper toweling.
3. Drain oil from frying pan. Wipe with paper towel. Add enchilada sauce. Heat until hot.
4. Set up assembly line: tortillas, enchilada sauce, ground beef mixture, cheese, and olives.
5. To fill enchiladas, follow steps below and refer to illustrations (on back):
    (1) Dip tortilla in sauce.
    (2) Place 2 tbsp. beef across middle.
    (3) Sprinkle beef with cheese and olives.
6. Roll each up and place, seam down, in oiled 13- × 9- × 2-inch baking dish. Pour remaining sauce over enchiladas. Place in 350-degree oven for 20 minutes or until cheese is melted.

Serves 6

Recipe Tips
- Do not overfry tortillas or they will become too crisp to roll.
- Raw onions may be placed in enchiladas for a stronger onion flavor.
- Top with additional cheese just before serving for a flavorful garnish.

Stir to moisten each grain. Cover tightly. *Do not peek.* Simmer for 20 to 25 minutes. Let stand for 10 minutes.

11. Transfer chicken to warmed serving bowl. Sprinkle with *cilantro*. Pour sauce into warmed pitcher. Serve chicken and sauce over hot cooked rice. Add vegetable topping.

Serves 6

Recipe Tips
- *The chocolate adds a distinctive—and delightful—flavor to this dish. The sauce does not end up tasting like chocolate.*
- *Do not peek while rice is cooking. The liquid will evaporate and the rice will burn.*
- *Warm serving dish and pitcher by placing in hot water.*
- *To divide preparation time of Chicken Molé into two days, complete Steps 1 through 5 the first day. Cover and refrigerate. Begin with Step 6 the next day.*

Chicken Molé (MOH-leh) is the national dish of Mexico. The word *molé* comes from the Aztec "mol-li," meaning a sauce flavored with chili peppers.

Legend tells us that the dish became famous after it was made by Spanish nuns in honor of an archbishop visiting their central-Mexico convent. The nuns chopped and ground every food available in the convent's kitchen—some 20 or 30 ingredients, including chili peppers, tortillas, toasted avocado leaves, onions, tomatoes, bananas, almonds, sesame seeds, raisins, lard, sugar, garlic, herbs, and spices. They cooked this mixture for hours and as a final touch added a bit of chocolate, an ingredient the local Indians used with game, which gave the molé its special character. The archbishop was delighted.

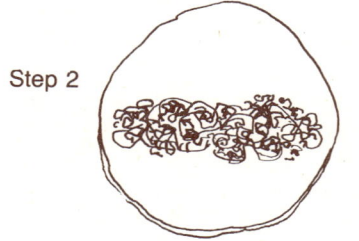

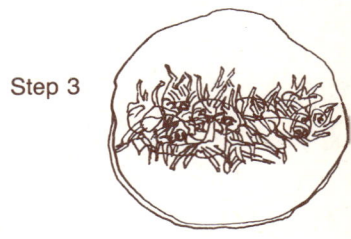

Step 1

Step 2

Step 3

Filling Enchiladas

Enchiladas (en-chee-LAH-thas) are made from fresh corn tortillas that have been dipped in a prepared sauce and then filled. Fillings may include beef, pork, chicken, cheese, eggs, beans, zucchini, carrots, potatoes, tomatoes, or almonds. Enchiladas are either rolled, folded, or stacked and topped with more sauce and baked. The hot enchiladas can be garnished with cheese. In towns such as Morelia in central Mexico, vendors assemble rolled enchilada dishes in griddles over charcoal braziers, omitting the baking step.

Purchased enchilada sauce comes in varying degrees of hotness. The traditional thin sauce contains the pulp of bland, red chilis and other spices; it is not hot. But you can add liquid hot-pepper seasoning or hot chilis to the sauce if you want a sharp, hot flavor. For a spicy sauce, buy one that has been made with *chorizo*, a Mexican pork sausage.

PORK STEW WITH TOMATILLOS

Food Category: Main Dish *High Cost*

Pork Stew

2½ lbs. lean boneless pork
2 tbsp. oil
1 large onion, chopped
2 cloves garlic, crushed
1½ cups canned tomatillos, drained and chopped
1 7-oz. can green chilis, seeded and chopped
1 tsp. marjoram leaves
1 tsp. salt
1 tbsp. dried cilantro
½ cup water
Hot cooked rice
1 cup sour cream

Rice

3 cups water
1½ cups long-grain rice
½ tsp. salt

1. Trim and discard fat from pork. Cube pork into 1-inch pieces.
2. Place oil in a frying pan over medium-high heat. Add meat a few pieces at a time. Brown lightly. Push meat to sides of pan. Add onion. Cook until onion is limp.
3. Stir in garlic, tomatillos, chilis, marjoram, salt, cilantro, and water.
4. Cover. Simmer until meat is *fork-tender*, about 1 hour. Skim off fat.
5. Prepare rice. In saucepan, bring water to boil. Add rice. Stir to moisten each grain. Cover tightly. *Do not peek.* Simmer for 20 to 25 minutes. Let stand for 10 minutes. Place in warmed serving bowl.
6. Transfer pork stew to warmed serving bowl.

Serve with hot cooked rice. Pass sour cream to spoon over stew.
Serves 6

Recipe Tips

- Pork must be cooked until done. Internal temperature must reach 140 degrees to destroy trichinae.
- Do not peek while rice is cooking. The liquid will evaporate and the rice will burn.
- When spaces appear between the grains of rice, it is done.
- Warm serving bowls by placing in hot water.
- To divide the preparation time of the pork recipe into two days, complete Steps 1 through 4, simmering for 20 to 30 minutes. Cover and refrigerate overnight. Begin with Step 4, simmering for 20 to 30 minutes the next day.

BUÑUELOS

Food Category: Dessert *Moderate Cost*

4 eggs
¼ cup sugar
2 cups flour
1 tsp. baking powder
1 tsp. salt
oil for frying
1 cup sugar
1 tsp. cinnamon

1. In a large bowl, beat together with electric mixer, eggs and ¼ cup sugar until thick and lemon colored.
2. Stir together 1½ cups of flour, baking powder, and salt. Gradually add to egg mixture. Beat until well blended.
3. Stir in ¼ cup flour.
4. Turn soft dough onto board coated with about ¼ cup remaining flour. Gently *knead* for about 5 minutes until dough is smooth and no longer sticky.
5. Divide dough into 16 equal pieces. Shape each piece into a ball. Cover each ball with waxed paper to prevent drying. When all balls are made and covered, allow to rest 20 minutes. Remove waxed paper.
6. On floured board, roll each ball into 5-inch circle. Stack circles between pieces of waxed paper.
7. Heat 1½ inches of oil in a heavy frying pan to 350 degrees. Use deep-fat-frying thermometer.
8. Mix 1 cup sugar and cinnamon.
9. Fry circles of dough, one at a time, in hot oil for 1½ minutes or until golden brown. Turn once.
10. Remove from oil. *Drain* on paper towels.
11. Coat thoroughly with cinnamon and sugar mixture.
12. Repeat until all buñuelos are cooked and coated. Makes 16

Recipe Tips

- An easy way to divide dough into 16 pieces is to cut dough into 4 equal pieces. Then cut each piece into 4 equal pieces again.
- The correct oil temperature is essential. If oil is too cool, foods will absorb it and become greasy; if too hot, foods will burn before they are cooked. Use a

Stews were the mainstay of the Indian diet. Wild game and domestic turkeys were tough. Long, slow cooking enhanced the flavor and tenderized the meat. A more tender meat, pork became popular after being introduced by the Spanish. Pork Stew similar to this dish is served today in southern Mexico with corn tortillas and lime wedges.

Tomatillos (toh-mah-TEE-yos) are *not* unripe tomatoes. However they are used in the green stage, and because their flavor does not develop until they are cooked, tomatillos are not used raw. The paperlike husk is removed before they are cooked, and their unique texture adds a distinct touch to sauces.

You can acquire a taste for chili peppers by purchasing one of the prepared varieties for this recipe. The flavor of California chilis—sometimes called "green" or "Anaheim" chilis—varies from mild and sweet to fairly hot. California chilis work well in this recipe.

Since all 140 varieties of chilis grown in Mexico do not grow in one region, the flavor of homemade Mexican sauces depends upon what chilis are available locally to the cook. After you have been introduced to the taste of Mexican-prepared chilis, you may want to experiment with any chilis found fresh in your area.

---

deep-fat-frying thermometer to check the oil temperature. If you don't have a thermometer, drop a 1-inch cube of bread into hot fat. Time 1 minute.

If bread is brown, oil temperature is correct.
- A cake pan works well when coating buñuelos with cinnamon and sugar.

Buñuelos (boo-NYUE-los), a fried, sweet bread, is a Christmas Eve supper tradition throughout Mexico. Making Buñuelos is a family project; many hands are needed to help stretch the dough and shape it into paper-thin rounds.

Uruapan, a village in central Mexico, is set in a lush, floral landscape. Here pine, cedar, and oak trees grow alongside tropical banana, avocado, and mango trees. In Uruapan the buñuelo is not just holiday food but a daily dessert served with hot chocolate. In the evening, everyone gathers in the central plaza by the buñuelo stand. It is the custom to purchase soft, just-cooked buñuelos doused with a hot, raw-sugar syrup flavored with cinnamon bark. Or you may buy crisp buñuelos, break them apart, and dip the pieces into hot syrup yourself.

FLAN

Food Category: Dessert   Moderate Cost

Caramel

1 cup sugar
¼ cup boiling water

Custard

4 cups milk
1 cup sugar
¼ tsp. salt
6 eggs, beaten
1 tsp vanilla

1. To make caramel, heat sugar in heavy skillet over low heat. Stir constantly until sugar is melted and turns light brown.
2. Remove pan from heat. Add water very slowly.
3. Return pan to heat. Cook and stir until sugar is thickened and dark brown.
4. Pour into 1½ quart glass *casserole*. Turn casserole to spread caramel evenly.
5. Combine ingredients for custard. Mix well with hand beater.
6. Pour egg mixture over caramel in casserole. Place casserole in pan of hot water.
7. Bake in 325-degree oven for 1 hour or until done.
8. Chill overnight. Run knife around edge. Unmold on platter.

Serves 6

Recipe Tips

- *Do not use an iron skillet when heating sugar. The black color absorbs heat and the sugar will burn.*
- *When a knife inserted in the center comes out clean, the custard is done.*
- *To unmold easily, dip casserole dish quickly in hot water.*

MEXICAN WEDDING CAKES

Food Category: Dessert   Moderate Cost

1 cup butter, softened
¾ cup confectioners' sugar
2 tsp. vanilla
2 cups flour
1 cup finely chopped walnuts
powdered sugar

1. In a large bowl, *cream* butter and powdered sugar. Stir in vanilla and a tbsp. of water.
2. In another bowl, mix flour and nuts together. Add to butter mixture.
3. Shape into small balls.
4. Place on ungreased cookie sheet.
5. Bake in 300-degree oven for 20 minutes.
6. Roll in confectioners' sugar.

Makes 2½ dozen.

Recipe Tips

- *These cakes do not brown during baking. When they feel slightly firm to the touch, they are done.*
- *Use a strainer to remove lumps from the confectioners' sugar. Flour sifters become clogged and do not work well.*
- *Finely chopped pecans, pine nuts, or almonds can be substituted for the walnuts.*

Flan (flahn) is the classic dessert of Mexico. *Flan* is Spanish for "baked custard." It was a popular dessert in Spain, and when the Spanish brought dairy cattle into Mexico, flan became a Mexican dish as well.

Spanish nuns made flan as one of the desserts for visiting dignitaries. In fact, when the Alcolman Convent just north of Mexico City was constructed, a round flan with grapes and other fruits and vegetables was carved on the stone arch of the main doorway. The nuns combined native vanilla with the custard recipes they had brought from Spain. Two popular variations of flan have coffee and orange flavors, but simple vanilla flan still remains the favorite in Mexico.

Sometimes called *bride's cookies*, Mexican Wedding Cakes are really more a shortbread cookie than a cake. One version calls for the cookie to be individually wrapped in tissue paper, which is bunched at each side and twisted, with the ends cut into shreds. This makes them look like bonbons.

These cookies are one of many desserts calling for *vanilla,* which is native to Mexico. This flavoring, an extract of the vanilla bean, is a major product from the south along the Gulf coast. Vanilla is found in the pods of the vanilla orchids harvested from vines by the local Indians. Also, flavorings such as orange and cinnamon are sometimes used for Mexican Wedding Cakes.

CHILAQUILES*

Food Category: Bread   *Moderate Cost*

24 corn tortillas
oil for frying
1 cup chicken broth
2½ cups grated jack cheese
1½ cups sour cream
salt
1 tbsp. dried cilantro
2 canned jalapeño chilis, chopped

Salsa Verde

1 10-oz. can tomatillos, drained
2 cloves garlic, crushed

1. Cut tortillas into ½-inch-wide strips.
2. Heat ½ inch of oil in frying pan over medium-high heat. Fry strips a few at a time until chewy but not crisp.
3. *Drain* strips on paper towels.
4. Put all ingredients for *salsa verde* in blender. Blend until smooth.
5. Remove remaining oil from pan. Add salsa verde and broth. Heat.
6. Stir in tortilla strips, cheese, and sour cream. Salt to taste.
7. Spoon into shallow, oven-proof bowls. Broil only until mixture bubbles.

Serves 6

Recipe Tips

- *Chicken bouillon cubes (one cube per cup of water) may be substituted for the chicken broth.*
- *If mixture is not moist, add more broth or sour cream.*

DEEP-FRIED MEAT BURRITOS*

Food Category: Appetizer   *High Cost*

3 tbsp. oil
1 large onion, finely chopped
3 cloves garlic, crushed
2 canned jalapeño chilis, seeded and minced
½ cup pinto beans
2 cups cooked and shredded beef
½ tsp. cumin
1 tbsp. vinegar
salt
16 6-inch flour tortillas
oil for frying
sour cream
guacamole
   (see Totopos con Guacamole)

1. Place beans in *Dutch oven*. Wash thoroughly. *Drain.* Cover with water.
2. Soak overnight.
3. Bring beans and water to boil. Cover. Simmer, adding more water as necessary until beans are tender, about 3 hours.
4. In a heavy frying pan, heat oil. Add onion and garlic and *sauté*. Drain beans reserving liquid. Add beans to frying pan.
5. Mash beans with onions and garlic. Add enough reserved liquid to make mixture slightly moist.
6. Add chilis, beef, cumin, and vinegar to bean mixture. Salt to taste. Heat.
7. Put 2 tbsp. filling in middle of tortilla. Fold in half. Keep filling inside tortilla while frying it by holding tortilla shut with tongs or small skewer or wooden pick.
8. In frying pan, heat 1 inch of oil to 375 degrees. Fry stuffed tortillas until browned on both sides. Drain on paper towels. Serve hot with guacamole and sour cream. *Makes 16.*

Recipe Tips

- *Pinto beans and pink beans are generally used for Mexican dishes because they are bland and provide a good base for heavy spicing.*
- *To wash beans cover them with cold water, then pour it off. Repeat process until water remains clear. Remove any floating beans or other foreign particles.*

Chilaquiles (chee-la-KEY-less) means "maize omelet" in Spanish, because the original recipe called for eggs. Now Chilaquiles is a catchall dish for leftover tortillas—a Mexican hash.

Because Mexicans like to eat tortillas the day they are made, leftover tortillas often become part of a delicious breakfast dish. Chilaquiles can be served at other meals, depending on what is on hand in the kitchen. Ingredients such as shredded chicken, red chilis, chorizo, and fish vary the flavor.

This modern Mexican version is a favorite. It is very popular in central Mexico's Pacific Ocean beach resorts.

- Beans increase in size as they cook. Be sure to use a large pan for cooking.
- The correct oil temperature is essential. If oil is too cool, foods will absorb it and become greasy; if too hot, foods will burn before they are cooked. Use deep-fat-frying thermometer to check oil temperature. If you don't have a thermometer, drop a 1-inch cube of bread into hot fat. Time 1 minute. If bread is brown, oil temperature is correct.
- Leftover burritos reheat very well. Wrap them in foil and place in 350-degree oven. Heat for 12 to 15 minutes from refrigerator or 25 minutes from freezer.
- To divide preparation time into two days, complete Steps 1 and 2. Begin with Step 3 the next day.

A *burrito* (boo-REEEE-to) is a snack specialty. It is made with a large flour tortilla that is filled and rolled up. Fillings include chili peppers, shredded cooked meat, scrambled eggs, and refried beans with cheese.

When burritos are fried crispy, as in this recipe, they become *chimichangas* (chee-mee-CHAN-gas). Deep-fried burritos are a favorite in the cattle and flour-milling region of northern Mexico. The Spanish originally brought wheat seed and beef cattle into this area in the 1500s.

FLAUTAS*

Food Category: Appetizer　　　　　　　　　　　　　　　　　　　　　　　　　　　　　　　　　　　　　**High Cost**

- 2 lb. ground beef or shredded roast beef
- 3 tbsp. chili powder
- salt
- pepper
- 1 tbsp. ground cumin
- 2 tbsp. flour
- water
- lettuce, chopped
- tomatoes, chopped
- cheddar cheese, grated
- sour cream
- guacamole (see Totopos con Guacamole)
- 20 6-inch flour tortillas

1. In a frying pan, over medium heat, *sauté* ground beef until lightly brown.
2. *Drain* fat. Add chili powder, salt, pepper, and cumin. Mix well so meat absorbs seasonings.
3. Sprinkle flour over meat. When flour is absorbed and none can be seen, add enough water to moisten meat mixture. *Simmer* for 5 minutes. Stir occasionally to blend flavors. Keep warm.
4. Heat tortillas in warm, ungreased frying pan for 30 seconds per side, turning only once.
5. Place 3 to 4 tbsp. of meat mixture across center of each tortilla. Cover with lettuce, tomatoes, and cheese. Roll up.
6. Top with guacamole and dabs of sour cream. Serve at once.

Serves 6

Recipe Tip
- *Chop lettuce just before using or it will become limp and brown.*

TACOS*

Food Category: Main Dish　　　　　　　　　　　　　　　　　　　　　　　　　　　　　　　　　　　　　**High Cost**

- 2 lb. lean ground beef
- 1 clove garlic, minced
- 2 onions, chopped
- 1 tsp. salt
- 2 tsp. chili powder
- ¼ cup Mexican red chili sauce
- ½ tsp. cumin
- oil for frying
- 12 corn tortillas
- 1 cup shredded iceberg lettuce
- 8 oz. sharp cheddar cheese, grated
- 1 or 2 tomatoes, chopped

1. In a frying pan, over medium heat, cook ground beef until lightly brown.
2. Add garlic and half of onions for milder flavor. *Sauté* until onions are limp. *Drain* grease.
3. Add salt, chili powder, and cumin. Mix well. Add chili sauce. *Simmer* uncovered, stirring until heated through.
4. In a frying pan, heat 1 inch of oil. Fry tortillas one at a time, until limp. Fold in half, leaving open enough so filling can be placed inside. Fry both sides until chewy but not crisp. Drain on paper towels. Keep warm in oven preheated to 200 degrees.
5. Spoon 2 to 3 tbsp. beef mixture into each tortilla shell. Top each with lettuce, cheese, tomatoes, and remaining onion.

Serves 6

Recipe Tips
- *Either purchased or homemade tortillas work well.*
- *Do not fry tortillas too long or they will become too crisp to fold and difficult to fill.*
- *Tortillas can be kept warm in 200-degree oven while waiting to be filled.*
- *Shred lettuce just before using, or it will become brown and limp.*
- *To peel tomato easily, dip into boiling water.*

Flautas (FLOU-tas), which is Spanish for "flutes," are one of the many snacks made from tortillas in Mexico. Flautas are made by rolling a filling tightly in a tortilla to form a tubular, flute shape.

This recipe, which uses the popular flour tortilla of northern Mexico, can also be made with shredded roast beef. Roast beef became a traditional ingredient after the Spaniards brought long-horned cattle into the region.

Some recipes call for frying Flautas. This is done by overlapping two corn tortillas, which are rolled around a filling of ground beef, bulk *chorizo*, pork, or chicken.

Popular throughout Mexico, the word *taco* (TAH-ko) means a rolled corn tortilla "snack." The taco, like most Mexican snacks, is eaten out-of-hand, usually after being purchased from a food vendor at a sidewalk cart. You can eat a taco without spilling a drop of sauce by holding the taco with one hand, tipping and eating one end, and curling the other end up with your little finger so that none of the sauce can run out.

Tacos can be made with almost any filling, but the most popular taco in Mexico is just warm, shredded meat doused with sauce and rolled into a warm, soft, freshly made corn tortilla. Although not as popular as the warm tortilla taco, another type of taco in Mexico is first filled and then fried.

In the United States, a taco—the most popular Mexican food—consists of a corn tortilla that is fried and then folded. The crisp shell is then filled with seasoned meat, different garnishes, and sauce.

TAMALE PIE*

Food Category: Main Dish · *High Cost*

- ¾ lb. ground beef
- 1 medium onion, chopped
- 1 green bell pepper, chopped
- 2 8-oz. cans tomato sauce
- 1 12-oz can whole kernel corn, drained
- ¼ cup ripe olives, pitted and chopped
- 1 clove garlic, minced
- 1 tbsp. sugar
- 1 tsp. salt
- 3 tsp. chili powder
- 1 cup cheddar cheese, grated

Topping

- ¾ cup corn meal
- ½ tsp. salt
- 2 cups cold water
- 1 tbsp. butter

1. In a frying pan, over medium heat, cook meat until brown. Add onion and green pepper. Cook until tender. *Drain* excess fat.
2. Add tomato sauce, corn, olives, garlic, sugar, salt, and chili powder. Simmer for 20 minutes or until thick.
3. Add cheese. Stir until melted. Pour into greased casserole.
4. Stir corn meal and salt into cold water. Bring to boil. Cook and stir until thick. Add butter. Mix well.
5. Spoon over meat mixture in narrow strips.
6. Bake at 375 degrees for 40 minutes or until top is brown. Serve hot.

Serves 6

Recipe Tips

- Cornmeal spatters very easily during cooking. Be careful.
- To divide preparation into two days, complete Steps 1 to 5. Cover and refrigerate. Begin with Step 6 the next day.

A traditional *tamale* (tah-MAH-le) consists of dried corn husks spread with *masa* dough—to seal in the flavor—topped with a flavored filling. The husks are then folded shut and steamed. Any number of fillings may be used—green chili pepper strips and cheese, pork, or chicken. A sweet dough variety is served for breakfast and supper.

Different kinds of tamales are made throughout Mexico. The more unusual tamales of the Yucatan region are wrapped and cooked in banana leaves and flavored with *achiote* (ah-chee-OH-teh), the seeds from the annatto tree, and *epazote* (eh-pah-SOH-teh), an herb.

Although they are eaten throughout the year, tamales are a special Christmas custom in Mexico. It is time-consuming but fun for a family to make tamales ahead of time so that visiting friends and relatives can enjoy them during the holidays.

To make the traditional version, you can purchase dried corn husks in the grocery store, or you can dry your own by leaving green husks in a warm, sunny spot for three to eight days and storing them in a dry place. Of course, you can use other wrappings—even aluminum foil. Tamale Pie tastes like the traditional tamale but is much easier to put together.

GLOSSARY

Achiote seeds of the annatto tree ground into a paste and used in ancient Mayan, Mexican, and Central American cuisine to give food a delicate flavoring and yellow color.
Al dente "to the tooth," a term for pasta that is slightly resistant to the bite; tender but firm.
Amaranth grain of the ancient Aztecs, eaten today in India, Pakistan, Nepal, Tibet, China, Central America, and Mexico.
Antipasto in Italian cuisine, an appetizer or light first course preceding the main meal.
Avocado a tropical fruit grown in Mexico, Florida, and California; varieties, from green to purplish-black, weigh from one to three pounds. Its soft pulp has a nutty flavor.
Bake to cook with dry heat, as in an oven.
Bamboo shoots young, tender growths of an edible bamboo plant, commonly used in Chinese foods.
Basil an herb commonly used in Italian dishes.
Bean curd processed, custard-like soybean milk, more commonly known in the United States by the Japanese name, *tofu*.
Bean sprouts sprouts of soy bean or mung bean, commonly used in Chinese dishes.
Beat to mix ingredients rapidly to incorporate air.
Binder the ingredient in a recipe that makes the mixture stick together (such as eggs).
Bland having a mild or dull flavor.
Blend to mix ingredients until they are combined completely.
Blender small electrical appliance for mixing, chopping, and liquefying.
Boil to cook in rapidly bubbling liquid.
Bolillos small, elongated rolls of bread.
Bone to remove bones from meat, fish, or poultry.
Braise to brown and then cook in a liquid.
Breadfruit a round, seedless fruit that, when baked, resembles bread in color and texture.
Bride's cookies Mexican cookies that are rich with butter, nuts, and powdered sugar. Also called Mexican Wedding Cakes.
Broil to cook uncovered under direct heat or over hot coals.
Broth a liquid in which meat or poultry has simmered.
Brown to make the outside of a food brown by frying, broiling, or baking.
Brown bean paste in Chinese cuisine, a thick, brown sauce made from fermented soybeans, salt, flour, and sugar.
Buñuelos fried sweet pastry puffs.
Burrito sauce-filled wheat-flour tortilla.
Cacao a tropical tree bearing beans used to make chocolate and cocoa.
Candy thermometer a thermometer for measuring the temperature of syrups and oils.
Capsaicin a heat-producing substance in chili.
Casserole covered pottery dish used for baking and serving; or a combination of foods baked in a single dish.
Cayenne pepper very hot pepper which must be used in small quantities.
Cellophane noodles in Chinese cuisine, translucent noodles made from ground mung beans.
Chayote pear-shaped, light-green squash whose edible seed and pulp are

delicately flavored.
Chicken molé a chicken-and-molé-sauce dish.
Chilaquiles a dish that uses leftover tortillas.
Chili peppers any member of the podded pepper family that is hot, pungent, or sweet.
Chill to refrigerate until cold, but not frozen.
Chimichangas deep-fried burritos.
Chinampas agricultural islands created by the Aztecs of Tenochtitlan of mud and aquatic vegetation layered onto woven frames and anchored by stakes and trees.
Chop to cut into small pieces using a sharp knife and a cutting board.
Chorizo a spicy pork sausage.
Cilantro fresh leaves of coriander, commonly used in Mexican foods.
Cinnamon spice from the bark of a laurel tree.
Coat to lightly cover or dust one food with another (such as covering meat with flour before frying).
Colander large hole-filled container for draining liquids from solids.
Cornstarch a fine flour made from corn, usually used for thickening.
Cream to whip or beat until frothy.
Croutons small cubes of toasted or fried bread.
Crush to flatten or break down by force.
Crusty having a hard exterior, as with most breads.
Cube to cut into pieces with six square sides; to dice.
Cumin an herb used in chili powder and many Mexican dishes.
Cut in to distribute fat evenly through dry ingredients using a pastry blender, a fork, or two knives.
Deep-fat fry to cook in fat deep enough for food to float in.
Diagonally at an angle.
Dice to cut into small cubes; to cube.
Dim sum "touch the heart," a term for Chinese foods not ordinarily served as main dishes.
Dissolve to turn from a solid into a liquid in combination with a liquid, as salt in water; also, to cause a solid to dissolve.
Drain to allow liquids, such as water or grease, to drip from a food.
Dry onions several varieties of onions which are harvested when the tops are dry.
Dry soup sopa seca, usually rice, pasta, tortillas, or dried legumes in which the liquid is absorbed in cooking.
Dust to give a light coating, usually of flour or sugar.
Dutch oven a heavy, large, covered pan.
Egg rolls pancake-like wrappers filled with a mixture of vegetables and seafood.
Empanaditas small, filled turnovers, baked or fried and served as appetizers.
Enchiladas name given to a tortilla dipped into a sauce and filled, usually with cheese or meat.
Epazote a pungent herb used in Mexico to flavor black beans, soups, fillings, and so on.
Espresso coffee brewed by forcing steam through finely ground, darkly roasted beans.
Fettuccini a spaghetti-like, long noodle.
Fillet to remove bones and slice thinly or to pound lightly between sheets of wax paper.
Flan a caramel custard dessert.
Flautas a variety of taco in which two overlapping tortillas form a tubular shape.
Florets the small flowers forming the head of a plant (for instance, broccoli).
Flute to decorate an edge with wide round grooves (as done with pie crust).
Focaccia flat bread.
Food mill a small appliance for grinding foods.
Fork-tender tender when pierced with a fork.
French carrots small, very sweet carrots frequently used whole.
Frittata an open-faced omelet.
Garnish to decorate one food with another.
Gelata Italian ice cream.
Ginger root the whitish-brown root of the ginger plant, used as a seasoning, especially in Chinese foods.
Gluten a protein formed when a liquid is

added to flour; used as a base for breads and cakes.
Gradually a little at a time.
Granulated sugar common refined table sugar; obtained from the juice of plants such as sugar cane or sugar beets.
Grate to make fine food particles by rubbing a food (such as cheese) over a grater.
Grease to brush a surface lightly with shortening, butter, or oil to prevent food from sticking to it.
Grissini breadsticks.
Guacamole a mashed avocado mixture.
Guava a tropical fruit served fresh or cooked.
Heat to raise the temperature.
Ice crusher small hand or electric appliance used to crush ice.
Jicama brown-skinned root vegetable with a crisp white pulp.
Julienne to cut a food into long, thin strips.
Kidney bean a large red bean.
Knead to press, turn, and fold dough to develop gluten and further combine ingredients.
La cena supper, or an evening Mexican meal.
La comida midday dinner, or the main Mexican meal of the day.
Ladle to spoon up with a large dipper-like spoon.
Lard white, semi-solid fat rendered from the fatty tissue of the hog.
Lasagna broad, flat noodles about one and one-half inch wide; also the dish made with the noodles.
Leeks very mild onions.
Legumes dried seeds from the pods of plants such as beans and peas.
Limp soft as a result of cooking.
Linguini thin, flat member of the pasta family.
Litchi nuts small, rough-skinned fruit used in Chinese cuisine, available canned or dried. Now grown in Florida and Hawaii.
Maize dried corn.
Mano a grinding stone used with a metate.
Marinade a liquid used for marinating.

Marinate to let a food stand in a liquid mixture to make it tender or to improve its flavor.
Marjoram an herb used especially in Italian foods.
Masa harina a granular flour made from corn.
Mash to make a food soft and smooth by crushing.
Medium hard crack the point at which a drop of syrup put into ice water instantly forms a hard sugar mass.
Melt to change a solid into a liquid by heating.
Metate a flat, rectangular tripod of volcanic rock used for grinding corn and chilis.
Millet ancient cereal grain of Italy, eaten today in India, China, Egypt, South America.
Mince to chop into very small pieces using a sharp knife and a cutting board.
Minestrone a thick vegetable soup.
Mix to combine ingredients.
Moisten to dampen or make slightly wet.
Molé a concoction or mixture; also a thick, rich sauce to accompany poultry or pork.
Mozzarella a mild cooking and snacking cheese native to Italy, commonly used in pizza.
Nachos con queso tortilla chips with melted cheese.
Nutmeg a spice often used in Mexican foods.
Oregano an herb often used in Italian foods.
Oyster Sauce a rich brown sauce made from thickened oyster broth, which does not taste fishy and adds a subtle smooth flavor to dishes.
Pancetta Italian bacon.
Panettone bread containing spices and dried fruits.
Parmesan a sharp cooking cheese native to Italy, usually used grated.
Parsley, Chinese fresh leaves of coriander, used to add flavor and color.
Pasta a dough of flour, water, and sometimes eggs, made into a variety of shapes and sizes; also a dish that is made

primarily of pasta.
Peel   to strip off the outer covering.
Peppercorn   a dried berry of the black pepper plant.
Pimiento   sweet member of the pepper family.
Pinch   the amount of an ingredient, such as salt, that can be held between thumb and index finger.
Pinto bean   a small pink and brown bean commonly used in Mexican cuisine.
Pit   to remove seeds.
Pizza   dough crust baked with various fillings, such as cheeses, vegetables, and meats.
Preheat   to heat an oven before putting in food.
Prewarm   to warm an oven, then turn it off before using, as with yeast.
Prickly pear   a cactus fruit with fleshy green leaves called pads or paddles; also called a nopal or a tuna cactus.
Prosciutto   Italian ham.
Pulmentum   grain, to the ancient Romans their staple diet.
Pulque   a drink made from the distilled milky sap of the agave plant.
Punch down   to force air from dough by pushing it with a fist.
Puree   to make a food into a pulp by forcing through a sieve.
Quarter   to cut into four pieces of roughly the same size.
Queso   cheese.
Rancid   having a bad, spoiled, very flat taste or odor.
Reduce   to decrease the amount by cooking.
Refried beans   beans thoroughly fried in a flavorful fat.
Reserve   to set aside for later use.
Residue   food left over from the cooking process.
Rice   to put through a ricer or strainer to remove lumps; also a grain which provides the principal calories in the Chinese diet.
Ricotta   a mild un-aged cooking cheese native to Italy, commonly used in lasagna.
Rinse   to wash in clear water.

Rise   to inflate, as when dough is let to stand in a warm place to increase in volume.
Romano   a sharp, granular cheese used for cooking and snacking.
Rosemary   a strong, pungent herb used both dried and fresh, especially in Italian foods.
Salarium   Latin for *salary*, from the Latin *sal*, meaning "salt."
Salsa verde   "green sauce," made from tomatillos, the tart green tomatoes of Mexico.
Sapote   a tropical fruit with a reddish-brown skin and a soft pulp that tastes somewhat like a pear.
Sauté   to brown lightly in a small amount of fat.
Scallion   an herb of the onion family, sold with edible green leaves attached to small bulb, often used in Italian and Chinese cuisine. Green onions are often substituted for scallions.
Seed   to remove the seeds.
Serrano chilis   very hot, long, green chilis that are used fresh, boiled, or toasted.
Sesame seeds   tiny flat seeds often used in Chinese and Italian foods. These are sometimes crushed to make a butter-like paste.
Shred   to cut or tear a food into thin strips.
Sieve   a bowl-shaped container made of screen, used for separating solids from liquids.
Sift   to put a dry ingredient through a sifter or strainer to remove lumps.
Simmer   to cook in a liquid below the point of boiling.
Skim   to remove from the surface of a liquid, as fat from the surface of a broth.
Skin   to remove the skin, as from chicken.
Slice   to cut into thin, flat pieces.
Soak   to place in a liquid so that liquid is absorbed.
Sopa seca   "dry soup," a rice, pasta, tortilla, or dried legume dish in which liquid is absorbed in cooking.
Sopa seca de arroz   a dry soup course of rice.

Soufflé cups fluted paper cups sized for individual servings (similar to those for cupcakes).
Soy sauce a sauce made from fermented soybeans, wheat, and salt; a seasoning in Chinese foods.
Spaghettini thin rod-shaped member of the pasta family.
Spongy light, porous, and absorbent.
Spring-form pan a deep pan with removable sides.
Sprinkle to shake a fine ingredient onto a food for a thin coating.
Steam to cook using the vapor of boiling water as the source of heat.
Stir-fry a quick Chinese cooking technique in which foods are cut diagonally in small pieces and fried in a small amount of fat over high heat until tender.
Strain to drain a liquid from a solid as with a sieve or strainer.
Taco a tortilla wrapped around a filling and sometimes fried.
Tamale a dough food made from ground corn and lard, steamed in a corn husk or banana leaf.
Tender easily pierced with a fork.
Tender-crisp slightly tender, but still a bit resistant when pierced with a fork.
Thaw to warm something that is frozen; to defrost.
Thicken to reduce the amount of liquid by cooking, or to add corn starch or flour.
Thin to make more fluid; to add liquid.
Thyme an herb often used in Italian dishes.

Tomatillos small green tomatoes used in Mexican foods.
Tortellini small stuffed pasta rings.
Tortilla flat bread of Mexico made from corn or wheat flour.
Tortoni a rich, frozen Italian dessert.
Tostada a flat, crisp, fried tortilla topped with meat and cheese.
Totopos con guacamole small triangular pieces of crisp-fried tortillas served with a mashed avocado mixture.
Translucent a term applied to foods that have been cooked until they have a nearly transparent quality.
Trattoria an Italian restaurant.
Trichinae tiny parasites found in raw pork that must be killed by thoroughly cooking the pork.
Tuna cactus edible pads of the nopal cactus or prickly pear.
Vanilla extract true (not artificial) vanilla flavoring, prepared by soaking fermented vanilla beans in alcohol.
Veal the flesh of a young calf.
Vermicelli small, rod-like member of the pasta family.
Well a space made in the center of dry ingredients in a bowl for the addition of another ingredient, such as an egg.
Wet soup sopa aguada.
Wok a cooking pan with a round bottom used by the Chinese for stir-frying.
Wontons filled and fried pockets of dough.
Zucchini dark green member of the summer squash family.

Glossary   245

INDEX

A

Amaranth, 169
Antipasto, 87, 109
Appearance
  Chinese food, 35
  Italian food, 117
  Mexican food, 199
Atole (hot chocolate), 169

B

Beans, Refried, 167, 181, 183
Bread, 95, 178
Bread sticks, 117
Breakfast
  Italian, 87
  Mexican, 168–169
Brunch, 169
Buffet settings
  Chinese, 26–27
  Italian, 108–109
  Mexican, 190–191
Buns, Pork Steamed, 19

C

Cacao, 164
Calzone, 82, 92–93, 118
Chayote, 164
Cheese
  in Italian meals, 87
Chili peppers, 164, 181
Chinese food
  appearance, 35
  baking, 15
  braising, 15
  buffet setting, 26–27
  chicken, 14
  Chinese meal cost sheet, 20
  chopsticks, 28–29
  colors, 15
  common ingredients, 7
  cookies and cakes, 7
  cooking in water, 15
  cooking techniques, 15, 36
  cost analysis, 20–25
  current practices, 5–6
  cutting, 36
  deep-fat frying, 15
  determining convenience of recipe, 18–19
  dining table settings, 27–28
  doughs, 14
  equivalent amounts, 22–23
  evaluating your Chinese meals, 34–38
  factors affecting, 4–5
  Fire Pot demonstration, 9–10
  fish and shellfish, 6
  flavors, 15, 35–36
  and the four major culinary regions, 5
  and guests, 7
  history, 3–5
  litchi nuts, 18
  meal patterns, 7
  meal planning form, 30–33
  meat and fowl, 6
  menu selection, 14–15
  nutrition, 16–17
  Onion Cakes demonstration, 11–12
  planning your meal, 13
  Pon Pon Chicken, 18
  pork, 14
  use of preserved foods, 6
  recipe cost analysis, 24
  refrigeration, 6
  rice, 7
  sesame seed paste, 18

247

Chinese food (continued)
    soup, 7, 14
    spices and seasoning, 6, 35–36
    Steamed Pork Buns, 19
    steamer, 19
    steaming, 15
    stir-frying, 15
    sweets, 14
    table manners, 28–29
    texture, 35
    timing, 36
    vegetables, 7, 14
    weights and measures, 21
chopsticks, 28–29
Color
    Chinese food, 15
    Italian food, 117
    Mexican food, 199
cookies and cakes
    Chinese, 7
    Italian, 88
Cooking techniques
    Chinese food, 15, 36
    Italian food, 83–84, 85–86
    Mexican food, 167

D

Desserts
    Italian, 88
    Mexican, 169–170
Doughs, 14

E

Empanaditas, 199
Enchiladas, 179
Espresso, 88

F

Fish and shellfish
    and Chinese food, 6
    and Italian food, 87
Flan, 169
Flautas, 162, 173
Flavor
    Chinese food, 15, 35–36
    Italian food, 87, 117–118
    Mexican food, 199–200
Frittata, 88
Fruit ices, 88
Frying, deep-fat, 15

G

Gelata, 88
Gnocchi, 95
Granite, 88
Guacamole, 169
Guavas, 165

I

Ingredients
  for Chinese dishes, 7
  for Italian dishes, 88
  for Mexican dishes, 169
Italian food
    antipasto, 87, 109
    appearance, 117
    bread, 95
    bread sticks, 117
    breakfast, 87
    buffet settings, 108–109
    butter, 95
    calzone, 82, 118
    Calzone demonstration, 92–93
    Cheese Ball demonstration, 90–91
    cost, 100–103
    cost analysis, 106–107
    Deep-Fried Rice demonstration, 90–91
    determining convenience of recipe, 99–100
    equivalent amounts, 103–105
    evaluating the meal, 116–120
    evening meal, 88
    espresso, 88
    first course, 95
    fish, 87
    flavor, 117–118
    frittata, 88
    fruit ices, 88
    gelata, 88
    Gnocchi, 95
    Granite, 88
    history, 83–85
    ingredients, 88
    Lasagna, 83
    macaroni, 87
    main meal, 87
    Marinated Vegetables, 109
    meal cost sheet, 101
    meal patterns, 87
    meal planning form, 112–115

meat, 87
meat course, 95
menu selection, 95–96
Minestrone, 84, 117
northern cuisine, 87
nutrition, 97–99
one-dish meals, 88
Panettone, 88
pasta, 83, 87
pizza, 117
planning your meal, 94
Polenta, 84
regional differences, 85–87
rice, 87, 88, 95
salads, 87, 96
shopping, 87
soup, 87
southern cuisine, 87
spaghetti, 83
special-occasion dinner, 87
spices and seasoning, 87–88
springform pan, 99
stew, 88
table manners, 84, 110–111
table settings, 109–110
texture, 117
Tortellini, 96
Tortoni, Biscuit, 99
trattoria, 108
Veal Scallopini, 99, 117
vegetables, 95
vegetables, stuffed, 88
weights and measures, 102

L

Lasagna, 83
Litchi nuts, 18

M

Macaroni, 87
Main courses
  Mexican, 179
Manners, table
  Chinese, 28–29
  Italian, 84, 110–111
  Mexican, 192–193
Manos, 165
Meal cost sheet
  Chinese, 20
  Italian, 101
  Mexican, 184
Meal evaluation
  Chinese, 34–38
  Italian, 116–120
  Mexican, 198–202
Meal patterns
  Chinese food, 7
  Italian food, 87–88
  Mexican food, 168–170
Meal planning form
  Chinese, 30–33
  Italian, 112–115
  Mexican, 194–197
Meat and fowl
  and Chinese food, 6
  in Italian cooking, 87, 95
  in Mexican cooking, 169
Menu selection
  Chinese, 14–15
  Italian, 95–96
  Mexican, 178–179
Metates, 165, 200
Mexican food
  amaranth, 165, 167
  appearance, 199
  appetizers, 178
  atole (hot chocolate), 169
  Aztec influence, 165–168
  Beans, Refried, 167, 181, 183
  bread, 178
  breakfast, 168–169
  brunch, 169
  buffet settings, 190–191
  cacao, 164
  chayote, 164
  chili peppers, 164, 181
  cost analysis, 184–189
  desserts, 169–170
  determining convenience, 182–183
  Dutch oven, 183
  Empanaditas, 199
  Enchiladas, 179
  equivalent amounts, 186–187
  European influence on, 167
  evaluating the meal, 198–202
  Flan (custard), 169
  Flautas, 162
  Flautas demonstration, 173
  flavor, 199–200
  fruits, 165, 170
  guacamole, 169
  guavas, 165
  herbs, 166
  history, 163–166
  influence on Europe and Asia, 167
  ingredients, 169

Mexican food (continued)
   lacena, 170
   la comida, 169
   light supper. *See* la comida
   maguey syrup, 166
   main courses, 169, 179
   main meal. *See* la comida
   manos, 165
   masa harina, 183
   Mayan influence, 163–165
   meal cost sheet, 181
   meal patterns, 168–170
   meal planning form, 194–197
   meat and fowl, 169
   metates, 165, 200
   molé dishes, 179, 199
   native cooking techniques, 200
   nutrition, 180–182
   planning the meal, 177
   pulque, 166
   regional differences, 168
   rice, 168
   sapote, 164
   seasonings, 185
   soups, "dry," 178
   soups, "wet," 178
   spaghettini, 182
   Spanish cooking techniques, 167
   Spanish foods brought from Europe, 166
   table manners, 192–193
   table settings, 191–192
   Tacos, 162
   Tacos demonstration, 175–176
   tamales, 166
   texture, 199
   tomatillos, 181, 183
   tortillas, 166, 181
   tostadas, 181
   vegetables, 166, 179
   vermicelli, 182
   weights and measures, 185
Minestrone, 84, 117
Molé, 179, 199

P

Panettone, 88
Pasta, 83, 87
Pizza, 117
Planning
  Chinese meals, 13
  Italian meals, 94
  Mexican meals, 177
Polenta, 84
Pulque, 166

R

Recipe demonstrations
  Chinese, 9–12
  Italian, 90–91
  Mexican, 173–176
Refrigeration
  and Chinese food, 6
Rice
  Chinese, 7
  Italian, 87, 88, 95
  Mexican, 168, 178, 179, 187

S

Sapote, 164
Sesame seed paste, 18
Settings, table
  Chinese, 26–27
  Italian, 109–110
  Mexican, 191–192
Soup
  Chinese, 7, 14
  Italian, 87
  Mexican, 169, 171, 178
Spaghetti, 83, 104
Spaghettini, 182
Spices and seasoning
  Chinese food, 6, 35–36
  Italian food, 87
  Mexican food, 185
Steaming, 15
Stew, 88
Stir-frying, 15

T

Tacos, 162, 175–176
Tamales, 166
Texture
  Chinese food, 35
  Italian food, 117
  Mexican food, 199
Tomatillos, 181, 183
Tortellini, 96
Tortillas, 166, 181
Tortoni, Biscuit, 99
Trattoria, 108
Tostadas, 181

V

Veal Scallopini, 99, 117
Vegetables
    Chinese, 7, 14
    Italian, 87, 89, 95
    Mexican, 169, 179
Vermicelli, 182